THE INTEMPERATE ZONE

Council on Foreign Relations Books

The Council on Foreign Relations, Inc., is a non-profit and nonpartisan organization devoted to promoting improved understanding of international affairs through the free exchange of ideas. The Council does not take any position on questions of foreign policy and has no affiliation with, and receives no funding from, the United States government.

From time to time, books and monographs written by members of the Council's research staff or visiting fellows (like this book), or commissioned by the Council, or written by an independent author with critical review contributed by a Council study or working group are published with the designation "Council on Foreign Relations Book." Any book or monograph bearing that designation is, in the judgment of the Committee on Studies of the Council's board of directors, a responsible treatment of a significant international topic worthy of presentation to the public. All statements of fact and expressions of opinion contained in Council books are, however, the sole responsibility of the author.

Overseas Development Council

The Overseas Development Council is collaborating with W.W. Norton & Company, Inc., in the dissemination of *The Intemperate Zone* in the belief that it is an insightful treatment of crucial issues in U.S. foreign policy towards the Third World. The ODC is a private non-profit organization established in 1969 to increase American understanding of the economic and social problems confronting the developing countries and to promote awareness of the importance of these countries to the United States. Richard E. Feinberg, who was an ODC visiting fellow while completing *The Intemperate Zone,* is now the director of its Foreign Policy Program.

Richard E. Feinberg

THE INTEMPERATE ZONE

The Third World Challenge to U.S. Foreign Policy

W · W · NORTON & COMPANY *New York · London*

LIBRARY
COLBY-SAWYER COLLEGE
NEW LONDON, N.H. 03257

E
840
.F44
1983

5/85

Published simultaneously in Canada by
Penguin Books Canada Ltd,
2801 John Street, Markham, Ontario L3R 1B4.

Copyright © 1983 by Richard E. Feinberg
All rights reserved.
Printed in the United States of America.

The text of this book is composed in Bembo,
with display type set in Columna and New Caslon Italic.
Composition and manufacturing by The Haddon Craftsmen, Inc.
Book design by Adrianne Onderdonk Dudden

First published as a Norton paperback 1983

Library of Congress Cataloging in Publication Data
Feinberg, Richard E.
The intemperate zone.
Includes index.
1. United States—Foreign relations—1945-
2. United States—Foreign relations—Underdeveloped areas.
3. Underdeveloped areas—Foreign relations—United
States. I. Title.
E840.F44 1983 327.73 82-18847
ISBN 0-393-01712-5
ISBN 0-393-30143-5 PBK

W. W. Norton & Company, Inc., 500 Fifth Avenue, New York, N. Y. 10110
W. W. Norton & Company Ltd., 37 Great Russell Street, London WC1B 3NU

5 6 7 8 9 0

96349

To my father who challenged me to think,
to my mother who instilled an appreciation for literature,
to my sister who keeps me honest,
and to Diane and Sonya always

Contents

Acknowledgments

Many individuals were kind enough to assist me in the production of this book. I owe special gratitude to Kenneth Oye, who first encouraged me to write the book, and then provided a continual stream of trenchant commentaries as each chapter spewed forth from my typewriter. Other individuals generously took time out from their own busy schedules to read and criticize an entire draft of the manuscript, including Philip Brenner, Moss Blackman, Stephen B. Cohen, Anton de Porte, Tom Farer, Brian Glade, Paul Kreisberg, William Leogrande, Richard Newfarmer, Robert Pastor, Susan Purcell, Ronald Steel, Kenneth Sharp, John Sewell, Tom Thornton, and Jennifer Whitaker. For their helpful comments on individual chapters, I am indebted to David Albright, Bruce Bagley, Stephen Daggett, George Lawton, Robert Legvold, John Mathieson, Earl Ravenal, Barry Rubin, and Scott Thompson. Jan Austin, Tamar Jacobi, and Ronald Weber provided invaluable editorial advice. Martha Stein, Amha Selassie, and Maureen Young were most able research assistants.

I would also like to thank the Council on Foreign Relations and the Woodrow Wilson Center, Smithsonian Institution, for granting me the necessary funding, and the Carnegie Endowment for International Peace and the Overseas Development Council for providing me with office space in their superb facilities.

Without the assistance of these colleagues and organizations, this book would not have been possible.

THE INTEMPERATE ZONE

Introduction

The seventh floor of the State Department is the exclusive preserve of the Secretary of State and his senior advisers. One day in early 1979, the seventh floor's central brain—the Policy Planning Staff—was meeting in one of the plush inner conference rooms to review U.S. global foreign policy. Together, the twenty-three staff members were responsible for devising policies across the full range of international issues of concern to the United States. The director of the planning staff asked each staff member briefly to summarize the major problems confronting the United States in his or her region of the world and explain the United States government's plan for resolving those difficulties. That day, the problem areas ranged widely and included civil war in Cambodia, instability in Iran, peace talks in the Middle East, the economy of Sudan, conflict in the Horn of Africa, arms sales to Morocco, the latest round of talks on Zimbabwe, foreign aid levels in the Caribbean, human rights violations in South America, and a series of issues involving Western Europe and the Soviet-Chinese relationship. As a staff member, I reviewed several international economic issues and the growing unrest facing Somoza in Nicaragua. This extensive menu covered most of the day's newspaper stories on foreign affairs and several that had not yet entered the public domain. But unlike the newspaper reader, the Policy Planning Staff was expected to provide detailed recipes for coping with each problem.

The director struggled to find a pattern in the kaleidoscopic swirl of ideas being presented by all of the staffers. At the end of the 90-minute *tour d' horizon,* the director noted the sheer mindnumbing quantity of it all and sighed: "Sometimes I wonder, if we put all the problems on a circular board, all the proposed solutions on an outer wheel, and just spun away, and implemented each solution wherever it stopped on the wheel, whether we wouldn't do as well."

The pace on the seventh floor is hectic; the pressures are intense. Officials try to maintain the sense that they are on top of the crises of the moment and that U.S. policy is molding history in the desired direction. Only occasionally, even to themselves, do they admit that events are spinning beyond their control. For instance, I remember drafting a cable with a personal aide of the department's second-ranking official, the Deputy Secretary of State, during an especially difficult moment in El Salvador. The cable instructed our embassy in San Salvador to deliver messages to various Salvadoran government officials, military officers, politicians, businessmen, and clerics to gain their support for our plans for their country. The aide suddenly collapsed in his chair and blurted, "We're behaving as though we push buttons in Washington and the Salvadorans jump. It's a fantasy, a self-delusion."

Looking Backward

Every day, the Third World moves further and further beyond the control of the United States. Formerly subservient nations now march to their own drummers. The central debate in U.S. foreign policy in the 1980s will be over how the United States should react. Can we reverse the course of history at reasonable cost? If not, how can we ensure that the forces unleashed in the Third World march alongside us rather than against us?

Since the years immediately after World War II, the Third World has been the chief locus of international tensions. The United States and the Soviet Union, separated by forbidding distances and restrained by the fear of mutual assured destruction, have concentrated their competition in "third areas." Europe retained its primordial importance, but its political systems were firmly established, and East-West boundaries were clearly drawn. With its political instabilities and localized wars, the developing world has provided a fertile, alternative battleground where the Great Powers could wage a shadow war by proxy, where each could seek to spread its own influence and deny or disrupt its opponent's ambitions.

Most of the major foreign policy crises since the Second World War have erupted in Asia, Africa, or Latin America. American attention and energies were consumed by veritable earthquakes in Korea, Cuba, and Vietnam, and by tremors in such places as Guatemala, Lebanon, Indonesia, the Congo, the Dominican Republic, and Chile. Today, Washington's attention is directed toward the rumblings emanating from the Middle East, Central America, southern Africa, the Horn of Africa, southwest Asia, and Indochina. The Soviet Union has sought to exploit some of these disturbances, while at the same time struggling to manage or cap explosions along a rim running from China through Afghanistan to the Balkans and Poland. Indeed, both superpowers find themselves embedded in "arcs" and "circles" of crises. Upheavals near to home are worrisome precisely because of their proximity, while those further away provoke anguish because greater distances are a barrier to influence.

In its dying days, the Carter administration was blamed for the worldwide decline of American power and prestige. As Henry Kissinger lamented, "We are sliding toward a world out of control, with our relative military power declining, with our economic lifeline increasingly vulnerable to blackmail, with hostile radical forces growing in every continent, and with the number of countries willing to stake their future on our friendship dwindling."[1]

The Reagan administration promised to reverse these trends. In a speech delivered one year later to the same audience Kissinger addressed, the new Secretary of State, Alexander Haig, affirmed that the administration's primary foreign policy objective was "to enlarge our capacity to influence events and to make more effective use of the full range of our moral, political, scientific, economic, and military resources in the pursuit of our interests."[2] This reassertion of American power could come about largely through an act of will. "Confidence in ourselves," Haig argued," [is] the crucial psychological element in any foreign policy." Increased military spending was also necessary, in order to stiffen our resolve, augment our capabilities, and make our threats and blandishments more credible.

Central America looked like a good place to begin to reassert the will and power of the United States. The countries were small, our supply lines were short, and the Soviet Union was far away. Secretary Haig announced that the United States was prepared to do "whatever is necessary" to prevail in El Salvador. Yet, Central America has refused to be pacified. Instead, the Caribbean Basin has become the United States' own circle of crisis. The winds of political change carry sparks across the firebreaks we have made, igniting brushfires in country after country.

In Central America, the United States is trying to recapture control over events by resorting with increased rigor and determination to old formulae. As befits the postcolonial period, the United States recognizes it cannot rule directly and is working instead to align itself with selected local elites. Military officers, businessmen, and cooperative, "moderate" politicians are the political vehicles we have chosen. Our policymakers hope that with decisive American backing these groups can maintain or gain power and install regimes that are aligned with the United States. We are employing a wide range of traditional instruments to accomplish these objectives: economic and military aid, large-scale training of intelligence and army officers, covert aid to friendly parties and media, persistent propaganda for "our" friends and against "our" enemies, and incessant diplomatic maneuvering. The United States has followed similar strategies in many other places. On occasion they have worked—at least momentarily. But, as is evident in Central America, these policies are increasingly ineffective and, even when they do seem to work, increasingly costly.

The fires continue to burn in Central America: economies are contracting sharply; violence is escalating; and tensions among states are rising. Declining per capita GNP withers the popularity of those governments Washington prefers. The local firefighters, whom we have been counting on to follow our prescriptions and restore stability, have been rejecting our advice and arguing among themselves. Guerrilla groups blaze up seemingly overnight. Cuba, whom we accuse of arson, is more influential than ever.

The setbacks in Central America are the consequences of policies based on false assumptions regarding American influence, the nature of Third World politics, and the imperatives of our national interest.

We are overestimating our ability to control events in other countries—even in small, nearby ones. Generals like Somoza in Nicaragua, Romero in El Salvador, and Lucas Garcia in Guatemala have ignored our best advice and resisted our pressures. Businessmen and centrist politicians have often acted against our preferred strategies or have been unable to organize themselves and win. Incantations of American will and self-confidence and increased military spending cannot readily reverse this historic trend.

We also forget that the U.S. government controls only a small percentage of the economic resources at stake. Private firms and banks —U.S. and Central American—have been removing much larger amounts of capital than our government has been able to pump in. Autonomous shocks in international commodity, capital, and export markets have also struck against official U.S. objectives.

Moreover, we frequently ignore or attempt to block the growing influence of other states whose policies and interests do not perfectly match our own. Other foreign governments can match our official aid efforts—but will not always place their capital behind Washington's purposes. Regional powers—Mexico, Venezuela—as well as interested Western European governments have become active agents in Central America. When we dismiss their influence, we are in danger of miscalculating the course of events. When we try to push them aside, we generate unnecessary bilateral conflicts and, more importantly, work against solutions in Central America that may not be optimal but that should be acceptable.

Too often, the United States has been trapped by ideological preconceptions. We react strongly against nationalist rhetoric, whether coming from the right or left. Regimes that prefer a strong state role in the economy are severely criticized and credits are withheld. Governments are attacked for failing to meet our democratic ideals. In particular, we have assumed that leftists are irreconcilably hostile and will inevitably seek alliance with Cuba and the Soviet Union. Only positively friendly governments are considered safe. No room is left for genuine nonalignment.

Not surprisingly, policies based on these assumptions increase conflict within Central America, and between groups in that troubled region and the United States. Efforts to assert U.S. control leave little room for the expression of local will. Worse still, the risk is great that the United States will fail. Even when the United States seems to win one battle, new troubles sprout elsewhere, and the cycles of violence are shortening.

These same misconceptions reappear in U.S. policy throughout the Third World:

- We overestimate our ability to control Israel, as Prime Minister Menachem Begin made clear when he rebuffed our protest for his annexation of the Golan Heights in late 1981:

  > What kind of talk is this, "punishing Israel?" Are we a vassal state of yours? Are we a banana republic? Are we 14-year-olds who, if we misbehave, we get our wrists slapped? . . . He who threatens us will find us deaf to his threats.[3]

- Similarly, we imagine that the U.S. government possesses the economic resources to stabilize friendly governments, such as those in Morocco and Kenya, only to find our aid programs overwhelmed by gyrations in the international prices of phosphate, coffee, oil, and capital. Private firms make their own decisions: shunning pressures from Washington, American-owned oil companies have refused to abandon Libya, and U.S. bank branches in Europe gladly accept Qaddafi's petrodollars and pay him market rates of interest.

- Just as we have brushed aside the advice of Mexico in Central America, so has the United States failed to listen carefully to Saudi Arabia. Preferring to follow its own gameplan for the Middle East,

> the Reagan administration largely ignored the peace plan forwarded by Crown Prince (now King) Fahd in late 1981; the promising proposal held out the possibility of Saudi recognition of Israel in the context of a settlement of the Palestinian question.
>
> Our ideological preconceptions have blinded us to the opportunities for working more closely with nonaligned nations like Iraq, Algeria, and India.

The Reagan administration holds no monopoly on mistakes in Central America and the Third World. The Carter administration and others before it committed their share. However, it is not enough to assign blame; it is more important to devise alternative approaches to interpreting and defending U.S. interests. There is a better way to define a place in the world for the United States that is safe for us and for others.

The National Interest

"Reassertionism," the Reagan foreign policy, responds to a heightened sense of threat to American interests and purpose. Reassertionists fear that radical forces in the Third World will take advantage of local instabilities, overthrow pro-U.S. governments, and build pro-Soviet regimes. One after another, these hostile regimes will gradually tilt the global balance of power away from Washington and toward Moscow. As Kissinger warned, "the seemingly marginal enroachments (of Soviet power) cumulatively now amount to a major erosion of the free world's security."[4] These pro-Soviet radical regimes are also seen as a threat to U.S. business and U.S. access to raw materials. As they multiply, they will work to isolate American capitalism and culture.

This gloomy vision derives from a worldview formed in the years following World War II, when the Soviet Union established military control over Eastern Europe and deprived the West of their markets. Then Communists triumphed in China, allied themselves with the Soviet Union, and largely withdrew from the international economy.

Both U.S. economic and security interests seemed to require the containment of change in the Third World. The world was locked in ice.

This Cold War vision was based on one definition of the U.S. national interest. A sense of the national interest, intuitive or explicit, lies behind any coherent foreign policy.[5] Many academics despair of arriving at a theoretically satisfying definition, and correctly point out that different groups within society have separate and sometimes conflicting interests. Nevertheless, policymakers—at least good ones—have a working definition in mind.

The Cold War doctrine of global containment held an expansive view of U.S. interests and the threats they faced. Any growth of Soviet power could pose a danger to world order. Since the Soviet Union was seen as being engaged in "piecemeal aggression," appeasement would only lead to "gradual withdrawals under pressure until we discover one day that we have sacrificed positions of vital interest."[6] Moreover, failure to honor commitments to one regime would shake the structure of our entire foreign policy. As Lyndon Johnson warned, "There are a hundred other little nations . . . watching what happens. . . . If South Vietnam can be gobbled up, the same thing can happen to them."[7] The mettle of American power could be tested at any place, any time.

Geopolitics and ideology were one. The Soviet Union was both our chief military adversary and the fountainhead of global Communism. The advance of socialist forces anywhere inevitably resulted in a gain for Soviet power. The defeat of an anti-Communist regime was therefore a loss for American power. The very existence of a Communist movement created a U.S. interest in that country, however distant or small it might be. Freedom was indivisible.

Global containment was a doctrine for the "high politics" of national security. Economics was "low politics" and left to bankers and technocrats. But the United States did have a foreign economic policy during the Cold War. Economic "liberalism" emphasized the free flow of commodities and capital across national boundaries. A stable, open and predictable international economic order was needed to permit the growth of both the national and global economies. The United States and Great Britain established the International Monetary Fund to uphold the new rules. Its basic document, the Articles of Agreement, commanded the Fund "to facilitate the expansion and balanced growth of international trade . . . to promote exchange stability . . . [to assist] in the elimination of foreign exchange restrictions which hamper the growth of world trade . . . [to provide countries with the] opportunity to correct maladjustments in their balance of payments without resorting to measures destructive of national or international prosperity." Nationalist impulses toward autarky were thwarted to ensure an ever-expanding global system.

Economic liberalism and global containment were mutually reinforcing strategies. Countries with liberal—that is, capitalist economies —were allied with the United States against the centrally planned Soviet bloc. Economic blocs neatly overlapped with military alliances.

Inside Third World countries, the United States sought allies favorably disposed to our security and economic visions. From our vantage point, local businessmen and military leaders seemed the most reliable allies. Internationally oriented businessmen extolled a liberal economic order, while local militaries were guarantors of our security interests. Although conservative or centrist civilian political parties were occasionally favored, the United States often felt they were too fragile or erratic to be reliable.

The meshing of global containment and economic liberalism began to unravel with the Sino-Soviet split. Countries with centrally planned economies became strategic enemies. Moreover, as Western Europe and then the United States began to expand trade and financial relations with Eastern Europe and even the Soviet Union itself, military opponents became economic partners. In addition, the actions of Third World states further undermined the assumptions that equated political conservatism with pro-Americanism, and economic nationalism with pro-Sovietism.

During the Cold War, the global containment doctrine was challenged by a diverse group of "realist" critics, including Walter Lippmann, Hans Morgenthau, George Kennan (in some of his writings), and George Ball.[8] While equally concerned to contain Soviet power, realists sought more refined and measured means of doing so. Distinguishing a continuum from vital to peripheral interests, realists sought to be more discriminating in their definition of the national interest. Since resources were limited, the United States should be more circumspect before entering into commitments to countries of secondary importance. Western Europe was vital—many areas of the Third World were not. The global containment doctrine had misused and squandered American power in attempting to impose a Pax Americana on six continents, beyond what was necessary to secure our territorial, cultural, and economic well-being.

Realists were not always comfortable with political change. Nevertheless, some recognized that even violent change in the Third World was not necessarily a threat to the United States. This was true because nonalignment and Third World nationalism can become bulkwarks against Soviet expansion.

Realists also sought to constrain the role of ideology in American foreign policy. It was a mistake to identify the "moral aspirations of a particular nation with the moral laws that govern the universe."[9] The United States should not be obsessed with projecting its own national experience onto the international arena.

Realists distinguished themselves from those who would make ideas, not power and alliances, the organizing element in American foreign policy.[10] The realists argued that the interwar years had demonstrated that a policy based on "Wilsonian idealism" was bound to produce disappointment and lead to cycles of activism and withdrawal. Such unstable emotionalism was ill-suited to a Great Power whose permanent responsiblity was to introduce some order into world affairs. "World order" idealists, who sought to reduce the role of power and even of nation states in favor of international law and cooperation, were also considered utopian. If they were believed, America might lower its guard, while other states would continue to play by the old rules of self-aggrandizement.

Today, a new approach is needed that would draw on the realist modification of global containment and on the virtues of economic liberalism. This construction—neorealism—must take into account the important changes in the capabilities of the United States, in the Third World, and in the international economy that have transpired over the last thirty years.[11] The elements of realism and liberalism that are dead wood must be pruned, and some new concepts must be grafted.

Neorealism

Stated succinctly, neorealism concentrates on defending the vital interests of Americans—their life, liberty and property. In the modern world, this translates into protecting our physical security by building (within the NATO alliance) strategic forces capable of deterring a Soviet attack, and designing a foreign policy that curbs the Soviet Union from gaining strength by expanding its control over other states. Our economic well-being can be secured by an open and growing international economy, and an American economy sufficiently robust to compete globally. The third vital American interest—the freedom of our political institutions—is guarded indirectly, by a successful defense of our physical security and economic welfare, and by a diplomacy that occasionally reaffirms, and does not generally contradict, our ideals.

Expressed at this level of generality, neorealism is not particularly new. More controversial, perhaps, than neorealism's definition of America's vital interests is its conception of the threats that face us in the Third World, and its prescriptions for dealing with them.

Like realism, neorealism recognizes that nation states remain the organizing units of world politics. Governments will continue to defend what they perceive as their national interests. Tensions and even conflicts among states will continue to provide the lead stories for the network news. The United States cannot be safe without a strong military, and must check the expansionist tendencies of the one nation that could physically threaten us—the Soviet Union.

Neorealism, however, notes that governments now have great difficulty in controlling many private agents, especially multinational corporations and banks.[12] Rather than treating these economic forces as threats to state power, neorealism considers them to be potentially positive elements for U.S. diplomacy. In this sense, neorealism is more supportive of liberal economics than are those reassertionists who would give government the power to marshall the nation's economic resources behind its immediate diplomatic objectives.

Neorealism places a greater emphasis on economics than did most realist forebearers. U.S. influence is still partly a function of military power, but armed force is of diminishing utility in many Third World contingencies. Changes in the world economy and polity have transformed economics into the strong suit of the United States. Indeed, security and economics can no longer be treated as separate realms.

The fundamental tenet of economic liberalism remains valid: an expanding and open international economy is still the system that best promotes prosperity for the United States. Moreover, the continued flow of capital and commodities between the industrial and developing states will not eliminate all differences, but will create important mutual interests. Today's liberal order, however, corresponds not to a 19th-century, laissez-faire model, but to a modern system where governments are active in influencing markets, and large corporations and banks are prime movers of resources.

Whereas realists generally focused on Europe, neorealism gives more explicit attention to the Third World. While they cannot typically affect the strategic military balance, Third World states have gained substantially in economic and even military strength.

In the neorealist view, the structure of the international economic system importantly affects many actions of Third World countries. Third World leaders frequently find that their nation's material interests contradict their professed ideology. Being generally rational, Third World governments eventually bow to necessity. Therefore, changes in the leadership, and even the domestic institutions, of Third World nations, do not necessarily pose a threat to the international economy.

Neorealism rejects the tendency in global containment strategy to identify U.S. interests with particular governments, and to seek to align them with the United States. We must not confuse U.S. interests in a country with the stability of a particular regime. The decline of our ability to shape events within a Third World state need not be seen *ipso facto* as a gain for Soviet diplomacy. A rigid and schematic "zero sum" view of the world must be replaced by the acceptance of a decentralized, pluralist world in constant flux. Edges are fuzzier, outcomes less definitive and relations more complex.

Global containment strategists sometimes behaved as though the United States needed to maximize its influence abroad. Only then could the United States rest secure that the Soviet Union and its allies would not fill "power vacuums." In the neorealist view, other forces, including nationalism and regional powers, have emerged beyond the superpowers capable of filling these spaces. The containment of Soviet power, therefore, can be accomplished with a less direct extension of American power.

Neorealism would constrain the role of ideology in American foreign policy. Neorealism emphasizes that foreign policy is a window, not a mirror. It is both unnecessary and often counterproductive for the United States to allow ideology to cloud its perception of events and foreign governments. The survival of our culture and economy do not require that other nations copy us. We can form useful ties with nations that have chosen other ways to organize themselves. U.S. foreign policy should be rational and pragmatic in responding to cultural differences with other nations.

At the same time, whereas some realists decried ideology altogether, neorealism accepts that ideas will inevitably influence history. While ideology should not dominate U.S. foreign policy, a carefully crafted human rights policy can assist American diplomacy in adapting to change in Third World countries, while serving, indirectly, to strengthen humanistic sentiments within the United States.

Neorealism, then, provides a description of the Third World, a method for interpreting events there and their likely impact on the United States, and general guidelines for U.S. policy.

HISTORICAL PRECEDENTS

The use of economic structures to protect U.S. interests in the Third World—on the reasoning that military force is generally unnecessary and often only amplifies tensions—clearly has its precedents. In announcing the Good Neighbor Policy, for example, President Franklin D. Roosevelt promised to place the "big stick" in the closet, to withdraw United States Marines from Haiti and not return them to Nicaragua, and to respect the sovereignty of the Latin American states. Financial credits became the preferred means for competing with the Axis powers for hemispheric influence. Direct intervention was seen as creating deep resentments and carving openings for Japanese and German penetration. As Roosevelt told his close aide, Henry Stimson, "Latin Americans would always be jealous of us," but "it was very important to remove any legitimate grounds of their criticism."[13] As an historian of the period has noted,

> The Good Neighbor policy was partly an admission that the United States should act more tactfully in its relations with weaker neighbors, and partly a realization that military intervention actually hindered the effective employment of American economic and military power. Nor was it morally consistent to condemn Japan's forward movement while continuing and initiating military intervention in equally doubtful circumstances.[14]

Of course, the Good Neighbor Policy labored under the paternalism inherent in the wholly asymmetric power relations between the United States and the Latin America of those days. When even the larger Latin nations ran into balance of payments difficulties, the U.S. government was often able to supply sufficient credits to alleviate the crises. A single U.S. firm, Pan American Airways, held a near monopoly over mail and passenger cargoes in many parts of the hemisphere. Still, the Good Neighbor Policy established a successful precedent in American foreign policy. By employing economic diplomacy rather than direct intervention, and by tolerating nationalism even when it took on anti-U.S. tones, FDR provided the foundation for securing the cooperation of most of the hemisphere during the Second World War.

THE CARTER EXPERIMENT

The Carter administration also contained the seeds of a neorealist diplomacy. Several of Carter's advisers recognized some of the global trends that make neorealism sensible. Vietnam had taught the difficulties of controlling events within Third World states. The United States not only failed to defeat the insurgents, but was repeatedly frustrated by the refusal of our clients in Saigon to follow our counsel. The Vietnam experience had also shown that Americans were hesitant to pay the costs of control. Especially in its early phase, the Carter administration sometimes viewed political shifts within Third World states more benignly. The administration believed that the strong pull of Western economic institutions, local nationalism, and Soviet bungling would combine to preserve U.S. interests in the Third World in the longer run. Although the human rights policy was an idealist reaction to the ready resort to force and coercion of the Kissinger era, it also recognized the inevitability of social change in the Third World, and the wisdom of the United States adopting a more flexible response. For the United States rigidly to ally itself with crumbling autocracies was not only nasty but self-defeating. The emerging winners of internal disputes in other countries would not necessarily be hostile to U.S. interests, but we might make them so. Although the appeal of the Soviet Union was declining in the Third World, an aggressive or rigid American posture could create opportunities for Moscow. It made no sense to lock the doors and windows and hand the burglar the keys.

Although it did represent an important shift, the Carter foreign policy also shared many more traditional assumptions regarding U.S. interests than its conservative critics allow. The Carter administration continued to try to work its will in the Third World through close relations with regional powers, and generally sought to guarantee American interests within Third World countries by supporting the same traditional elites. While the administration was less likely to engage in covert action, or to intervene massively in the event of an impending unfavorable outcome, it continued (with some notable exceptions) to try to manipulate events according to more or less traditional criteria. Moreover, the continued attention paid to the rhetoric of Third World leaders and movements betrayed lingering concerns regarding a traditional view of U.S. prestige and power in the world. Most importantly, the Carter neorealists' relatively sophisticated view of political currents was not matched by a sophisticated awareness of developments in economic institutions. The division of the world into "free market" and "socialist" economies persisted.

Finally, the Soviet Union's drive for influence in the Third World was never sufficiently taken into account in their analysis. Cuban activities in Africa, and then the Soviet entrance into Afghanistan, severely undermined their position. Moreover, the downfall of the Shah in Iran and of Somoza in Nicaragua was widely perceived as the result of faulty Carter policies that had needlessly created openings for the Soviet Union. Carter seemed to be yielding helplessly to aggressively anti-American, and manifestly or potentially pro-Soviet, forces. With no other recourse prepared, the alternative choices seemed to be appeasement or a return to the Cold War.

To be fair, the neorealists were few in number, and they never even controlled the State Department, let alone the rest of the foreign policy bureaucracy. Nevertheless, the lack on their part of a comprehensive and integrated view of the world and of U.S. interests impeded consistent action and advocacy, and left the neorealist faction exposed to criticism. Because neorealism signified a marked shift away from the assumptions undergirding U.S. policy since the late 1940s, its practitioners would have to have had a consistent set of priorities based upon a comprehensive view of the world. A new strategic vision had to be articulated and vigorously defended within the bureaucracy and before the wider public. Instead, neorealists in the Carter administration responded on a case-by-case basis. They yielded in a series of compromises on policy and on public pronouncements until the administration appeared to be sailing without a compass. Uncharted reefs suddenly appeared in familiar seas. The actors themselves generally failed to see how these compromises undercut their ability to project a strategy—until it was too late. By the time Secretary Vance resigned in early 1980, the critics—both inside and outside the administration—were in full offensive. They, at least, seemed to offer a consistent, ordered, and familiar set of principles based on an interpretation of current history.

With its stark emphasis on power projection and military might, the Reagan administration represents a sharp rejection of neorealism.

International economics is downgraded, while laissez-faire liberalism is extolled as a model for all nations. Like their Cold War ancestors, the Reaganites are ideological maximalists. In strategic affairs, Reaganism embodies that more aggressive branch of containment strategy: that which seeks security not through a balance-of-power equilibrium but through superiority over an untrustworthy foe.

LOOKING AHEAD

My intention here will be to pick up where the Carter administration neorealists left off. No book can possibly anticipate all the crises that will confront future administrations and present a detailed blueprint of responses. But it is possible to paint a picture of the Third World in the 1980s, to outline the nature of the problems posed for the United States, and to construct some appropriate policy guidelines that will best defend our national interests. This framework for analyzing future events must be clear and complete enough so as to provide an alternative to falling back on old instincts when domestic pressures and foreign troubles mount, as occurred during the second half of the Carter experiment.

The central message of this book is that the world has actually become safer for the United States—if we can learn to seize the opportunities presented to us. A new order has emerged, and it is characterized by an integrated but pluralistic economy, where nation states are both more fragmented and more resistant to control by the Great Powers. It is a world in which threats that once loomed so large are no longer so forboding. Those national interests that are still pressing are within our reach to preserve.

This book is organized around a series of questions regarding the current state of the Third World and of U.S.-Third World relations. Why has the Third World been escaping from our control? Does the decline of political influence necessarily pose a threat to the United States? What does the global economy look like in the 1980s, and what potential advantages does it offer to U.S. diplomacy? How is the Soviet

Union faring in this new environment? Is Moscow being more successful in shaping the ambitions, rivalries, and growing strength of Third World states to its own profit? In seeking to respond to social change and to contain Soviet power, is the United States using its diplomatic tools wisely and spending its economic resources efficiently? (Many of the particular "global village" issues—exploitation of the seas, food supply, energy resources, poverty alleviation, migration—are not directly addressed, although the broader issues discussed here affect the general climate in which these problems are debated.)

The final chapter offers a neorealist prescription for U.S. policy that seeks to define the genuine threats we face in the Third World, and proposes strategies to surmount them. Economics is integrated into U.S. security policy to form a coherent strategic vision for the U.S. role in the Third World of the 1980s.

1 *A Less Controllable World*

Many State Department officials devote much of their time to efforts to influence the internal affairs of Third World states. In our well-staffed Asian, African, Middle Eastern, and Latin American bureaus, officials spend their day gathering and processing information on the latest developments *within* their assigned countries. They read embassy and CIA cables, and occasionally meet face-to-face with foreign government officials, businessmen, and politicians. Lower-level officials assemble and collate this information, and then pass it up the bureaucratic ladder where decisionmakers use it in devising plans. Once policy has been formulated, individuals and groups in the target country must be persuaded, cajoled, intimidated, or forced into acting their assigned roles in Washington's script. Higher-level U.S. government officials will meet with target-country leaders, while lower-level State Department bureaucrats will seek to influence the more junior actors. Embassy personnel will be cabled their instructions and dispatched into field action.

The American public knows little about this elaborate machinery for stage-managing the history of other nations. As every State Department official recognizes, many news stories on U.S. foreign policy are replete with information provided on "background" to reporters, with planted "leaks" to favored journalists, and with carefully crafted official statements. This controlled flow of data is designed to mobilize and maintain public support for policy, not to inform the electorate. When an enterprising reporter learns too much, the seventh floor of the State Department, or the White House itself, will raise an outcry and demand the sealing of these "unauthorized" leaks.

Yet, it is difficult to pretend that the smell of dead fish is anything other than the smell of dead fish. Eventually, the public comes to learn about the more spectacular failures of American foreign policy, and these have been mounting. More recently, the apparent defeats in Cuba, Angola, Iran, Ethiopia, and Nicaragua have shaken American confidence. Americans could see their flag being burnt, figuratively and literally, on the nightly news. Even more puzzling and frightening has been the actual collapse of American-backed regimes, and the victory of apparently hostile factions, with the U.S. government a helpless witness. The seizure of the U.S. embassy in Teheran and Washington's inability to free its own hostage diplomats displayed America's new weakness before the whole world.

Ronald Reagan campaigned against this decline in American power as though he were a football coach addressing his team in the locker room before the Big Game. He promised to recoup America's greatness, to make America number one again in the arena of foreign relations. There would be no more American hostages, no more forsaken, friendly governments. Americans at home would once again be comfortable and secure, while their diplomats quietly rewarded friends and punished enemies abroad. Our control over history would be restored.

President Reagan and his supporters have blamed America's declining fortunes in the Third World on several factors.[1] The loss of American superiority in strategic nuclear weapons meant that Washington could no longer demand, as Kennedy had done in the Cuban missile crisis, that the Soviet Union back down in a Third World theater or face nuclear attack. With less to fear, the Soviets had become bolder in supporting forces hostile to the United States. Détente and the "Vietnam syndrome" also supposedly undermined the U.S. position. Détente, the reduction in tensions between NATO and the Soviet bloc, lulled the West into dropping its guard, while the Soviets purportedly took advantage of European peace to divert their resources into operations in the Third World. The Vietnam syndrome meanwhile prevented the United States from aiding friendly governments abroad who were under attack by Soviet-supported forces. The fear of another costly and bloody intervention paralyzed Washington. Finally, the naïveté, fecklessness, and incompetence of the Carter administration institutionalized America's decay.

As the Reagan Administration has discovered, engaging in a nuclear buildup, scrapping détente, and rejecting the Vietnam syndrome will not automatically reverse our fortunes in the Third World. The Soviets are still in Afghanistan; the Vietnamese occupy Cambodia; Mugabe, Frelimo and the Popular Movement for the Liberation of Angola (MPLA) rule in Southern Africa; and Fidel Castro remains in Havana. The Rapid Deployment Force could not save Sadat; and "our side" in Central America continues to lose ground. Even allies in our traditional "sphere of influence" such as Brazil and Argentina have not foresworn their ties to the Soviet Union, disappointing those who had placed great faith in a more forceful U.S. posture.

A closer look at our problems in dealing with the Third World suggests that a hardening of our attitudes and a change in personnel at the State Department will not be sufficient antidotes. Nor will more competent policy planners and a greater volume of cable traffic enable Washington to press buttons and make history happen. These traditional remedies are closer to snake oils than to magic bullets. Our problems in the Third World originate in a profound series of developments that have transformed the international environment over the last generation.

The Third World Challenge

The economic and social landscape of Latin America and much of Asia and Africa has changed with blurring rapidity as the train of modernization has accelerated during the postwar period. Traditional, vulnera-

LIBRARY
COLBY-SAWYER COLLEGE
96349 NEW LONDON, N.H. 03257

ble, agrarian societies have been transformed into diversified economies with modern, commercially organized, agricultural and industrial sectors. Simultaneously, governments have grown stronger with the recruitment of new generations of trained technocrats and managers, the creation or enlargement of national security forces and intelligence services, and the expansion of state control over the economy. In some countries, civil society has become more vibrant with the emergence of cohesive and representative interest groups, or of mass-based political movements. In the lesser developed countries, these trends have been superimposed upon the most fundamental stage of "modernization," a process that witnesses the disintegration of communal, tribal, or regional cultures, and the integration of the nation's farmlands and towns into a national market.

Compared to the situation that the colonial powers found in the heydays of imperialism, when a small flotilla of gunboats could manhandle an ancient civilization or conquer disorganized territories, many of today's Third World states wield much more formidable degrees of organized power. The French, for example, were able to subdue Algeria with only thirty thousand soldiers in 1830, whereas a force twenty times as large was inadequate by 1960. Examples to the contrary can be found in areas of deepening poverty and disorganization, especially sub-Saharan Africa, but these are exceptions. While most Third World states may not yet be powerful enough to guarantee their own sovereignty, it has certainly become more problematical for foreign powers arbitrarily to impose their will upon them.

Many American analysts attributed the success of the Vietnamese communists to their ability to expropriate the banner of Vietnamese nationalism. Innumerable other instances, from the anti-Americanism of post-Shah Iran, to the plebiscite won by Chilean President Augusto Pinochet against foreign "human rights" criticisms, have confirmed the force of nationalist sentiments when they are harnessed by mass movements or strong leaders. American policymakers have learned from experience to pay at least lip service to the dangers of opposing Third World nationalism. This particular awareness, however, is no longer enough. A number of additional trends have deepened and accelerated the problems that await any foreign power attempting to control events in the Third World.

Economic developments abroad and at home have complicated the task of controlling the Third World. Political events in the developing world are heavily influenced by economic conditions, and now that the global economy has become unhinged, politics are even less predictable and harder to control. Moreover, the economic resources under the direct command of the U.S. government have shrunk compared to the expansion of global resources, further reducing our government's ability to manipulate overseas events. We are no longer the only big kid on the block. Just as our ability to resist Soviet pressures depends significantly on the successful coordination of policies with our NATO allies, so our ability to act in the Third World is conditioned by the actions and attitudes of the other Western powers. Yet underlying trends in the world economy, such as increased competition for export markets and for access to raw materials, are driving wedges between their interests and ours.

President Nixon and Secretary of State Kissinger had hoped to preserve world order, as they defined it, by allying closely with regional "influentials." The underlying assumption was that nations such as Iran, the Philippines, Saudi Arabia, and Brazil shared our basic interests and would protect them in their respective regions. In the interim years however, these nations have demonstrated that their fidelity is far from assured. Indeed, these new power centers are often wary of U.S. influence and intentionally seek independent courses based upon increasingly self-defined national interests. Given the legacies of colonialism and the attendant rise of Third World nationalisms, it isn't safe even for friendly governments blindly to follow U.S. policies. Moreover, if we are unwilling to pay the price of being the "world's policeman," why should others assume the risks of being labeled America's mercenaries?

Yet even when direct military intervention became less viable after Vietnam, the United States persisted in believing that it could maintain its influence within Third World states by allying with certain domestic forces. Remaining in power, these forces would presumably protect

U.S. interests both within their country and in the region. In most cases, the chosen allies were either local business or military elites. History has already proven that this strategy cannot guarantee U.S. objectives. Too often we have lacked the leverage to keep such allies in power, and even when they prevail, they may turn against us.

The United States is not devoid of influence, but unless we modify our ambitions and retune our policies, each successive scoreboard will record fewer successes and more failures. This chapter will elaborate the nature and consequences of the centrifugal forces that are pulling the Third World further from our control and to which we must now adapt.

Many of the country examples that follow will be from Latin America. If the United States cannot decisively influence the course of events in its own backyard, it can hardly hope to do so in more distant regions. Similarly, chapter 3, which analyzes the often parallel difficulties that the Soviet Union is experiencing in the Third World, will draw most of its illustrations from Asia and Africa, where Soviet influence is greatest.

Uncertainties in the Economic Environment

In the years between the end of World War II and the early 1970s, the international economy expanded at a rather steady rate. Third World governments therefore enjoyed an external economic environment relatively propitious for their own development. To the degree that steady economic growth will make governing easier, political stability was also more certain. The United States could earmark a portion of its own substantial economic assistance to further improve a friendly government's economic prospects, and thereby help keep it in power. While the scorecard on such attempts to use economic aid for political purposes was spotty, there were many successes.

Today, the international economic climate is ridden with hazards, and the U.S. government lacks the resources to right all of the miniature Titanics it sees succumbing to icebergs of external economic shock.

The skyrocketing costs of oil and other essential imports, the fluctuations in export earnings resulting from uneven growth in the Organization for Economic Cooperation and Development's (OECD) markets, and the uncertainties in financial markets have thrown many Third World economies into disarray. Their developmental paths cannot be predicted to any useful degree. Economic instabilities often lead to social unrest, which can further dampen economic prospects, and so initiate a descending cycle. The power of these economic maelstroms often dwarfs our best efforts to keep ships of state afloat or to otherwise control the political process.

A host of examples could illustrate how international economic turmoil has frustrated U.S. foreign policymakers in the late 1970s and early 1980s. U.S. efforts to stabilize the governments of Mobutu in Zaire and Kenneth Kaunda in Zambia, and to guarantee the liberalization process in Peru were all hampered, although not fatally, by the fluctuating and generally weak international copper market. The military overthrow of the American-backed democracy in Turkey in September 1980, was partially inspired by an economic crisis. The Turkish economy was severely wounded by an oil bill that was bleeding off over half of the nation's export earnings. In addition, the situation was aggravated by the economic slowdown in Western Europe that reduced the flow of earnings from Turkish "guest workers" who were laid off. The political liberation processes in Brazil and the Dominican Republic were threatened by externally induced economic disappointments. Poor economic performances, resulting from unfavorable swings in the terms of trade and from the fickle policies of private capital markets, were endangering democratic institutions throughout the English-speaking Caribbean. The decline of coffee prices in 1980–81 severely affected the economies of Central America, including that of the U.S.-supported junta in El Salvador. Conversely, high oil prices made antagonists such as Libya's Colonel Qaddafi less vulnerable to actual or potential American pressure. A full listing of the countries where political objectives were threatened by economic trends would be almost endless. Unless the international economic environment unexpectedly regains its balance in the 1980s, the political aftershocks are likely to become increasingly widespread and severe.

Unfortunately, these international economic instabilities have been deepening just as the resources at the command of U.S. foreign policymakers have been in relative decline. U.S. economic assistance, bilateral and multilateral, has fallen from 0.53 percent of the nation's gross national product in 1960 to 0.27 percent in 1980.[2] Moreover, the U.S. government's control over its aid contributions has been receding. The proportion of American financial assistance allocated to multilateral institutions (for example, the World Bank and the regional development banks) had risen from an average of 14 percent in 1969–71 to 30 percent in 1978–80.[3] To compound the trend, U.S. influence within these multilateral organizations, while still significant, has been perceptibly declining. We are no longer the overwhelming power in international finance that we were in an earlier era; no longer do we own all of the marbles.

The Reagan administration intends to offset this trend by shifting emphasis to bilateral aid, thereby hoping to regain political control of aid resources. The shift, however, will be only gradual and marginal. The administration agreed to honor existing commitments to the multilateral agencies, and the Office of Management and Budget has limited the expansion of bilateral aid.

The declining ratio of official aid to private capital flows has been even more disabling. During the 1970s, the eurocurrency and other international markets exploded, and the ratio of private to public financial resource flows to the developing world rose from 44 percent in 1970 to 64 percent in 1979.[4] The leverage of the U.S. government over these private flows is generally small. Banks, even when U.S.-owned, are rarely willing to alter their lending decisions to serve "the national interest" as interpreted by the State Department. Indeed, many bankers are suspicious of the political judgments of Washington bureaucrats.

In fact, during the Carter years, Latin American policy was frequently undercut when decisions of private U.S. lenders and investors ran counter to official policy. For example, the U.S. government sought to stabilize Jamaican democracy by sharply increasing bilateral aid flows, and the multilateral institutions also increased their commitments, but the U.S. private sector decided to decrease its exposure. Private business was responding to the deteriorating economic situation in Jamaica, as well as to the fears that the Manley government might turn further leftward. Despite very high per capita official aid inflows, the negative private-capital account played an important role in producing successive years of economic recession. Similarly, in 1979–80, the U.S. government poured economic aid into El Salvador to prop up a series of military/civilian juntas struggling against a strong leftist challenge. The decisions of U.S. lenders and investors to withdraw their lines of credit and other liquid assets more than offset these official inflows. Fearing political change in El Salvador, private banks and firms acted to protect their own interests in ways that harmed official U.S. efforts to rebuild the country's tottering political stability.

The Carter administration's efforts to improve the human rights performance of the Western Hemisphere's Southern Cone states—Argentina, Chile, and Uruguay—were undermined by the private international capital markets. The small amounts of bilateral economic or military aid that were withheld paled in comparison to the hundreds of millions of dollars each of these governments was borrowing from private creditors. Of course, the United States Treasury Department understandably was pleased to see these Latin states improve their credit ratings and become more integrated into the international financial system. But there was only silence over the fact that Washington's leverage against the political practices of the Southern Cone's governments had declined noticeably. Another balloon had popped and no one wanted to be caught holding the pin.

While he served as Secretary of State, Edmund Muskie lamented the decay of our official economic instruments. "Are we willing to commit sufficient resources to the defense of our interests and the promotion of our ideals abroad?" he asked in a speech before the Foreign Policy Association on 7 July 1980. Muskie surveyed our bilateral and multilateral economic assistance efforts, found them alarmingly wanting, and issued this warning:

> With [these programs] we have an opportunity to influence events in crucial areas of the world. Without them, our power to shape events is drastically diminished. All of us are concerned—and rightly so—that we not slip into military weakness. We are steadily modernizing our military posture. Yet cutting back our other international programs contributes to another kind of weakness, every bit as dangerous. It cuts back our arsenal of influence. Our support for liberty in the world—our defense of American and Western interests—cannot by mounted with military weapons alone. The battle for American influence in the world requires more than rockets, certainly more than rhetoric. It requires the resources that make diplomacy effective.

The future is likely to see a deepening of the trends of the 1970s. The economic resources under the direct command of U.S. foreign policymakers are likely to continue receding compared to those under private control, or compared to the probable growth of multilateral agencies. These agencies' structures will increasingly reflect the diffusion of global power and the relative decline of the United States in the world economy. Ironically, this will reflect the success of a major, postwar American foreign policy goal—the rebuilding of the shattered economies of Western Europe and Japan.

Competition among Industrial States

The United States' ability to work its will in Third World states often depends heavily on the cooperation of the other industrial countries. Such cooperation occured between the United States and France in 1979, when the two powers (together with Belgium) aided Zaire's President Mobutu to regain control over rebellious Shaba province. The United States supplied the airlift, while France, Belgium, and Morocco provided troops. All agreed that it was in their mutual interests to sustain Mobutu, and the economic costs for the limited military operation were small. In other cases, however, where the potential economic burden of cooperation has been much higher, our

European and Japanese allies have been less enthusiastic. When the United States refused to sell Libya commercial jets to protest Qaddafi's terrorism, France seized the opportunity to market its Airbus. Compliance with our economic sanctions against Iran following the November 1979 seizure of U.S. embassy personnel was reluctant and partial. Nor did our allies rush to join us in reducing economic ties with the Soviet Union following its military intervention into Afghanistan.

Competition among industrial states for export markets is accelerating at the same time that Third World markets are becoming more significant. By 1977, 37.6 percent of the European Community's exports were earmarked for the developing countries (up from 28.5 percent in 1973), and many nations outside of OPEC were included among the expanding markets.[5] By 1980, meanwhile, the developing world (including OPEC) was absorbing more than one-third of all U.S. exports. During the 1970–78 period, U.S. exports of capital goods to developing countries more than quadrupled, jumping from less than $5 billion to more than $22 billion. As export drives intensify, and the domestic stakes get higher (fewer jobs and a lower rate of internal growth), the Europeans and Japanese will be less receptive to exhortations from the United States to use economic sanctions to achieve political purposes in third areas. In fact, our allies are reluctant even to take diplomatic positions that might jeopardize relations with trading partners. European willingness to move closer to Arab views on the Palestinian question clearly reflects both their dependency on Middle Eastern petroleum and their intentions to maintain or increase their shares of the profitable OPEC markets.

Already American efforts to alter Third World states' behavior by restraining certain types of exports have been undercut by other industrial countries. When the United States sought to halt nuclear weapons proliferation by embargoing certain categories of nuclear technology in the absence of sufficient safeguards, this valiant policy was undermined repeatedly by other suppliers' willingness to sell with lesser safeguards.[6] The United States has also tried to dampen the Latin American arms race by refusing to sell the more sophisticated conventional weapons in our own arsenal. This policy's intent was thwarted when enthusiastic European and Soviet merchants rushed to fill the vacuum and to benefit from American scruples. While U.S. restraint may have reduced overall Latin arms purchases, the visible result was a sharp decline in the U.S. share of actual Latin weapons procurements.

The United States has tried using the international development banks to alter Third World states' political behavior. In the mid-1970s, Congress mandated that the administration vote against development bank loans to governments committing "gross and flagrant" violation of human rights. Carter administration officials voted against approximately one hundred loans on "human rights" grounds, but nearly all still received the required majority of votes. The Europeans, who command a major share of the voting power in the development banks, refused in almost all cases to inject "political" considerations. Instead, they emphasized that the banks should concentrate on their essential functions—the financing of economic development and industrial-country exports in Third World markets. With few exceptions, the Third World's representatives, sometimes fearful that their country might one day be guilty of human rights violations, agreed with the European view. To be sure, U.S. lobbying within the banks did kill some loans before they could reach the boards of directors for formal voting. On the whole, however, the European accent on maintaining the "economic integrity" of the banks defeated the U.S. efforts to alter the banks' lending patterns away from governments that were denying human rights.

Since the increased importance of Third World markets raises the commercial costs of using economic instruments as leverage for political or diplomatic ends, coordinated diplomacies among the industrial states will become more difficult. Each nation will temper its positions to appeal to countries with growing purchasing power; no one wants to be excluded from cooking for the banquet. This increased ability of Third World states to play the industrial countries off against each other will make economic sanctions less enforceable and generally complicate our diplomacy. The trend toward increasingly fierce competition among the industrial "allies" for shares of the Third World's lucrative markets should accelerate, at least through the end of the century.

The Regional Influentials

During the Vietnam War and its immediate aftermath, many Americans concluded that the number and the nature of our overseas commitments exceeded our capabilities to honor them. President Kennedy's inaugural pledge to "pay any price, bear any burden, meet any hardship, support any friend, oppose any foe," had lost its appeal to a war-weary nation. Even before the economic trends discussed above were fully apparent, some Americans were arguing for redefining our interests to coincide with our ability and willingness to defend them.[7] Instead, the Nixon administration reaffirmed our existing commitments and searched for new strategies to secure them.

In 1969, on Guam, President Nixon proclaimed the "Nixon Doctrine," which included a plan gradually to withdraw U.S. troops from Vietnam and strengthen the South Vietnamese military (ARVN). The direct U.S. presence would be replaced by a friendly local force. In other areas of the world, the analogy to "Vietnamization" was reliance on friendly regional powers whose vision of their security interests presumably accorded with our own. As Secretary of Defense Melvin Laird stated: "America will no longer play policeman to the world. Instead we will expect other nations to provide more cops on the beat in their own neighborhood."[8] In return for our support and out of their own convergent motives, regional powers would protect our interests in their own spheres of influence.

Vietnamization collapsed when the ARVN troops disintegrated before the final NLF/North Vietnamese offensive. Like a cat with nine lives, the Nixon Doctrine survived to be applied to other areas of the world. In fact, it even survived Nixon's resignation in disgrace. The doctrine was adopted and broadened in considerable measure by the Carter administration under the slogan of "integrating the upper-tier developing nations into the global system." Yet the inadequacies of the doctrine as a means to secure U.S. interests as traditionally defined have become increasingly apparent. Four difficulties have plagued the policy. First, the rulers of the regional influentials were often themselves unstable partners in power. Second, "special relationships" with one nation dragged the United States into regional rivalries, making our allies' enemies our own. Third, the chosen regional powers have not always been able to prevail in local crises. And finally, the influentials have not always shared American security concerns.

UNSTABLE ALLIES

The fall of the Shah of Iran unmasked the fragility of some of our Third World friends. Other friendly regional powers with less-than-stable governments as of early 1983, included: Guatemala, Argentina, and Brazil in Latin America; Egypt, Morocco, Saudi Arabia, and Zaire in Africa and the Middle East; and Indonesia, Pakistan, and the Philippines in Asia. Secondary powers whose existing governments were endangered included: Somalia, Sudan, Tunisia, South Korea, and Thailand. Our security arrangements are subject—even prisoner—to the stability of individual rulers in many of these lands. Although such personal alliances seem to offer the most certain rewards (one need rely only on the word of a strongman who can enforce his will) the dangers are also magnified. Should this single leader fall, who or what will fill the vacuum?

Nowhere was this more apparent than in Iran. Contrary to the popular perception, the United States tried desperately to help the Shah retain power: we continued to the last to supply him with both modern weaponry and crowd control equipment; we sent a special military emissary to bolster the resolve of his military officers; President Carter repeatedly voiced our firm support for the Shah; and we persisted in offering him our best advice.[9] Just two months before the Shah fled Teheran, Carter's assistant for national security affairs, Zbigniew Brzezinski, informed the Shah by telephone that the United States would support him if he used whatever force was necessary to quell the gathering revolution.

Our inability to save the Shah had many roots. Some may have been embedded only in Iranian soil, but several can be seen extending to other unhappy moments in the history of U.S. policymaking. Certainly this would include Vietnam, Nicaragua during Somoza's last days, and the unnecessary intervention in the Dominican Republic in 1965. For example, in Iran and elsewhere our information about "what was happening on the ground"—local social and political trends—was faulty.[10] Few embassy political officers spoke the native language or had contacts outside of a narrow circle of upper-crust Iranians. Additionally, for its data the CIA relied heavily on the Shah's own security force, SAVAK, which was neither an objective nor an especially perceptive source. Consequently, we failed to grasp the depth and breadth of the opposition. Incredible as it now seems, a comprehensive study written by the CIA the year before the Shah's demise concluded that: "Iran is not in a revolutionary or even a 'prerevolutionary' situation."[11]

Even when the intelligence was solid, the bureaucracies' ability to interpret information and to deliver honest and objective analyses to top policymakers was sometimes hampered by the fear of displeasing superiors who did not want to hear bad news. The White House was particularly loath to receive assessments that the Shah's government was crumbling. Our government feared negative political fallout at home and was under pressure from friendly governments, such as Saudi Arabia and Morocco, who worried that the Shah's fall could foreshadow their own. American policymakers, preferring to indulge in shadow-casting and wishful thinking, screened out information that failed to confirm their chosen views. Such "cognitive dissonance" is especially common—and disastrous—in moments of extreme stress.[12]

These decision-making problems are compounded by the inherent difficulty of trying to control events occurring thousands of miles away. In crises, decision making typically rests in the hands of the president and his chief advisers. One ingrained difficulty immediately suggests itself. With responsibilities for endless strings of important issues, top officials cannot possibly be well informed on the historical background and local complexities of each sudden Third World crisis.[13] Moreover, it is very hard for them fully to grasp the political mood in a distant nation fast enough to devise appropriate strategies. This certainly occurred in Iran, where the images policymakers held of a complex political dynamic lagged several days or even weeks behind the events. In such crises, the tendency is to select prescriptions that events have already rendered obsolete. Our failures in this regard have become so common that the Washington bureaucracy has coined a phrase for them: "being behind the power curve."

Even if fewer mistakes had been committed in intelligence collection, information processing, and decision making, the United States could not have saved the Shah. By 1978, virtually all of the major Iranian social and political groups had turned against him. Each grouping had its own accumulated grievances, but all were now united in the common cause of unseating the hated Shah. When we finally turned in desperation to the Iranian military to crush the rebellion, the armed forces simply disintegrated. They too had been permeated with, and radicalized by, the same sentiments that had turned the rest of the population against the *ancien régime.*

Given the number of less-than-stable, friendly governments in the Third World, the probabilities are high that our best efforts will again fail to prevent the collapse of some of them. In fact, efforts to fortify Third World regimes can even be counterproductive for both patron and client. The visible presence of the United States can sometimes strengthen a regime's resolve or intimidate the opposition. It can also deepen the national perception that the country's rulers are "tools of imperialism." This possibility is especially damaging where the legacy of colonialism has sensitized public opinion to the presence of foreign influences. Certainly, the Shah's public image was marred by the massive U.S. military presence in Iran. Over time, it seemed that not only the guns, but the leaders, were stamped "Made in the U.S.A." Moreover, where such a weakened regime is overthrown, the succeeding rulers are likely to remember vividly the U.S. role in their nation's recent history. In some cases, such bitter memories will poison relations for at least the near-term future. And the added danger exists that the dictum, "The enemies of my enemy must be my friends," will drive the new rulers into the arms of the Soviets. This would be the ironical result of a policy whose chief aim was the avoidance of just such an outcome.

LOCAL RIVALRIES

Security commitments extended to Third World states have proven to be two-way streets. Just as we have looked to Third World states to help protect our regional interests, so our friends have asked us to protect their interests. These states' regional rivalries (often the outgrowth of historical, geographic, or ethnic squabbles) may seem insignificant to us. Yet they can force the United States into choosing between being dragged into interstate disputes or letting down an ally. For example, as we drew closer to the government of Mohammed Siad Barre, President of Somalia, he tried to draw us into providing both political and military support for Somalia's effort to annex the Ogaden region—homeland for many ethnic Somalis but legally a part of Ethiopia. At first, the Carter administration avoided establishing a large-scale, military-supply relationship with Siad Barre. But, when the United States began to seek military facilities or bases in the Persian Gulf vicinity, the abandoned Soviet base at Berbera looked so appealing that Somalia's bargaining position was suddenly strengthened. We proceeded in 1980 to offer to supply Somalia with weapons, albeit with the proviso that Somali troops be withdrawn from the Ogaden. Beleaguered Ethiopia was not reassured and its suspicion of the United States deepened. Moreover, U.S. relations were strained with otherwise friendly Kenya, which was at odds with Somalia over similar border and ethnic conflicts.

Just as ties to Somalia have threatened to draw the United States into Somalia's disputes with Ethiopia and Kenya, other commitments to our Third World allies will inevitably harm our relations with a new set of states. Our longstanding tie to Pakistan was one reason for India's tendency to look to the Soviet Union for military equipment and diplomatic support.[14] In the complex web of the Middle East, our ties to the Shah of Iran deepened the hostility of Iran's neighbor and rival, Iraq, toward the United States. In Latin America, the Nixon administration's tilt toward Brazil preoccupied Brazil's traditional rival for South American primacy, Argentina. In Africa, our faithful support for Zaire's President Mobutu made us party to his off-again, on-again disputes with Angola. The decision to supply sophisticated aircraft to Saudi Arabia angered our major Middle Eastern ally, Israel, albeit not decisively. Most obviously, U.S. ties to Israel, and now to South Africa, vastly complicate our diplomacy throughout the Middle East and Africa.

In many such cases, our allies' local rival looked to the other global superpower to offset a potentially threatening U.S. presence. From the previously mentioned perspective of New Delhi, a Soviet presence counterbalanced the hostile array of Pakistan, China, and the United States. Meanwhile in Africa, the Popular Movement for the Liberation of Angola (MPLA) turned to the Soviet Union and Cuba for stepped-up military assistance in response to escalating U.S. and South African involvement on behalf of its domestic enemies; continuing fears of external invasion or harassment from neighboring states has deepened and legitimized Angola's dependency on the Russians. Argentina's cultivation of Soviet ties (under the ideologically diverse governments of General Alejandro Lanusse, Juan Peron, General Jorge Videla, and General Roberto Viola) was partially motivated by an interest in counterbalancing the traditional U.S. preference for Brazil. Rather than excluding Soviet influence from a region, our very presence has tended to invite a countering Soviet presence. This tendency has increased as Moscow has demonstrated its heightened capability and willingness to match our moves in the global chess game. It is especially frustrating since the Soviet presence often occurs not through illicit aid to subversive guerrillas, but from a legitimate government's invitation.

An offended country may still work with the United States in the pursuit of common objectives. Its overall national interest will often dictate cooperating with us on particular issues. In such cases, the anger elicited by our commitment to its rival may be an acceptable price for us to pay, but only if the gains from that commitment are demonstrably real.

FAINT FRIENDS

On numerous occasions, our Third World allies were unable to fulfill their part of the bargain—they failed to preserve our mutual interests in their region. Such disappointments have been most glaring in the Middle East. For example, Saudi Arabia failed, at least until recently, to prevent oil price rises. At the very best, it acted as a relatively "moderate" brake on the OPEC "radicals." Saudi Arabia has also been unwilling to lend its weight to the Camp David peace process—the 1979 treaty between Egypt and Israel that was intended as a first step toward resolving the major issues in the Arab-Israeli conflict. Afraid of being labeled an American "tool" by the other Arab states, the Saudis refused to carry our brief for us. Subsequently, the "rejectionist" states successfully lined up the Arab world against the Camp David accords.

One of the more spectacular uses of a regional influential to secure American interests was the 1978 U.S. airlift of Moroccan troops into Zaire's copper-rich Shaba province. Many of the province's inhabitants felt that President Mobutu had been draining its wealth for the benefit of the distant capital, Kinshasa. They had not resisted—and some had even welcomed—the invasion of the Katangese gendarmes, who had been living in neighboring Angola since their defeat in the secessionist wars of the early 1960s. Mobutu's troops proved to be too undisciplined to subdue the Katangese. So, first French and Belgian troops, and then Moroccan, were flown in to restore Mobutu's control over Shaba. By "Africanizing" the rescue operation, the Moroccans gave it greater legitimacy on the continent.

However impressive this use of "proxy" troops, the operation failed to address the source of Zaire's growing instability: the arbitrary and flagrantly corrupt rule of President Mobutu. The temporary presence of foreign troops could not halt the decay of Zairean public institutions or the depressing decline of living standards. The airlift could only rescue a leader whose continuance in power clearly depends upon outside aid.[15]

DIVERGENT INTERESTS

If regional powers have sometimes been unable to defend our interests, in other cases they have simply refused to try. Third World powers have failed to react to particular challenges that Washington has viewed as ominous, thereby negating the primary condition for a working alliance—agreement on what constitutes a serious threat to common interests. For example, Nigeria not only refused to condemn Cuban assistance to the MPLA, but considered such aid a justifiable response to South African intervention into the Angolan civil war on behalf of a second faction, UNITA. Even more shocking to Washington was Brazil's immediate recognition of the newborn MPLA government. In fact, Brazil was the first nonsocialist government to do so. Brazil was more interested in currying favor in Black Africa than in expressing disapproval of the Cuban military involvement.

In the Middle East, the United States has come to rely upon Saudi Arabia to advance U.S. interests. The Saudis have been willing to join with the United States in extending financial aid to strengthen governments in Turkey, Pakistan, and Morocco. Yet, policies in Washington and Riyadh have often diverged. In the 1960s, the United States backed the Republican forces in North Yemen, while Saudi Arabia aided the opposing Royalists. In 1977, Saudi Arabia argued for aid to Somalia, while the United States opposed Somalia's designs on eastern Ethiopia. Whereas Washington has generally sided with Israel, and centered its Middle East security policy on reducing Soviet influence, Riyadh has assisted the Palestine Liberation Organization and insisted that the greatest threat to regional stability is the unresolved Palestinian question.

A dramatic instance of the unreliability of Third World influentials occurred just as the Sandinistas were staging their final and successful drive against President Somoza in Nicaragua in June 1979. The United

States called for a special meeting of the Organization of American States (OAS)—a meeting of Consultation of Foreign Ministers—to consider the Nicaraguan crisis. The four regional influentials—Argentina, Brazil, Mexico, and Venezuela—were, of course, in attendance. None of these states were as openly tied to the United States as, say, Iran under the Shah or the Philippines under Marcos; but they were all conservative, capitalist states with anti-Communist internal politics and a confirmed stake in the international economic system. The United States hoped to receive at least the passive support of Brazil and Mexico, and counted on receiving the active cooperation of Venezuela and Argentina in resolving the Nicaraguan situation favorably.

The primary U.S. objective in Nicaragua was to prevent a Sandinista military victory; but at the time the OAS meeting convened in Washington on 21 June, the Sandinista offensive was gaining ground. This presented Washington with an immediate dilemma. The United States could not back Somoza. His presence in power only fueled the Sandinistas' appeal within Nicaragua, and few Latin governments were willing to associate with the tottering dictator.[16] No, Somoza had to be forced to resign and an alternative government had to be constructed that would limit the Sandinistas to a minority position within a broader coalition.

In his opening address to the twenty-seven-nation assembly, Secretary of State Cyrus Vance warned that "we must not leave a vacuum" in Nicaragua: shorthand for saying that a government needed to be installed before the Sandinistas could seize power. Vance proposed the "formation of an interim government of national reconciliation acceptable to all major elements of [Nicaraguan] society." To assist this process, a ceasefire between the rebels and the Nicaraguan government should be declared, all nations should cease to ship weapons to either side (Vance specifically accused Cuba of involvement), and a special OAS delegation should be dispatched to Nicaragua. This delegation would remove Somoza and select a transitional government. In addition, Vance called for an OAS peacekeeping presence—that is, a military force—"to help establish a climate of peace and security and to assist the interim government in establishing its authority."

The State Department had warned the White House that the Latins were unlikely to agree to an Inter-American Peacekeeping Force. However, National Security Adviser Brzezinski persuaded President Carter that the United States ought at least to begin to float the idea publically, with a view toward perhaps winning eventual approval later. Whatever the initial doubts, the State Department, and certainly the National Security Council, were not prepared for the widespread rejection of the other main elements contained in the U.S. proposal.

The Mexican Foreign Minister, Jorge Castañeda, took the lead in dissenting from the U.S. position. Whereas Vance saw only a dark "war of national destruction," Castañeda praised "el pueblo de Nicaragua" for exercising "the sacred right of rebellion against tyranny, just as el pueblo Mexicano had done seventy years before." Castañeda declared that he carried explicit instructions from the President of Mexico to oppose any plan for an OAS team to negotiate with Somoza. The Mexicans feared that the result would be "somocismo sin Somoza," the maintenance of the basic structures of the old regime. This amounted to a rejection of the U.S. proposal for an all-inclusive government of national reconciliation. Finally, Castañeda maintained that the civil war was an internal affair and that the OAS had neither the "legal, nor the political nor moral right" to intervene in Nicaragua's internal affairs. In essence, the Mexicans welcomed a Sandinista military victory and opposed any OAS mission, much less a peacekeeping force.

The Venezuelan foreign minister spoke on behalf of the entire Andean Pact, which included Bolivia, Colombia, Ecuador, and Peru. At that time, all of these countries either had elected governments or were in the process of moving from military to civilian rule. While less aggressive than Mexico, the Venezuelans also differed with the United States on essential points and failed to endorse other elements of the U.S. proposal. Whereas the United States proposed a "government of reconciliation including all sectors," Venezuela's solution called for the "definitive exclusion of the Somoza regime," which was to be replaced by a government "representing the democratic sectors of the country." Rather than asking for a ceasefire and an end to weapons shipments, Venezuela reaffirmed the Andean Pact's declaration of a state of belligerency in Nicaragua that was issued a few days before and that effectively recognized the Sandinistas. The Venezuelans did not endorse an official OAS mediation as the United States wanted, but they did accept the principle of international action to help resolve the crisis.

Brazil chose to maintain a low profile and did not even send its foreign minister to the meeting. While they supported the concept of a mediated solution, the Brazilians privately expressed their skepticism that such an outcome was possible. Of the four "influentials," only Argentina—Brazil's chief rival in South America—supported the spirit of the U.S. position. Argentina seconded the ideas of a ceasefire, an end to arms shipments, and the formation of a new government that included all sectors. They even suggested that they might support a peacekeeping force. However, the Carter administration, because of its human rights policies and its support of a democratic solution for Nicaragua, could not ally itself closely with authoritarian Argentina. In any case, the influence of strife-torn Argentina was at an ebb within the Latin community, and its usefulness as an ally was limited.

Mexico and the Andean states carried the day. To save face, the United States voted for the final resolution, which called for the resignation of Somoza and for the installation of a "democratic government including the principal representative opposition groups": that is, it included the Sandinistas. The resolution failed to call for a ceasefire, a halt to arms shipments (which were flowing from Cuba, Panama, and Costa Rica to the rebels), or the establishment of a formal OAS mediation team. The resolution did, however, allow individual states "to take steps . . . to facilitate an enduring and peaceful solution." The United States would use this phrase to legitimate its last-ditch diplomatic effort to establish a non-Sandinista transition government. When that failed, the resolution would be used to justify trying to alter the composition of the Sandinista-backed provisional government. But the continual flow of weapons to the Sandinistas, plus the speed and the ferocity of the insurrection, left the U.S. efforts OBEd—a State Department abbreviation for "overcome by events."

Why did Mexico, Venezuela, and Brazil fail to line up behind the United States? In explaining the outcome of the OAS meeting to a congressional subcommittee, Assistant Secretary of State Viron "Pete" Vaky offered two reasons: first, "A majority of OAS members clearly and openly sympathize with the opposition now fighting Somoza and are increasingly showing it—by breaking relations with the Somoza government and supporting the Sandinistas"; second, the denial of an OAS peace force "reflected how deeply the American states were sensitized by the Dominican intervention of 1965, and how deeply they fear physical intervention."[17] Basically, U.S. perceptions about the opposing social forces in Nicaragua and the legitimacy of an OAS military intervention differed sharply from those of key Latin states.

Beyond these general explanations for the Latins' behavior, Mexico and Brazil had additional reasons for not supporting the United States. Mexico's own history caused it to view social revolution as legitimate and fiercely to oppose U.S. military intervention in Latin America. Moreover, the recent discovery of vast oil deposits gave Mexico greater confidence to assert itself in world affairs. Mexican nationalists, whose opinions weighed heavily in Castañeda's foreign ministry, saw volatile Central America as a region where Mexico would exert greater influence. Since the region's conservative forces traditionally had been allied with the United States, the avenue to greater Mexican influence was through processes of change that would bring new social forces to power.[18] Mexico believed it could help create a new order out of Central American revolution and mold the new regimes in its own image. Like Michelangelo's portrait of the Creation, Mexico's finger would touch and animate the new governments germinating in Central America. This was, after all, Mexico's natural geographic sphere of influence.

Brazil was not interested in competing with the United States in distant Central America, but Brazil was equally emphatic about pursuing a foreign policy independent from the United States. Viewing itself as an emerging world power, Brazil was following a policy of "automatic nonalignment," sometimes referred to as "responsible pragmatism." The rationale for a policy of nonalignment flowed in part from the Brazilian belief that U.S.-Soviet competition was motivated more by selfish national interests than by ideology. The Brazilians also feared that the United States, sometimes in a "condominium" with the Soviet Union, wanted to maintain the status quo by repressing emerging centers of power like Brazil. U.S. efforts (with varying degrees of Soviet support) to limit the spread to South America of nuclear technologies and sophisticated conventional weaponry reinforced these suspicions.

Brazil's enthusiasm for siding with the United States on East-West issues was certainly dulled by the fact that 7 percent of its exports were flowing to Eastern Europe by 1977. Indeed, Brazil's obsession with finding new export markets in order to pay its oil bill and to remain current on its debt service made East-West concerns largely irrelevant and potentially bothersome. As one Brazilian policy planner said, matters such as the East-West nuclear balance sounded like "fiction" in Brazil's industrial cities.

Brazil also feared that the appearance of being a willing instrument of the United States would jeopardize access to its fastest-growing export markets. The developing countries, which had accounted for 13 percent of Brazil's merchandise exports in 1960, were importing 26 percent by 1978. The OPEC countries' share had zoomed from a negligible figure to over 7 percent. In fact, to court favor in the Middle East, Brazil had moved from a pro-Israeli stance toward a pro-Arab posture in official communiques and U.N. votes. Nor did Brazil want to endanger its newly won markets in Black Africa by too visible an alliance with U.S. interests.[19]

In practice, Brazil has been willing to reach agreement with the industrial states on specific economic matters. This is evident in Brazil's pragmatic and active participation in the multilateral trade negotiations during the Tokyo Round (GATT). Brazil has even continued to side diplomatically with the United States on such issues as the Soviet invasion of Afghanistan and the seizure of American diplomats in Iran. At the same time, however, Brazil has been unwilling to participate in activities that could prove costly to it, even indirectly. Nonaligned

Brazil does not want to find itself embroiled by the United States in "adventures": the term used by a topranking Brazilian diplomat in late 1980 to describe U.S. policy in El Salvador. Had the Sandinistas been active in neighboring Uruguay, the Brazilian military would have seen them as a threat to Brazil's own internal security. But open collaboration with the United States in Central America did not fit Brazil's overall conception of its national interests.

U.S. recognition of the growing importance of these new influentials, the newly industrializing countries, is a positive step toward coming to grips with emerging realities in the Third World. Solid and lasting alliances, however, should neither be demanded nor anticipated. The instability of many Third World rulers makes them too uncertain a foundation upon which to construct our basic strategy. Most of the more important Third World states have developed definitions of their national interests and these frequently differ from U.S. interests. Even when we are in agreement, the emergence of other regional forces may overwhelm the efforts of our regional allies, causing events to spin out of their control. And even amenable regimes may hesitate to make a slavish display of loyalty to the United States, not wanting to lose their domestic credibility. Of course when regimes do display their loyalty to the United States, they will expect some return payment. The commitments exacted from us may be greater than the return on the investment.

The Unreliability of Local Businessmen and Military Officers

In contemporary diplomacy, alliances between states are only one form of international bond. Major powers like the United States also form transnational links with social groupings within states. The Soviet Union, of course, has a long history of experience in this area via its ties to local Communist parties. For its part, the United States typically looks to local businessmen and to military officers to advance U.S. interests in regional and global affairs. We do seek ties with other groups (such as labor unions, the media, and intellectuals), but we generally do not expect these groups to run their government. Where democracy exists, we may invest in political parties; but even then, we have routinely counted on business or the military to guarantee our interests.

Why have we looked to these two forces; what do they and we have in common? An alliance with local business groups seems only logical. They normally advocate sound fiscal and monetary policies, oppose socialist ideologies, and understand the language of "the bottom line." In addition, businessmen in many Third World countries tend to look and talk like us. They dress in familiar Western-style suits; they speak English or French; and they share at least a superficial interest in Western cultural trends. More importantly, direct commercial ties have in some cases forged common economic interests and personal friendships between local business elites and their Western peers. If this doesn't amount to cultural and political cloning, it does suggest that entrepreneurs selectively adapt in order to succeed in the larger economic system.

Our attachment to local militaries is less comprehensible in cultural terms, given our own political system's emphasis on keeping our military outside of politics. There are, however, other explanations. American officials often admire Third World militaries as the most coherent and modern institutions in otherwise backward societies. Sometimes their officers are educated in the United States or Western Europe and therefore seem to understand our interests. Perhaps most significantly, our foreign policy often places a premium on stability, and the military frequently appears to be the most effective and dependable guarantor of order.

From the perspective of American foreign policy, alliances with foreign elites have to accomplish two ends if they are to be considered useful. First, such domestic allies should be willing to act with us on most key issues of mutual concern. Second, they should also possess sufficient power to impose their views within their own countries. The question, then, is whether businessmen and military officers in the Third World are in fact reliable and powerful allies.

THE MYTH OF SHARED INTERESTS WITH LOCAL BUSINESS

Third World businessmen no longer fit the caricature sketched in the 1960s and early 1970s by some *dependencia* theories and by some American conservatives.[20] They can no longer accurately be accused of, or praised for, being the cats' paws of multinational corporations. These local business elites do not spend each day busily selling out their *patria* to foreign interests, nor are they blind adherents of free markets. They are not reflexively opposed to statism or to nationalism. Third World businessmen have grown in experience and power; they are maturing. Their firms have gained some degree of technological and organizational sophistication and have captured significant shares of growing domestic, and in some cases even foreign, markets. Moreover, their knowledge of international markets increases their ability to either successfully compete or negotiate with foreign firms. Most important of all, they have learned how to use their own government's leverage to bolster their positions vis-a-vis foreign competition.

Traditionally, the U.S. government has identified the overseas expansion of American firms as furthering the national interest.[21] At times, the United States has even pressed its corporations to invest abroad and has pressured host countries to receive them. The Carter administration backed away from actively stimulating foreign investment, but it did try to persuade less developed countries (LDCs) at least to avoid discriminating against U.S. subsidiaries.[22] Even this limited neutrality has been reversed, however, by the Reagan administration, which has been an enthusiastic advocate of multinational investment in developing countries.

Within the Third World, opposition to the U.S. assumption that unfettered foreign investment was beneficial to everyone has not been confined to left-wing intellectuals and politicians. By the late 1960s, local entrepreneurs in many Third World countries were challenging foreign investments in raw materials and in public utilities, and were supporting the partial or complete nationalization of foreign firms operating in these basic sectors.[23] The restricted terms under which foreign firms continue to operate in the natural resource sectors (whether through joint ventures or service or management contracts) are the product of hard-nosed bargaining. More recently, nationalist businessmen, especially in the more rapidly industrializing countries of Asia and Latin America, have successfully advocated rules that limit multinational investment in manufacturing. Third World governments want to assure their domestic firms' profitability by drafting regulations that carefully circumscribe the areas where foreign firms are permitted to enter. After close consultation with domestic entrepreneurs, governments have entirely barred foreign corporations from sectors where local firms are active but fearful of competition. Governments have also provided discriminatory treatment for national companies with regard to credit access, government procurement, and tax incentives. National businessmen are using this leverage either to dominate their markets or to maintain at least a competitive edge over foreign investors.

Not surprisingly, local businessmen tend to demand more protection and official advantages as foreign corporations increasingly penetrate the local country's industrial sector. This threshhold has been crossed in South Korea, Taiwan, Brazil, Mexico, and Argentina, where national businessmen have engaged their government's assistance in competing against the large, foreign corporate presence. When, as in Venezuela, this presence mushrooms overnight, domestic tidal waves rise demanding rapid governmental action. Thus, as a study of Latin American business attitudes concluded, "The open transnational embrace [that is, between foreign corporations and local businesses] of the 1940s has become a far cooler handshake in the late 1970s." The emergence of a stronger domestic entrepreneurship, "far from leading to a harmony of interest with the United States, has created . . . a hell [for U.S. policymakers.]"[24]

Moreover, the area of conflict between U.S. interests and those of Third World businesses has expanded beyond domestic conflicts and into the arena of international trade. Under the old international division of labor (when developing countries produced raw materials and the developed states provided the world's industrial goods), the "complementarity" of products allowed for frictionless interchange. Today, the firms of newly industrializing countries (NICs) are poised to assault the U.S. market with a wide variety of manufactured products from electronics, to polyesters, to steel, to automobiles, to petrochemicals. With their roles reversed, some American corporations and unions, already suffering from excess capacity and unemployment, will be demanding protection just when the NICs are becoming competitive. Conversely, at a time when many U.S. firms are turning away from the sluggish U.S. market toward the more buoyant foreign ones, many LDCs will be restraining imports because of unsustainable balance-of-payments deficits. Having to allocate scarce foreign exchange to essential oil imports and to service the accumulated foreign debt, many LDCs will be limiting the growth of food and industrial imports—the very areas in which the United States is most competitive.

All of these trends suggest that foreign businessmen will not be doormats for a U.S. open door policy for overseas investment. Third World entrepreneurs have supported the nationalization of American subsidiaries in natural resource extractions and lobbied with their own governments to adopt rules disadvantageous to foreign competitors. They will increasingly be at odds with U.S. firms as each seeks access to the other's home markets, and their professed faith in capitalism and international trade will not prevent them from further using their governments' power to discriminate against foreign competition. Local businessmen, then, have learned to negotiate with the United States and its businessmen in setting the rules of the game for the international transfer of capital and for the exchange of commodities. Deals are still made, but only after a stiff bargaining process: all a far cry from the kowtowing envisioned by those who see Third World businesses as starving men grateful for any crumbs that fall from the table of the industrialized world.

POLITICAL DIFFERENCES

Economic disputes need not preclude agreement on the preferred strategies to adopt in moments of crisis when the political futures of Third World states are at stake. Indeed, important sectors of local business communities have often lent their support to political projects favored by the United States. For example, U.S. interventions in Guatemala (1954), Lebanon (1958), the Dominican Republic (1965), and Vietnam were among those that were approved—even induced—by local business interests. Brazilian business and the United States were enthusiastic supporters of the military government and its "economic miracle" of the late 1960s and early 1970s. In 1978, the businessmen of Santiago Province in the Dominican Republic joined the United States in successfully pressuring President-General Joaquin Balaguer to honor the election of businessman Antonio Guzman. In the Jamaican general elections of 1980, both local business and the United States favored Edward Seaga against Michael Manley. This suggests that local businessmen and U.S. representatives can still peer through the same window to see common dangers that require common action.

In numerous other cases, however, local businessmen refuse to see U.S. interests reflected in the glass. Two recent examples occurred in Nicaragua in 1979 and in El Salvador in 1980. In a classic case of "popular front" politics, Nicaraguan business made an alliance with leftist guerrillas. On the other hand, as has often happened before in the Third World, El Salvador's business community resisted U.S.-backed social reforms that were designed to enhance the country's long-term political stability.

BUSINESSMEN IN NICARAGUA[25]

Anastasio Somoza successfully repressed the first uprising against his regime in September 1978; but the United States concluded that Somoza's days were numbered (he was overthrown in July 1979). The United States undertook a mediation effort aimed at removing Somoza through an orderly and controlled transition before leftist forces could regroup and gain wider support for insurrection. Our intention was to transfer power to a coalition of the traditional political parties, the National Guard (purged of the Somozas), and the business elites. The United States looked to the Nicaraguan business sector as the most promising political force for post-Somoza Nicaragua; it was modern, dynamic, and friendly to the United States. Many of these Nicaraguan businessmen had been educated in the United States and had maintained close contacts with U.S. embassy officials in Managua.

Possibilities of an alliance seemed promising, since the United States and Nicaraguan businessmen shared the basic objective of removing Somoza from power. What was not immediately apparent was that both parties did not share the same rationale. The businessmen felt that Somoza, increasingly arbitrary and grasping, was impinging on their commercial interests. In addition, some were morally repelled by Somoza's venality, arrogance, and brutality. Similarly, the Carter administration was unhappy with Somoza's human rights violations, but it was even more fearful of a leftist revolution.

When the U.S.-sponsored mediation failed, both the United States and the Nicaraguan businessmen were frustrated. Somoza and his combative National Guard simply refused to yield power. The business sectors and the traditional opposition parties had participated in two lengthy general strikes against Somoza and were exhausted. Only a counter-force could unseat the dictator.

When the second and final insurrection was launched in June 1979, the Sandinistas announced the creation of a provisional revolutionary government (PRG) that would temporarily be situated in Costa Rica. The five-member junta consisted of one Sandinista, two leaders associated with Sandinista-front groups, Violeta Chammorro (the widow of the assassinated businessman, Pedro Joaquin Chammorro), and Alfonso Robelo of the business-led Nicaraguan Democratic Movement. To the shock and dismay of the United States, two prominent symbols of the business sector had cast their lot with a Sandinista-dominated government. The United States feared that if such a provisional junta came to power as the result of a violent overthrow of Somoza, the Sandinistas and their army would be the dominant political forces in the new Nicaragua. The United States, therefore, maneuvered desperately to find prominent Nicaraguans, especially businessmen, willing to serve in a "centrist" junta that would replace Somoza and take command of the National Guard. The United States could legitimately lend its assistance to such a centrist, non-Somoza government, which would then be able to negotiate with the Sandinistas from a position of strength.

The United States was unable to convince more than one or two opposition figures of any stature to even consider its plan. Instead, the influential association of Nicaraguan businessmen, The Superior Council of Private Business (COSEP), pledged its adherence to the Sandinista-backed provisional government. The United States was leading a charge up a hill only to turn around and discover it was leading a shadow army. The U.S. plan was, in bureaucratic parlance, a "non-starter," and had to be abandoned.

Why did the Nicaraguan businessmen fail to respond in this last chance to forestall a Sandinista victory? Three contributing factors are worth mentioning. First, their furious hatred of Somoza drove them to align with almost any force, including guerrillas, capable of removing the tyrant. Second, the collapse of the earlier mediation caused the business sector to lose faith in the United States. Since the United States had failed in the most essential task of removing Somoza, it could no longer be counted as a reliable ally. The unspoken and unanswered question was: If the United States could not depose a tyrant it had historically protected, how could it protect the new government from a popular revolution? Third, many businessmen differed from Washington in their view of the Sandinistas. While the Carter administration's analysis was not univocal, the White House's dominant view was that key Sandinista leaders were Cuban-trained Marxist-Leninists who were intent upon eventually establishing a one-party socialist state. While most Nicaraguan businessmen were wary of the guerrillas, many were hopeful that they would seek to rebuild an open, pluralistic Nicaragua; they hoped that the new Nicaragua would resemble Mexico rather than Cuba. In fact, they had reason to feel encouraged since the Tercerista faction of the Sandinistas consciously had sought an alliance with the business sector, and since the program of the Sandinista-dominated, provisional government guaranteed property rights. Finally, many Nicaraguan businessmen had sons, daughters, and nephews in the Sandinistas, and hoped that these kinship ties would moderate the radicalized youth once Somoza was gone and they were enjoying the fruits of power.

Thus the priorities, the perceptions, and the emotional reactions of Nicaraguan businessmen differed from those of the United States. In what was the single most important political problem to culminate under the Carter administration within a Latin American country, the Nicaraguan business sector undercut our strategy and allied itself with the very political forces that Washington most feared.

Such an outcome should not have been altogether unexpected. From the French, to the Chinese, to the Nicaraguans, businessmen have sided with revolutionaries much more often than even the most lurid nightmares of American conservatives might allow. Moreover, recent events in Iran suggest that the U.S. policy in Nicaragua was probably foredoomed. In Iran, too, important segments of the business elite abandoned a despot and the U.S. policy that supported him. Many Iranian businessmen had come to hate the Shah and his secret police; and while they may not have liked the religious mullahs or the Marxist opposition parties, they were willing to coalesce with them in the first-priority goal of unseating the tyrant. Most businessmen, those in the modern sector and the traditional merchant classes, were unwilling to support us in upholding the Shah. When that effort failed, they were also unwilling to support a successor government installed by the Shah and headed by Shahpur Bakhtiar. Consequently, the Bakhtiar government was soon overrun by more revolutionary forces. It would seem that if the United States wishes to use shadow governments to block a popular revolution, the shadows had better be more substantial, and the army behind them had better be real.

BUSINESSMEN IN EL SALVADOR

In Nicaragua and Iran, local business interests and the United States differed both on the priority assigned to political stability and on the dangers of insurrection. In El Salvador, domestic business elites also viewed their society in ways that caused them to oppose U.S. policies, but this time the impetus was toward resisting change.

For decades, the United States accepted the military (with the open support of the business sector) as the true governors of El Salvador. The Carter administration, however, was less enchanted with military rule for both moral and *Realpolitik* reasons. The increasingly repressive rule of the latest president-general, Carlos Romero, clashed with the Carter administration's human rights policy: which had been given highest priority in Latin America. More importantly, as unrest became more apparent in El Salvador and throughout Central America, the administration concluded that polarization and violence would spread unless political systems were opened up and modernized.

The Carter overview was that, in the last two decades, industrialization and economic modernization had formed new socioeconomic groups that were now being politically gagged. Specifically, the enlarged middle class and the industrial unions were being systematically denied power through electoral frauds and increasingly overt repression. Previously reformist parties and unions were being driven toward the left and toward the acceptance of armed struggle as the only viable route to power. The Roman Catholic Church, once a leg of the ruling army/business/church triad, was now being pulled by an increasingly militant clergy and congregation toward revolution.

The Nicaraguan Revolution triumphed in July 1979, and the security situation in El Salvador continued to worsen. Alarmed at President Romero's passivity, reformist colonels ousted him on 15 October 1979. They immediately declared their intentions to democratize the country's political and economic life. The United States did not directly instigate the military coup; but the participating officers correctly inferred from our disappointment in Romero that we would welcome a change in government. The new junta was composed of two army colonels, two center-left civilians, and a conservative businessman. The junta was supported by the center and the center-left, and hoped to incorporate at least some elements from the leftist "popular organizations" (unions of white-collar, blue-collar, and rural workers). Here was the opportunity to develop a more broadly based regime capable of opening the political system to the newly emerging social forces, while drawing support away from the more radical left.

But the junta itself was deeply divided, and its civilians were unable to rein in the security forces, whose officer corps remained essentially intact. The military officers resisted and postponed the economic reforms advocated by the more progressive civilian members of the junta and its cabinet. Simultaneously, the number of assassinations perpetrated by the security forces and the rightist, paramilitary "death squads" actually multiplied.

The Salvadoran business elite believed that repression, not reform, was the most effective means to maintain stability. As Romero's Foreign Minister, Antonio Rodriguez Porth, a large coffee grower, explained to the author, "The example of Frei in Chile once again demonstrated that 'Kerensky' reformers only destabilize society and open the door to Marxism." The Salvadoran businessmen remembered well the dominant event in modern Salvadoran history—the successful destruction in 1932 of a popular rebellion by the massacre of some ten thousand peasants—and urged the military to take yet more forceful action to deter subversion.

Most of the Salvadoran business elite were appalled at the junta's composition and by its social rhetoric. To many businessmen, the junta was either Communist-inspired or had inadvertently opened the gates to communism. Soon, these businessmen began to subvert the junta's reformist tendencies by strengthening the resolve of the more conservative officers and by purchasing, when possible, the obstructionary capabilities of others. One effective tactic for splitting the junta, beyond mere public opposition to reform, soon emerged. It was as blunt as a blackjack and as politically sublime as a discourse by Machiavelli. The security forces would escalate their violent terrorism against both centrists and leftists. This violence would make the reformers uncomfortable with their governmental participation, tending to drive them from power. It would also undermine their efforts to initiate a meaningful dialogue with the left. One side is unlikely to listen while the other talks with bastinados and guns.

While businessmen used their influence to sharpen disagreements within the government and to increase violence against centrists and leftists, they also continued to remove their capital from the country. This had the effect of disrupting the economy and of making it that much more difficult for the reformist government to finance reform or to govern. In contrast, the United States was urging compromise within the government, emphasizing the importance of reducing official repression, and considering ways to increase official economic assistance to El Salvador. The U.S. government and the Salvadoran business community chose divergent strategies because they disagreed on how best to create political stability. This disagreement was partially the product of dissimilar historical experiences and political values. It also reflected the unequal sacrifice each party was being asked to make. The United States was, in effect, counseling the Salvadoran businessmen to surrender a portion of their power in order to prevent a socialist revolution. The only U.S. sacrifice was the provision of economic aid.

The rightists finally succeeded in driving the two center-left civilian members of the junta and most of the civilian cabinet to resign. A second military-civilian junta was formed in early 1980, with the more conservative Christian Democrats providing the main civilian component. However, this drift to the right was countermanded to some extent, since the United States had dispatched more dynamic and liberal envoys—first James Cheek, then Robert White—to head its mission in El Salvador. With energetic U.S. backing, major reforms were promulgated: the banks were nationalized; the major export crop, coffee, was placed under the control of a state marketing board; and the largest agricultural estates were expropriated. The business sector felt betrayed.

Ambassador White worked hard to convince them that their essential economic interests were being preserved and that reform was the only alternative to a "Pol Pot," radical-left victory. Under the constant barrage of U.S. arguments, the business sector split. One group remained implacably hostile and continued to work for an overt rightist coup, while a second faction decided to work with and within the junta in the interests of steering it rightwards. The differences were partly tactical, although the latter faction reconciled itself to accepting at least some of the reforms as faits accomplis. But even this "moderate" position was opportunistic and temporary and did not reflect a conversion to the Carter administration's reformist convictions. Following Ronald Reagan's election, the more conciliatory businessmen rejoined their more overtly rightist colleagues in working to halt the junta's reformist program.

The second junta collapsed in December 1980; and although the Christian Democrat Napoleon Duarte agreed to head the successor government, the elimination of the second junta's reformist military symbol, Adolfo Majano, signaled another rightward shift. This had the effect of further narrowing the government's base of support. Many centrists joined the left, convinced that the military government was again captured by the conservative oligarchy. The alliance of center-left and left, the Democratic Revolutionary Front, grew strong enough to challenge militarily the security forces—the very eventuality the United States had worked so hard to avoid. The United States had to inject rising amounts of economic and military aid to sustain the less-than-popular regime.

In El Salvador, as in Nicaragua, local business sectors consciously undercut U.S. strategies at crucial moments in their nation's histories.[26] The business elite's differences with the United States were not only over tactics; they also reflected fundamental conflicts about the acceptability of particular outcomes. In Nicaragua, many local businessmen not only saw armed insurrection as a legitimate tactic but decided that they could live with the results. The Salvadoran businessmen believed that repression, not reform, was the path to stability. They were unwilling to accommodate themselves to the reformed El Salvador envisioned by the United States, where political liberalization and agrarian reform would reduce—but not eliminate—their power. Although their courses of action were different, Nicaraguan and Salvadoran businessmen pursued their own self-defined interests first. Not surprisingly, they evaluated U.S. wishes in the context of their being either effective or ineffective tools to secure their own aims: not as commandments from on high.

BUSINESSMEN'S FAILURES

Businessmen can be unreliable allies even when their objectives coincide with ours, if they are unable to impose their will upon their nation. Very frequently in the Third World, the business class lacks sufficient size and cohesiveness, or enough popular legitimacy, to maintain power.

The private sector is relatively well developed in the more advanced Third World states. Even there, however, business has often failed to govern successfully. For example, in the southernmost Latin American states—Chile, Argentina, and Uruguay—the political instability of the 1970s can be found rooted largely in the business sectors' previous failures to provide effective and credible leadership. In all three countries, the resulting economic stagnation, inflation, and political alienation provoked political breakdowns in the mid-1970s. Ultimately, the respective militaries in these countries were able to assert control and defend U.S. interests as defined by presidents Nixon and Ford. They were not as successful in defending the interests of more than a portion of local businesses. Moreover, these "acceptable" outcomes were neither certain nor (as will be discussed below) necessarily stable.

The case of Chile illustrates the inadequacies of business as a Third World governing force. Most Chilean businessmen had supported the import-substitution-industrialization model, whereby domestic industry expanded behind a wall of highly protective tariffs. This "hothouse" industry used imported, capital-intensive technology that failed to provide enough jobs for new entrants to the urban labor force. The emphasis on industry did, however, divert resources away from agriculture, preventing food production from keeping pace with domestic demand. Finally, the impact of the new industries on the balance of payments was disappointing; since they were too inefficient to export, but required large amounts of imported inputs.

While the economic program of Chile's bourgeoisie failed to meet the country's needs and expectations, the main business-oriented political party proved unable to capture the voters' trust. The National Party, formed in the mid-1960s by a merger of the declining traditional Conservative and Liberal Parties, was unable to muster much more than 20 percent of the vote. The Conservatives and the Liberals had supported the successful candidacy of Arturo Alessandri in 1958, but his victory was attributable to the popularity of his family name in Chilean history. The National Party again backed Alessandri in the fateful 1970 elections, but he lost to Salvador Allende, the candidate supported by the Socialists and the Communists.

Some businessmen in Chile supported such centrist parties as the Radicals and the Christian Democrats (CDs). The Radicals, however, declined in importance in Chile as they did in other Latin American and Western European countries. Meanwhile, the Christian Democrats won the presidency for the first and only time in 1964; and during Eduardo Frei's six-year presidency, the Chilean CDs' internal contradictions and tensions surfaced with crippling intensity. These discords contributed to the substantial drop in the CDs' popular vote in the 1970 presidential elections. The Chilean Christian Democrats also failed thereby in their central objective—the major reason for their business support—to keep the Marxists from power. Frei accelerated a process of grassroots mobilization that he was unable to control, while his rhetoric raised a wildfire of economic expectations that the poorly performing Chilean economy could not extinguish.

Having failed to retain power themselves, Chilean businessmen and their major political parties—the Nationals and the Christian Democrats—turned in desperation to the military to end what they perceived to be a Marxist threat. But Allende's overthrow in 1973 had the additional effects of destroying Chile's democratic institutions and thereby the means of expression for Chile's business class. Political power was transferred to the military; political parties were placed "in recess." As a penalty for the businessmen's past inability to promote economic growth and political stability, the military opened the Chilean economy to foreign imports. Not only were their parties "in recess," but many domestic industries also went bankrupt. The military was determined to construct an entirely new political and economic model.

Under the military government headed by Augusto Pinochet, a new breed of businessmen is being created. Their activities center in an active import-export trade and in the expansive financial sector. These businessmen lack political coherence, however, and they fear that they and the monetarist economic model that produced them will require many years to gain widespread legitimacy among other Chileans. For this reason, they must continue to rely on the military and Pinochet to maintain political stability. This is of course only a different kind of "hothouse."

Almost everywhere in Africa and Asia, private businessmen have been too new and weak to establish and dominate a stable political order. Instead, power has fallen into the hands of either the multiclass political parties that led the struggle for independence (for example, those of India, Algeria, Zambia, Tanzania), or into the hands of military institutions. Often the political parties and the military have been grafted onto the state bureaucracy to form a hybrid, middle-class government. Business interests may have considerable access to and influence over such regimes; but they lack sufficient political organization and popular trust to govern either openly and directly or through political parties that would act as their surrogates.

THE UNRELIABILITY OF LOCAL MILITARIES

A survey of the recent political role of Latin American militaries reveals the difficulties that the United States inevitably encounters when it wants Third World armies to protect American interests. The Latin American militaries received much of their training and, during the 1950s and 1960s, most of their weapons from the United States. Of course this should have made them ideal allies and much more amenable to Washington than their African and Asian counterparts. And in fact, since the mid-1960s, the United States—with the exception of the Carter administration—has looked to Latin militaries as the Western Hemisphere's most important political actors and our most reliable allies.[27]

Many times, the United States has not been disappointed. For example, we supported the 1964 military coup in Brazil; and for the rest of the 1960s, Brazil had a stable and very pro-American government. The coup that toppled Salvador Allende's government ended a perceived threat to U.S. interests in Chile, and the subsequent Pinochet junta has generally supported U.S. policies.[28] In Central America, the militaries have for many years preserved at least the appearance of political stability and have loyally supported U.S. foreign policy goals. The beauty, however, is in the eye of the beholder, and many of these alliances have had their day: their allure belonging to an idealized past rather than to present realities.

In fact, Latin militaries have usually proven to be less than reliable long-term allies. Sometimes they have abandoned the United States on matters of mutual interest. In other instances, they simply have been unable to retain power.

CLASHES OF INTEREST

The military takeover in Peru in 1968 rudely upset the myth that the Latin militaries were reliable allies. The Peruvian military's first act was to seize the local subsidiary of the International Petroleum Corporation (IPC), an explicitly "anti-imperialist" nationalization that was followed by several others. General Velasco Alvarado's government soon took a leading role in galvanizing wider Latin American sentiment on what later came to be labeled "North-South" issues: the drive for greater equity between the industrialized nations of the Northern Hemisphere and the developing nations of the Southern Hemisphere. This incipient drift toward neutralism was given impetus when Peru joined the Non-Aligned Movement in 1972, at a time when the United States looked dimly upon this organization. Most shockingly of all, the Peruvians turned to the Soviet Union for large-scale purchases of modern military equipment, a package that arrived complete with Soviet advisers.

The Peruvian military believed itself to be starting a long-delayed process of national modernization and social integration. The old landed and financial elites, with their ties to American corporations, were seen as blocking these transformations. Moreover, this transforming role isn't an invention confined to Peru. Militaries have taken on similar revolutionary, nationalistic mantles in the Middle East and Africa. In fact, the most visible example, Colonel Qaddafi, seized power in Libya at about the same time that the Peruvian generals were seeking to remake their society. Some of these militaries, Ethiopia for one, have even become allies of the Soviet Union.

A pattern of increased independence has been evolving in many countries over the past two decades. When the Brazilian military first took power in 1964, it was so anxious to please the United States that Brazil was one of the few countries willing to send troops to reinforce the U.S. Marines in the Dominican Republic in 1965. But, as was discussed earlier, Brazil gradually redefined its national interests in the hemisphere and in the world. It has even become increasingly self-sufficient in weaponry, which provides a more solid foundation for that independence.[29] By the mid-1970s, Brazil was consciously following a path separate from that of the United States. The Nigerian military has undergone a similar transformation from a pro-British to a more nonaligned posture. For instance, the Nigerian military government nationalized British Petroleum's assets in retaliation against Great Britain's policies toward South Africa.

Although this drive for greater independence has accelerated recently, it does have precedents. A nonaligned foreign policy might be relatively new to the Brazilian military, but the Argentine military has long harbored a strain, not only of independent, but of outright anti-U.S., sentiment. Rightist nationalists sympathized with Nazi Germany, lobbying successfully to keep Argentina out of World War II. More recently, the Argentine military government has crossed swords with the United States on Third World economic issues, nuclear nonproliferation, and grain sales to the Soviet Union. When the United States sought to deny grains to the Russians following their intervention in Afghanistan, Argentina shunned U.S. appeals. Instead, Argentina took advantage of our embargo and sharply increased grain exports to the

Soviets. Admittedly, Argentine motives were essentially commercial, but their action had the effect of mitigating the impact of the attempted embargo.[30]

So, despite their historical rivalry, the Brazilian and Argentine military governments have shown remarkable convergence in their foreign policies. These similarities reflect their shared status in the world economy as newly industrializing states, their need for non-politicized trade, and their interest in developing an independent capacity to protect their own national security. All of these factors are present to some degree wherever the military comes to power in the more advanced countries of the Third World.

THE STAYING POWER OF THE MILITARY

In the late 1950s and early 1960s, some analysts looked for the institutional powers that could enforce political stability and achieve economic development in the Third World. This drive led them to extoll the influence of Third World militaries.[31] Admittedly, these militaries seemed likely candidates; they were coherent institutions that appeared relatively honest and technically competent. Our rose-tinted glasses, however, were to be shattered in Latin America and elsewhere. The economic performance of military governments has failed to surpass the performance of their civilian predecessors.[32] Once in power, even such a monolithic unity as the armed forces is splintered by ideological cleavages, interservice and generational rivalries, and personal ambitions; nor were military officers above common corruption.

The simple fact is that the military's monopoly of brute force has been insufficient to authorize continued military rule. For example, militaries in Peru and Ecuador restored civilian rule in the late 1970s, while the Honduran and Brazilian militaries were gradually loosening control and allowing the popular election of at least some government officials. The Bolivian military aborted the electoral process with a bloody coup in 1980, only to be compelled to relinquish power to the people's choice in 1982. All five of these democratization processes in

Latin America occurred because of the widespread and deeply felt conviction, both within the armed forces and the entire society, that the military regimes were exhausted and increasingly isolated. Civilian elections offered the promise of a rejuvenated and legitimate government, better able to mobilize public support for the sacrifices required by modernization.

Each case naturally had characteristics peculiar to it, but some patterns were recurrent in the five countries.[33] For instance, all of the militaries tended to disdain and distrust civilian politicians and to close themselves off from pressure groups and other forms of external influence. The underlying belief that all problems are technical and that politics implies selfish factionalism isolated the armed forces from civilian society. Moreover, the resultant absence of this "feedback" made it difficult for the militaries to correct mistakes. The separation of "state" from "society" was perhaps most extreme in Peru, where the military lost the support of virtually every major social grouping.[34] In the more complex and developed nations like Brazil, the problem has been exacerbated; military rule is too rigid a system for governing over a protracted period. More decentralized mechanisms, which permit the articulation of the wide range of societal interests and the resolution of recurring conflicts, become necessary. In Brazil, such different groups as business, unions, the Church, and intellectuals all felt that those in authority were paying insufficient attention to their problems.

Four of the five military governments (the exception being Honduras) also confronted mounting economic difficulties after an initial period of success. In fairness, these economic crises during the late 1970s reflected conditions common to many Third World countries. Balance-of-payments deficits from high oil prices and a weighty foreign debt accumulation were not problems invented by military governments. Nonetheless, Latin militaries proved that such governments were no magic remedy against economic mismanagement, excessive consumption, over-borrowing, or poor investment planning.

The Latin militaries have also been unable to develop a self-justifying ideology for permanently exercising power.[35] The doctrine of "national security," which concentrates on internal and external subversive threats, tends to lose force over time. The memory of such dangers—whether real or imagined—inevitably recedes. Moreover, the national security doctrine is essentially negative, and does not provide a positive blueprint for governing in more normal times. In Latin political culture and throughout much of the Third World, military rule is not expected to be a permanent state of affairs. Rather, it is seen as a temporary *deus ex machina,* required to break a civilian stalemate or to repress a subversive outbreak. Since the "national security" doctrine has not provided the military with a rationale for permanent rule, militaries necessarily feel obliged to promise an eventual return to democracy and to fulfill that promise as the strength of the military regime erodes.

In the Southern Cone states of Uruguay, Argentina, and Chile, the military juntas that seized power in the mid-1970s initially succeeded in silencing organized opposition; but this was accomplished more through force than through a co-opting of diverse interests. None has been able either to build a firm base of majority support or to move military rule beyond *de facto* status into institutionalized, legitimate authority. In 1980, the Uruguayan military suffered a stunning defeat when it lost a plebiscite to ratify a new constitution that was intended to legalize its political power. The Argentine military were badly tarnished by their humiliating defeat in the 1982 Falklands war with the British. If civilians are unable to mount viable alternatives, these regimes may continue for some time. Nevertheless, if they do not create a more solid institutional foundation—imbued with a popular and positive ideological mystique—they will join the long list of temporary, Latin American interludes of military rule.

Ironically, dramatic illustrations of the fragility of military rule can be found in Central America, the region where such regimes have been most persistent. In Nicaragua, El Salvador, and Guatemala, military governments had ruled, with some brief interruptions, since the 1930s. The decades of nonaccountability, corruption, and inefficiency, and the failures to attend to social organization and to construct a positive ideology began to catch up in the 1970s. In Nicaragua in 1979, the National Guard and the remnants of Anastasio Somoza's Liberal Party were isolated and destroyed by a broad-based popular insurrection. By 1980, the Salvadoran military, while somewhat less isolated, confronted the most impressive and deeply rooted guerrilla movement that Latin America has seen since the Mexican Revolution. And in Guatemala, the majority Indian population began, for the first time, to swell the ranks of guerrilla bands at the same time that the urban middle and working classes were becoming alienated and polarized. As it stands, even a massive inflow of foreign assistance may not suffice to enable the Salvadoran and Guatemalan militaries to retain power.

None of these defeated or endangered Central American militaries can be classified as modern military institutions. The Iranian case, however, suggests that even large and well-equipped armies can disintegrate when exposed to intensive social pressures. The Shah's army was not militarily defeated; it simply refused to defend an isolated regime and to massacre tens of thousands of civilians. In such cases, it is not even a question of ideology. The hard-pressed Afghan army would also have collapsed had the Soviets not massively intervened.

By the beginning of the 1980s, the results of military rule in Latin America were mixed at best. In the Andean region, the military had stepped down from power in disgrace (Peru, Ecuador, and Bolivia). In Brazil, power was gradually being transferred to civilian institutions. In the Southern Cone states of Uruguay, Argentina, and Chile, military governments were stumbling in their efforts to reconstruct a new political order. In Central America, traditional military governments were seriously threatened by insurgencies, with the Nicaraguan army having already been destroyed. Clearly, a U.S. policy that relies heavily upon Latin militaries will be in for some rocky times, and possibly for some traumatic failures. If such a policy cannot work in our own "sphere of influence," what can its prospects be in other regions of the Third World?

THE MILITARY AS A SOURCE OF INSTABILITY

Greek tragedies are formed around a common motif: out of pride and arrogance, men who would be great destroy themselves. Whatever their claim to greatness, Third World militaries too often damage their own and the nation's interests by radicalizing moderates. The likelihood of such eventual outcomes may not immediately be apparent: especially to U.S. officials accustomed to sanctifying the military as the main and perhaps only source of immediate order. Yet militaries do produce this instability, if inadvertantly, in several ways. Military regimes that seize or maintain power by force may not reflect a country's actual balance of political forces. After all, rape is not love, and such governments are unstable almost by definition. Had the Dominican military proceeded with its attempts to perpetrate fraud and deny Antonio Guzman and his majority Dominican Revolutionary Party (PRD) power in the 1978 elections, civil strife and continuing instability would have been inevitable. In both Bangladesh and Bolivia, feuding army factions have fueled chaos by repeatedly evicting promising civilian governments.

An exclusionary military regime that indiscriminately destroys civilian institutions, political parties, and leaders forfeits acceptable alternative futures. An amorphous environment of opposition is created that radical forces may be able to shape to their advantage. When repressive military governments deprive moderates of effective tools of opposition, they create desperate men, who will be more likely to adopt extreme methods or develop questionable alliances. These phenomena are only too apparent in the recent Central American upheavals. They were also at work in Vietnam and are waiting to surface again in South Korea if the military continues to deny liberalization.

This is not to say that Third World militaries can never maintain power, even over considerable intervals of time. It is to say that the United States should be aware of the dangers of equating military discipline with consensus and of perceiving short-term control as equivalent to long-term legitimacy. Too often, militaries have failed to design durable institutions. Too often, they are the destabilizers and the polarizers, the inside agitators that unravel a nation's fabric.

Conclusion

Awareness of how the post–World War II world has changed explains why Washington is no longer able to determine events in distant lands. U.S. policy-makers pay lip service to this new "diffusion of power," but they behave as if this were the same comfortable old world. The result is a wedge between means and objectives and a chronic sense of frustration. Administrations that visibly fail despite their best efforts to work their will in Third World states expose themselves to charges of incompetence, lack of fortitude, and even betrayal. Having placed U.S. "credibility" on the line, they find themselves without the means to defend U.S. interests as they themselves have defined them.

Our ability to dictate winners and losers in internal power struggles, or to alter the behavior of the victors, has been disrupted by the anarchy in the international economy and by the U.S. government's declining economic influence. Our leverage is restrained by our allies' interest in pursuing commercial advantage. Too many other nations, or groups within nations, are defining their interests differently from ours. Mexico and Brazil disagreed with us about the Nicaraguan Revolution's implications for hemispheric security. Argentina placed its commercial interest in grain sales above our need to punish the Soviets for their intervention in Afghanistan. Iran, even under the Shah, sought ever-higher oil prices. Saudi Arabia failed to support the Camp David peace accords. Nigeria accepted and even praised the Cuban presence in Angola. Nor have groups within nations been more cooperative. Businessmen in El Salvador, Nicaragua, and Iran disrupted our efforts to arrange political settlements. Third World militaries in Peru, Brazil, Ethiopia, Libya, and elsewhere have adopted nationalistic policies contrary to our wishes.

Our ability to persuade or coerce these nations or groups into accepting more accommodating policies is restricted and in many cases declining. Even in Central America, our traditional sphere of influence, where a history of U.S. military and other forms of influence have engendered a deep psychological dependency, local business sectors no longer agree to play Tonto to our Lone Ranger. These rejections have been especially damaging in moments of political crisis, as occurred in Nicaragua and El Salvador.

Nor have we found the antidote in local armies. For those who saw in Third World militaries an instrument of stable "authority" and a loyal ally, the decade of the 1970s was especially disappointing. Those who have blamed President Carter's human rights policies for the failure of Third World militaries to follow the U.S. lead were deluding themselves. Historical forces with much deeper roots were at work. President Reagan demoted the human rights theme, but Argentina and Brazil proceeded nonetheless to sign major trading agreements with the Soviet Union in 1981. Rejecting Reagan's personal appeal, Argentina invaded the Falkland Islands in 1982, and Haig's exhausting shuttle diplomacy was unable to convince the Argentine generals to withdraw peacefully from the British colony.

When we have been able to find a congenial leader, his regime has sometimes proven less than durable and our capabilities for saving it inadequate. Even military governments have been unable to endure. Nor can we expect to be able to find another local power in the region willing and able to intervene and establish a more malleable government. And when we do, we may discover that instead of resolving the problem, we have only exported it to a new friend.

Among the many regimes we have supported, some have survived for a generation or more. In a world of incessant political change, our diplomats understandably label these "success stories." Nevertheless, as Somoza and the Shah illustrate, regimes that may once have been solid can quickly disintegrate. Exactly because of the long record of good fortune, the United States may be caught off guard by the fall, and resist adapting to the adverse turn of events.

The complexities and uncertainties of the Third World are frustrating both policymakers and the American public alike. We cannot count on regional powers to protect our interests, but they on their part will inevitably try to entangle us in age-old, local conflicts. More nations are able to supply weapons to various disputing parties. The increasing likelihood of a Soviet presence at first glance seems to clarify our interests, but in fact adds a complicating dimension to already difficult situations.

These theaters of operation are littered with broken props, debris left over from our efforts to stage manage events in the Third World. When we see the failure of the Nixon "regional influentials" doctrine, the disloyalty of old friends, the non-reliability of businessmen, generals, even of our NATO allies, we understandably experience anxiety. A reflexive response is to revert to the familiar, to try again the rejected policy to which these now failing policies were a response; we can, for example, try to enforce our will through the direct use of U.S. arms. Thus, the Carter administration, frightened and frustrated by events in the Persian Gulf, announced the "Carter Doctrine," whereby vital U.S. interests in the region would be protected by U.S. military might, some of which would be stationed nearby in a string of military facilities. This represents the reverse of the Nixon Doctrine. How this military presence, which the Reagan administration has sought to deepen, would solve the actual problems at hand was unclear. The problems seemed to stem from the instability of local rulers, intraregional rivalries, the recalcitrance of regional states, and the play of new international economic forces. These problems are not unique to the Middle East nor are they easily resolved by the use of military force. In fact, in most other regions we will have neither the option, nor the resources, to establish a direct U.S. military presence.

It is as though we were stuck in a nightmarish, closed-reel tape of the Gunfight at the O.K. Corral. We reach for our Colts and find cap pistols. We persist in the dream because we confuse who we are with how we must behave. It is time to awaken to the real implications of this seeming loss of control over our own destinies. In the next two chapters, we will begin to examine how U.S. interests might be redefined to take advantage of the newly emerging international economic and security orders and our place within them.

2 *A Safer Economic World*

High-level Washington officials, buttressed by some academic experts, have painted a stormy picture of future economic relations between the Third World and the industrialized West.[1] Radical, antimarket forces are gaining ground in developing countries, according to these alarmists. Third World governments are building directed economies that are squeezing private initiative. Many Third World states want to dismantle the international economic system, which they blame for their underdevelopment, and the much touted "New International Economic Order" is their blueprint for a revolutionary future. The image is that of a beleaguered American island isolated from essential trade and investment opportunities and deprived of crucial raw materials.

As Secretary of State, Alexander Haig delivered an ominous warning to the American Bar Association that "the internal stability [of Third World states] is threatened by sudden social, political and economic change. Simultaneously, the West has become increasingly dependent on their natural resources."[2] Hammering on this theme in a key policy speech, Assistant Secretary of State for African Affairs Chester Crocker then reaffirmed U.S. support for "open market opportunities [and] access to key resources," specifically admonishing that in southern Africa, "important Western economic . . . and political interests are at stake." Moreover, economic development would be stalled if Africans pursued policies "which bloated government's role in the economy" and failed to grant "much greater opportunity to the private sector, both within these countries and from abroad."[3]

The implications of these official forebodings are alarmingly clear: the Third World is swarming with dangerous forces and vital United States economic interests are at risk. To counter these threats, the United States must regain its dissipated influence over events within Third World countries. Shirking aside the "Vietnam Syndrome," the United States ought to confront the hostile elements, aid their enemies, and prepare to intervene when all else fails.[4]

It should not surprise us that Third World nationalism is economic as well as cultural. Countries do not want merely to be clients of the United States, and they will bargain out of self-interest for more advantageous economic arrangements. For those American policymakers who still want to control the Third World, or for those who demand ideological conformity to free markets at home and abroad, such signs of nationalism are indeed harbingers of disaster. Whatever the imagined dangers, however, most Third World nationalists are not in fact a threat to basic United States economic interests. The loss of control over Third World politics does not necessarily translate into economic defeat.

This conclusion is drawn from the recognition of three interrelated trends. First, the structure of the international economy has changed in ways that make basic U.S. economic interests relatively secure whatever happens politically in Third World states. American traders and investors can do business in conservative nationalist Argentina, socialist Algeria, and revolutionary Angola. Second, economic structures in the 1980s vary less from country to country than ideological labels would suggest. Governments everywhere play a key role in their economies, while formerly centralized states in Eastern Europe are experimenting with market mechanisms. Finally, despite their corporatist, Marxist, or antiimperialist rhetoric, Third World leaders are increasingly aware of the limited options open to them if they wish to pursue economic development and maintain the needed economic links to the West.

Nations, like individuals, are not motivated solely by economics; political ideology and physical security are important, and sometimes overriding, concerns. However, conflicts over economics can amplify differences over ideology and even themselves seem to pose a threat to national sovereignty. Conversely, economic ententes between the United States and Third World states would open a new prospect for reduced tensions over ideology and security.

As we shall see in later chapters, the failures of American policymakers to understand the political economy of the Third World leads, again and again, to self-generated diplomatic disasters. Exaggerated American notions of a threat from the Third World induce unwarranted anxieties approaching paranoia. The tone of U.S. policy becomes surly and aggressive. Like the boastful but insecure schoolyard bully, the U.S. needlessly picks fights with smaller boys who mean no harm but simply refuse to kowtow. As a result, our image and our diplomacy suffer; the Soviets are handed easy opportunities to pose as the selfless defender of Third World sovereignty. Equally important, the obsessive fear of the Third World has detracted attention from the primary danger to U.S. economic interests. The true challenge to economic stability lies less in the Third World's political turbulence than in the possible mismanagement of the global economic system by the United States and its developed allies.

The Boom in Banking

One of the most dramatic developments in international economics in the past decade has been the explosion in banking. In the course of only a few years, the commercial banks of the industrial states have evolved from being a secondary source of finance for developing countries to being their most significant creditor. By 1981, commercial banks had outstanding claims against the developing world exceeding $265 billion and the sum is still growing.[5]

As a result of this expansion, the banks—based in the United States, Western Europe, and Japan—have replaced the multinational industrial corporations as the major source of private foreign capital for developing countries. In 1970, investments by multinational corporations (MNCs) in less developed countries (LDCs) were $3.5 billion, while new loans (extended primarily by banks) totalled $2.7 billion. By 1979, the banks' loan disbursements of $48 billion had far surpassed the MNC capital flows of $13.5 billion (see table 1). The actual disparity was even larger since a portion of the MNC investment represented reinvested earnings rather than new flows from the industrial states. The World Bank projected that by 1990 annual net private loans to LDCs may reach $55 billion and possibly as much as $95 billion, while direct investment by MNCs will fluctuate between $19 and $24 billion.[6]

As the volume of outstanding bank loans accumulates, interest income will become the dominant form of earnings for the developed nations from the Third World. By the end of the 1970s, income earned by U.S. financial institutions in the Third World had already surpassed the profits of all manufacturing subsidiaries. In 1980, income earned on

TABLE 1: TRENDS IN INDUSTRIAL COUNTRY DIRECT INVESTMENT AND BANK LENDING TO DEVELOPING COUNTRIES, 1970–1979 (In Billions of Dollars)

Years	1970	1971	1972	1973	1974	1975	1976	1977	1978	1979
Direct Investment[1]	3.5	3.6	4.5	6.7	7.1	10.5	7.6	9.5	11.2	13.5
Financial Markets[2] (disbursements)	2.7	3.9	6.0	8.7	11.6	15.5	20.9	27.2	41.0	48.1

[1]SOURCE: 1970–1976: K. Billerbeck and Y. Yasugi, *Private Direct Investment in Developing Countries,* World Bank Staff Working Paper 348 (Washington, D.C.: World Bank, 1979), table SI.3, p. 63.
1977–1979: OECD *Development Co-operation Report 1980* (Paris: OECD, 1980), table A.1, p. 177.

[2]SOURCE: 1970–1972: World Bank, *World Debt Tables: External Public Debt of Developing Countries,* vol. I (Washington, D.C.: World Bank, 1979), table B, p. xxi. Figures based on sum of Private Banks and Others categories.
1973–1979: ibid., vol II (1980), Table 4–G, p. 73.

interest reached $10.4 billion, outstripping the $7.6 billion in profits earned by nonpetroleum investments.[7] This gap between interest and investment income will probably widen in the 1980s. This shift represents a fundamental restructuring in the economic relations between the North and the South.

Why have the commercial banks been so enthusiastic in lending such vast sums to the developing world? The answers are simple and boil down to bankers' calculations of risks, profits, and opportunities. At first glance, nations lacking a track record on international capital markets and suffering from chronic balance of payments crunches might be considered poor credit risks. Zaire, for example, had only gained independence in 1960 and was heavily dependent upon copper, an unstable revenue earner. Yet, in Zaire as elsewhere, the bankers saw opportunity. The developing world's large number of potential clients would widen the breadth of bankers' portfolios, thereby diversifying risk across an expanding set of borrowers. Where the risk in one country was judged to be high, banks charged higher interest rates and other "fees." Banks also tried to reduce potential hazard by lending to governments and by having central banks, or official development agencies, guarantee loans made to private firms. Thus, loans to Zaire were made to government corporations, including the national power and copper companies, and often guaranteed by the export insurance agencies located in the lenders' home country.

Banks recognized that a severe shortage of hard currency would periodically prevent some countries from meeting their foreign obligations. The international banking system devised numerous schemes, or instruments, to keep such temporary balance of payment crises from precipitating actual defaults. Some of these mechanisms are little more than sleight-of-hand; but in the magical world of banking, appearance is the hat that holds the elusive rabbit, the all-important "confidence." For instance, a country can be rescued from the edge of bankruptcy by being granted a "rollover." The banks in this case simply inform the country that as soon as payments are received on the debt, the country can immediately borrow the same amount. "Refinancing" can also redeem a nation by making available new loans to repay old ones. When Zaire fell upon hard times as copper prices tumbled in the mid-1970s, the banks offered to open new credits once Zaire made deposits in a special "set-aside" account to be filled with copper revenues. In the most desperate instances, banks permit a formal "rescheduling," allowing the debtor to complete payments at a later date. When Zaire proved unable to meet the terms of the "set-aside" agreement, the bankers agreed in 1980 to stretch out maturing debt over a ten-year period. All of these devices serve both the lender's and the borrower's interests, since both wish to avoid the damage that accrues to reputations and financial balance sheets when loans go sour.

The banks also felt comfortable doing business with LDCs because they believed that in the worst case the United States government would bail them out. Generally, the United States would try to keep friendly governments solvent on "national security" grounds. The U.S. supported a series of loans by the International Monetary Fund (IMF) and the World Bank to keep Zaire alive, although the U.S. government, suffering under budgetary constraints, failed to supply the additional resources needed to cure the chronically ill African economy. Should a country default, the Federal Reserve Board would act in the interests of domestic financial security to minimize the impact on the U.S. banking system. Presumably this might require an injection of government funds into the wounded banks.

These profit-versus-risk calculations provided the banks with the safety nets they needed to justify what they already wanted to do for a more compelling reason. Deposits were gushing in from OPEC, from industrial nations holding surplus currency, and from the multinationals; but the demand for loans was sluggish in the stagnant industrial economies. The more rapidly growing LDCs were the most promising markets for these excess funds.

As the debt levels of the LDCs rose and the balance-of-payments positions of many countries deteriorated in the 1970s and early 1980s, the banks repeatedly revised their criteria for lending. Again and again, acceptable ratios for such key variables as debt service versus export earnings and debt outstanding versus gross national product (GNP) were revised upward.[8] These trends caused occasional anxieties, but they were always rationalized as necessary adjustments to changing circumstances. Actually, bankers had little choice. The more cautious banks would have found themselves losing market shares as their competitors expanded. Perhaps more important, without repeated injections of new loans, the banks' LDC clients would have been forced into default and bankruptcy. The doctor was dependent on the health of his patients.

From the perspective of the developing world, the banks' interest in them came at a fortuitous time. Oil price hikes, global inflation, and slow growth in exports to the industrial states contributed to burgeoning trade and current-account deficits. Zaire's current account turned from a positive $50 million in 1968 to a negative $204 million in 1973, while Brazil's deficit widened from $526 million in 1968 to $7 billion in 1974.[9] The oil-importing developing world as a whole needed an immediate inflow of $38 billion to cover its 1975 deficit. Official lending agencies, such as the World Bank and IMF, and the traditional source of foreign private capital, the MNCs, were not adequately equipped to meet this demand. Only the banks had the cash, the flexibility, and the interest.

The relative shift from multinational corporate investment to commercial lending had several advantages for the developing world. Direct foreign investments posed distinct liabilities to the host nation. MNCs, with their oligopolistic or controlled markets, often made super profits; and it was extraordinarily difficult for LDCs to supervise a subsidiary's complex financial transactions. This was especially true when the transactions were in-house with the other arms of the subsidiary's parent corporation. It was like trying to follow an octopus playing a shell game. Even more frustrating was the linkage between a multinational firm's investments and foreign ownership and control of assets. These assets often included natural resources—bauxite, copper, iron ore, oil, sugar—strategically located in the local economy. Inevitably, MNC investment transferred important decision-making powers to institutions whose first loyalty lay with home offices in the United States, Western Europe, or Japan. Finally, MNCs brought with them a particular technology, a form of work organization, and a culture that were not always harmonious with the traditions of the host country. Tensions naturally increased between MNCs and developing nations, and produced a rash of nationalizations in the 1960s and the early 1970s. The 1971 takeovers by Salvador Allende of the Anaconda and Kennecott Copper subsidiaries, together with the highly visible ITT, were perhaps the most notorious. The sharp reactions by the MNCs and the U.S. government, which contributed to the brutal overthrow of the Chilean regime, were decried throughout the Third World. These conflicts led to a slowdown in direct investment by the MNCs.

The rise of the commercial banks as the chief channel for capital transfer alleviated many of these problems. In the past, LDCs were at a disadvantage in bargaining with MNCs because LDCs had to compete against each other in offering favorable investment climates. With the arrival of the banks, the tables turned. Central bankers in the Third World could afford to leave executives from international banks waiting in anterooms, as the bankers bid against one another to "sell" their money. Whereas the profit levels of multinational investments, highly variable and often difficult to pinpoint, were a constant source of dispute, the interest rates charged by the bankers were more uniform and precise. Compared to the differentiated markets of the multinationals, where a few firms often dominate, international capital markets are populous and competitive. Dozens of large banks and investment brokers are hawking the same basic product—money. Market conditions set the rates of return (the interest rates) and these are public knowledge. Some LDCs may have to pay one or even two percent more for money, but this differential is small when compared to the variance in profit rates (15 percent and more above normal rates) enjoyed by some MNC subsidiaries.

Approximately two-thirds of the loans to LDCs are made to governments or to other banks.[10] For example, of the $13.6 billion lent by U.S. banks to Brazil at the end of 1979, $4.1 billion were to government entities, $4.6 billion to other banks; of $4 billion lent to the Philippines, $1.2 billion were to the public sector, $1.4 billion to banks. These capital transfers give the foreign banks no ownership rights and little direct control over particular sectors of the local economy. Bank loans are invisible flows existing on teletypes and in ledgers and encapsule little technology or culture. With the high-visibility issues of cultural penetration and economic control displaced, the emotions aroused by the process of capital transfer cooled. The dangers of irrational outbursts against foreign capital diminished sharply.

Developing nations have often gained partial ownership over a local mining or manufacturing subsidiary. but rarely over the MNC itself. Yet LDCs have gained in recent years leverage over the international banks through bank deposits. These claims against the multinational banks have reached $160 billion for the OPEC countries and have surpassed $90 billion for the rest of the developing world.[11] The largest depositors can even distort the inner deliberations of the banks. Furious at criticism of one of Chase Manhattan's major depositors, bank chairman David Rockefeller reportedly repressed an unfavorable analysis of Saudi Arabia by a country risk specialist. The discouraged analyst resigned shortly afterwards.

Developing countries also have welcomed the banks' flexibility in defining "political risk." Far from fearing state participation in economies, the banks have preferred to lend to governments, or at least to have their loans guaranteed by governments. International banks seek this government involvement because governments often control hard currency, especially in moments of crisis. It is in hard currency that banks generally wish to be repaid.

Bankers, it is true, often demonstrate a preference for authoritarian regimes of the Right or the Left. Strong governments are in the best position not only to guarantee hard-currency repayment, but also to control the levels of internal consumption and demand for imports. Wages and public expenditures must be restrained if hard currency is not to be spent on imports to the detriment of meeting payments on external debts. Banks were so confident of the Eastern European governments' ability to control internal consumption and meet their debt service that they had $60 billion in outstanding loans by the end of 1980 (see table 2). At the same time, banks have lent generously to South Korea, the Philippines under Marcos, Chile under Pinochet, and Argentina after the military takeover in 1976. In each country, the dictatorship stood armed to repress popular pressures for higher living standards that could drain scarce foreign exchange. Banks will of course also lend to liberal democracies if they appear capable of balancing their budgets and containing domestic consumption. What bankers fear most are weak governments unable to control public and private expenditures —the bankers' definition of "instability." If a government can guarantee stability, its particular organizational and ideological characteristics are secondary concerns.

This does not mean that individual bankers do not have personal preferences for certain ideologies or even rulers. For example, David Rockefeller developed personal attachments to such clients as the Shah of Iran and Argentine Finance Minister (1976–81) José Martínez de Hoz. The survival of these regimes may be important to the interests of individual banks or bankers. Their demise, however, need not affect the interests of the banking system as a whole. Thus, Chase Manhattan lost Iranian deposits when the Shah fell, but the funds were promptly redeposited in the Bank of America.[12]

TABLE 2: OUTSTANDING COMMERCIAL CREDITS EXTENDED BY WESTERN FINANCIAL INSTITUTIONS TO EASTERN EUROPE, End-1980.

COUNTRY	BILLIONS OF DOLLARS
USSR	10.8
Bulgaria	3.2
Czechoslovakia	4.2
German Democratic Republic	11.2
Hungary	8.1
Poland	14.8
Romania	7.8
Total:	60.1

SOURCE: Information provided to the author by the U.S. Department of Commerce, International Trade Administration, Office of East-West Policy and Planning.

It is true that bankers prefer regimes that pay extraordinary interest rates and fees and that allow wide-open opportunities to establish local branches that can take in deposits and engage in full-service banking. But these are preferences, not requirements. As the Third World matures, banks are recognizing that they cannot expect patsies for partners. Moreover, some banks have learned the hard way that the Shahs and Mobutus are unsteady associates. The banks by now are well accustomed to doing business with mature governments, even when domestic banking has been nationalized, as in Algeria, Cuba, Costa Rica, Gabon, India, and Romania.

Table 3 shows the long list of developing countries that have borrowed over $100 million from the world's banking system. Countries with economical and political structures and ideologies as diverse as Algeria, Argentina, Cuba, Guyana, Indonesia, Jordan, Kenya, Mexico, Tunisia, Zaire, and Zambia were all active users. While the better off ("upper tier") developing countries had absorbed the bulk of the finance, an increasing number of lower-middle-income countries were gaining access to international credit.

In sum, because the banks were less visible than the MNCs, more eager to do business, organized in a more competitive market, more politically flexible, and willing to work with governmental institutions, the central process of capital transfer was smoothed. Avenues were open for countries with differing resource endowments, levels of development, economic models, and political persuasions to participate on terms acceptable to both lender and borrower. As capital flows rose dramatically, decibel levels lowered in international financial disputes. What had been a shouting match became a debate.

More recently, the rate of increase in bank lending to developing countries has slowed. Sluggish export markets occasioned by the global recession, and high interest rates have made it more difficult for countries to service foreign debt. A more gradual buildup of debt was, in any event, desirable: some LDCs were borrowing more than they could efficiently invest. As we shall see, however, reforms in the international financial system are required to assure that a useful correction does not become a cumulative contraction that could threaten both the solvency of the banks and the growth prospects of the Third World.

The Survival Instincts of Multinational Corporations

Even if banks have become the primary vehicle for transferring capital to the Third World, multinational companies (MNCs) continue to find or create lucrative business opportunities. Political and economical turbulence, nationalizations, public-sector interventions, and monetary and exchange-rate instabilities have not prevented U.S. firms from expanding their Third World operations. In fact, the trade and international investment activities of U.S. firms have been growing more rapidly than their purely domestic operations. The MNCs have been drawn to the more rapidly expanding markets of the developing nations.

Size and dynamism account for much of the multinational success story. MNCs control global marketing and information networks, and their large-scale production gives them an added competitive edge. Many MNCs can generate massive amounts of capital within their own organizations while simultaneously enjoying preferential access to bank financing. Their superior research and development facilities assure them of control over technological innovation. Combined, these advantages create "barriers to entry" that protect the established giants against new challengers.

Multinationals may be large and omnipresent, but they are not dinosaurs. Their ability to be highly adaptive to changing circumstances in the Third World has contributed to their success. When many LDCs erected tariff walls against MNC products, the MNCs leapfrogged the barriers by successfully establishing local subsidiaries. Multinational pharmaceutical firms, for example, set up shop in dozens of LDCs, including Costa Rica, India, Pakistan, and Sri Lanka. As governments began to demand an equal voice through participation, MNCs learned to live profitably with joint ventures.[13] Where LDCs created state monopolies (as Brazil, Mexico, India, and Turkey did in steel), MNCs

TABLE 3: DEVELOPING COUNTRIES WITH ACCESS TO INTERNATIONAL CAPITAL MARKETS. (Cumulative Medium And Long-Term Disbursements From Private International Financial Markets, 1973–79)

COUNTRY	MILLIONS OF U.S. DOLLARS
Algeria	10,284
Argentina	17,031
Bangladesh	346
Bolivia	2,842
Brazil	31,339
Cameroon	1,273
Chile	6,770
China (Rep. of)	3,454
Colombia	3,776
Congo	210
Costa Rica	1,021
Cuba	1,830*
Dominican Republic	1,258
Ecuador	3,705
Egypt	856
El Salvador	272
Gabon	3,580
Guyana	466
Honduras	390
Indonesia	13,562
Iran	8,351
Ivory Coast	2,475
Jamaica	596
Jordan	732
Kenya	373
Liberia	286
Malawi	191
Malaysia	2,699
Mauritania	262
Mexico	36,710
Morocco	8,846
Nicaragua	475
Nigeria	2,657
North Korea	580*
Oman	687
Pakistan	939
Panama	5,669
Papua New Guinea	666
Paraguay	350

COUNTRY	MILLIONS OF U.S. DOLLARS
Peru	11,438
Philippines	3,288
Senegal	966
Singapore	2,013
South Korea	6,864
Sudan	2,264
Tanzania	183
Togo	594
Thailand	1,879
Trinidad & Tobago	1,105
Tunisia	2,325
Turkey	3,664
Uruguay	2,622
Venezuela	20,870
Zambia	2,415
Zaire	1,474

SOURCE: World Bank, *World Debt Tables,* vol. 1, (Washington, D.C.: World Bank, 1980) Table 1–G, p.13–14.

*Data for Cuba and North Korea, which includes short-term liabilities, is from the Bank for International Settlements; the liabilities are not cumulative, but rather are the countries' positions at the end of 1980.

entered into licensing, managing, and trading arrangements. Where countries have pressured firms to increase the use of local components, or to export, the multinationals' purchasing and marketing networks have expanded and often become more aggressive.

Indeed, the multinationals have been able to turn each successive set of demands, even those that at first appeared onerous or prohibitive, into advantages. Forced by tariffs to substitute local production for trade, MNCs proceeded to establish a solid presence in the host-countries' economy and society. Under the old regime, LDCs could curtail imports of consumer goods when foreign exchange was scarce; but once local production was in place, thousands of local jobs were dependent upon the firms' good health. Governments became obligated to supply the subsidiary with the required intermediate imports so that local production could continue. The network of workers and consumers that surrounded the subsidiary acted as a local pressure group on the firm's behalf.[14] Thus, in Allende's Chile, while the old-fashioned copper subsidiaries were confiscated outright, manufacturing subsidiaries were treated with care and the MNCs were often encouraged to maintain their operations.

A rising percentage of foreign investment is being concentrated in such manufacturing firms. They are less visible than large natural resource complexes and so are less likely to become the target of nationalist ire. Even where pressures mount on manufacturing subsidiaries to export a portion of their production to earn foreign exchange, it ultimately benefits the firm: since the subsidiary—and the host country—only become more tightly integrated into the MNC's global operations.

Firms that do operate in highly visible natural resource extractions and in public utilities, and who are forced into joint ventures, have found that the new relationship calmed local resentments. As a result, the risks of hostile, politically motivated legislation decreased. Chilean ruler Augusto Pinochet offered Exxon 100 percent ownership of a large copper complex, but the diversifying multinational actually suggested that the Chilean government might want to be a joint partner! Exxon felt that a joint venture arrangement would be protection in the event of a change in political regimes. Association with state firms not only reduces negative political exposure, it also can be used to guarantee official favors and to secure oligopolistic charters and privileges.

Naturally, multinationals complain loudly about host-country policies on taxation, performance criteria, price fixing, credit restrictions, limitations on the amount of profits that can leave the country, and a whole variety of other regulations. Nevertheless, as long as the investment is sufficiently profitable and the business climate is stable, the firms will generally try to accommodate the host-government's stipulations. As a study of MNCs conducted for the business-oriented Committee for Economic Development concluded, "Multinational corporations now tend to be less ideological and more pragmatic and flexible in their approach to operations in the developing world. . . . By and large, the multinationals understand and accept this [interventionist] role for the governments of developing countries."[15]

The multinationals have also learned to do business in countries with a wide variety of political institutions and ideologies. The Committee for Economic Development study, which surveyed 400 subsidiaries, found that "the transnationals said that if the terms of operation are clear and stable, they can operate in almost any situation, no matter how stringent the regulations, as long as some margin for profit exists. As an example, they pointed to their subsidiaries in Eastern Europe."[16]

The multinational oil companies' pragmatism in Angola is a dramatic example of this accomodation to shifting politics. Gulf Oil has not only maintained operations on its investment prior to the ouster of the Portuguese, but it has planned an additional $115 million in capital improvements. Gulf and the several other foreign oil firms operating in Angola have convinced the U.S. Export-Import Bank to lend $85 million, and Morgan Guaranty to help raise another $50 million in commercial money, to finance a gas-injection project for offshore wells. Gulf's general manager in Angola, Tom King, explained his firm's willingness to do business in a country ruled by self-defined Marxists: "One of the buzzwords floating around the world is pragmatism. I think it works here. . . . We are here on a business relationship." Nor does King object to the government oil company, Sonangol, owning a majority share in their joint venture: "We have a good rapport at the senior management level. This is not the first time we've done this kind of thing."[17] The oil companies also understandably haven't balked at the decision by the Angolan government to assign Cuban troops to protect their oil wells against raids by dissident guerrilla factions.

Of course, today some MNCs still are able to grasp a monopolist's share of benefits from international investment and trade. In many LDCs, profit margins are now much higher than those in the United States. Even taking into account the extra risk associated with the developing world, such profits are well in excess of what might be considered a "normal" return on capital.[18] As developing countries gain expertise and bargaining power, MNC profit levels will tend to decline. Initially, firms will feel threatened, but they have already demonstrated an ability to accommodate to new rules of the game. There is enough slack in the system so that conditions can tighten considerably in the developing world and firms will still enjoy "bottom line" profits as auspicious as those generated in the industrial states.

In the worst case, a combination of widespread instabilities, resurgent nationalism and slower LDC growth could reduce foreign investment opportunities. From the perspective of the United States' national interest, a slowdown in the rate of overseas investment might be beneficial. Instead of relying on cheap, Third-World labor and new markets for outmoded products and technologies, U.S. firms would be forced to compete more aggressively to win larger shares of the U.S. market and other markets where innovation is a necessary quality.[19] Firms could concentrate their resources on gaining and maintaining technological superiority, and on increasing labor productivity. In the long run, the firms might benefit from having to invest in the reindustrialization of America.

The U.S. economy can respond to a less favorable overseas climate for direct investment either by increasing investments in the United States, or by shifting capital flows to the international banking system. (Relative profit rates or government regulations would determine how much is invested in each market.) The rise of commercial banking means that overseas outlets for U.S. dollars are not foreclosed when direct investment opportunities are narrowed. This new flexibility means, from the perspective of some Marxists, that, once more, capitalism has found new channels to dispose of surplus capital. The great crisis has again been postponed. From the perspective of the State Department and liberal internationalists, arteries remain open to unite the world system. Investors and bankers are simply pleased to add to their portfolio choices.

The Complex Drama of International Trade

Just as the operating environments for commercial banking and multinational corporations have undergone tremendous changes, the arena of international trade has also been transformed. Once again, many of these alterations open the system to developing nations. This is true in the traditional area of tariffs, where systematic reductions in industrial-country duties have allowed many developing nations to increase dramatically their industrial exports to the United States and Western Europe. LDCs no longer simply produce raw materials and food. The North is being flooded by clothing, processed leather products, toys, sporting goods, television sets, and ships made in the South. The international trading system also has evolved to permit Third World countries with active public sectors to participate more fully.

The structure of international trade is an increasingly complex drama of private and public activity, of "free" and "administered" trade. International trade follows an intricate dialogue where private and public actors have parts to play at both ends of the transaction. Moreover, the transaction itself may occur not under the invisible hand of an unknown auctioneer (as orthodox economists would have us believe), but may be scripted by a government agency acting as an intermediary merchant.

Governments can be deeply involved in the production of export goods by the private sector. In countries as distant geographically and ideologically as Zaire, Chile, South Korea, and France, governments target industries as prospective exporters. These governments then extend tax breaks, provide research-and-development funds, build roads and port facilities, assure credit—often at subsidized rates—and may even assist in training skilled labor. Targeted products may be traditional (copper mining in Zaire), nontraditional agriculture (fruit and wines in Chile), light-industry consumer goods (textiles and electronics in South Korea), or high-technology industry (aircraft and nuclear power in France).

This extensive government role in the production and the sale of goods is justified in various ways. Developing countries argue that only the state can marshal the necessary resources and provide the required incentives to give the initial boost to such industries so that they can break into world markets. Even industrial states increasingly engage in such anti–free trade practices since their competitors are already doing so. As the tempo of world competition increases, the pressures for government assistance to export-oriented industries will continue to mount.

Governments have also traditionally used tariffs and exchange-rate regimes either to promote or inhibit international trade. Quotas and orderly marketing arrangements (OMAs) now distort the movements of such products as textiles, consumer electronics and some foodstuffs. Today, many governments play direct roles in arranging international trade transactions. Governments market their nation's products through embassies and trade fairs, sponsor teams of salesmen, and provide official credit guarantees to secure financing. Socialist countries are not alone in having ministries of trade to purchase their nation's products for export. Government-chartered trading companies, such as the quasi-public Samsung Group of South Korea, have been modeled after Japan's *zaibatsus*. The Canadian Wheat Board, the Salvadoran Coffee Board, and the Gabon Cocoa Bureau are all charged with the task of maximizing revenues for their domestic producers. In the United States, the Defense Department and the Department of Agriculture play an active role in marketing domestic production abroad. Sometimes the foreign client has already signed a contract and the U.S. government is just providing bridge financing. In other cases, a government agency acts as a broker to find outlets for production that is in surplus, or for goods that must be made and sold if firms are to operate at efficient production levels.

Socialist countries typically engage in "administered" or barter trade. Increasingly, nonsocialist states are involved not only in export production, but also in arranging two-way packages. Sometimes the partner is a second government. For example, Mexico has agreed to a long-term, petroleum-supply contract with France in return for imports of French technology. Other times, the partner may be a multinational corporation. The deal may be a straight-forward swap (the simplest form of barter), a "buy-back" or an "offset" agreement. In one "buy-back" agreement, Levi-Strauss sold Hungary equipment and expertise, while agreeing to purchase a portion of the plant's bluejean production and market it in other countries. An "offset" agreement occurs when a company agrees to buy products unrelated to its normal business. For example, McDonnell Douglas has sold DC–9s and DC–10s to Yugoslavia for substantial amounts of crystal glassware, cutting tools, leathers, and canned hams.

Socialist countries pioneered these forms of barter, but many LDCs now try to use foreign governments and multinational corporate trading partners to help them market their products abroad. General Motors alone is working presently with twenty-six countries in various forms of barter, or "countertrade" deals. Some analysts predict that such nonmarket transactions will account for 20 percent or more of international trade in the 1980s. Indeed, this may already be the case.[20]

Apparently then, capitalist-oriented governments are involved deeply in international trade from production through sales, and are using their exports as leverage to guarantee desired imports. Such governmental activity is intended to increase competitiveness and bargaining power, or to insure the supply of essential foodstuffs, raw materials, or other strategic commodities. Sometimes government action is aimed at countering the distorting effects that giant multinational firms can have on perceived national interests and on otherwise open markets. Since these goals respond to trends imbedded deeply in the global economy, it is reasonable to assume that governmental activity in international trade will intensify.

What this means is that to divide the world into the "good" free traders and the "evil" government intervenors is both dated and uninformed. "Free trade" can still serve as a rallying cry to contain protectionist pressures, but the slogan should not be confused with reality.[21] In fact, the existing pragmatic nonsystem for the exchange of goods is the most realistic answer to the pressures of austerity and nationalism in the 1980s. Nations can participate in international trade without sacrificing their nonnegotiable economic interests or their ideological preferences.

Government and Private Enterprise

The perceived threat from the Third World partly derives from a Manichaean image of what its economies are, or ought to be. The preferred, liberal ideal is an economy where goods and capital move freely and efficiently in markets that set prices by supply and demand.

In this frictionless world, governments—inherently uninformed, bureaucratic, and political—are restricted to perfecting the functioning of market mechanisms and to providing for national security.

President Reagan's secretary of the treasury, Donald Regan, invoked this vision before a gathering of world leaders and bankers. He recommended that other nations ought to follow his administration's philosophy, saying: "As I mentioned, the United States is embarked on a comprehensive new economic program. It rests on the fundamental premise that market mechanisms and individual effort, operating with a minimum of governmental impediments, are the driving forces behind sustainable economic growth."[22]

At the other extreme is the closed centralized economy where all the means of production are owned by the state, and all decisions are made from the center by the state planning commission. The socialized economy, operating under the premise that only autarky will ensure the independence needed for economic development and self-determination, withdraws intentionally from the international economy.

In past decades, the world did seem to be sharply divided into two hostile camps—one capitalist, one socialist—each seeking to realize its own ideal. Stalinist Russia was highly centralized and largely self-sufficient, and socialist China initially followed a similar path. Although many capitalist economies, developed and developing, have long been a more complex mix of public and private initiative than idealized models would suggest, many people thought the paragon of the free market was a relevant goal.

As so often happens, concepts have persisted after the conditions that produced them have changed. The world today is much more blurred than yesterday's ideologies ever thought possible. Everywhere, capitalist economies are a hodgepodge of private and public decision-making. In the United States, the share of GNP that passes through official hands has reached 30 percent (including federal, state, and local expenditures), while official incentives, subsidies, loan guarantees, tax preferences and regulations affect the allocation of additional resources. Despite its rhetoric, the Reagan administration can affect only marginally the government's impact on resource allocation. Administration officials would like to see federal spending fall from 22 percent to 19 or 20 percent of the GNP, but escalating defense spending actually increased the weight of federal outlays in 1981 and 1982. Efforts to cut government spending could also be frustrated by decisions of the states and local municipalities to increase their activities when federal services and subsidies actually do drop.

In many other nonsocialist countries, state activity is even more widespread. In LDCs, and to varying degrees in the Western European nations, the state is usually active in raw materials production, infrastructure (electricity, transportation, communication), and basic industry (steel, oil). Governments may also play a role in wholesale commerce, finance, and export production, and may participate in large-scale farming and high-technology industries such as computers, aircraft, and nuclear power. Petty commerce, real estate, construction, and most consumer-goods industries frequently remain in private hands. Additionally, many LDCs typically employ a variety of direct instruments such as price controls, foreign exchange rationing, and official credit allocations, as well as indirect instruments such as tax incentives, to influence the destinies of privately owned firms.[23]

In many countries, the public and private sectors recognize the advantages of a marriage that is mutually supportive.[24] In the earlier stages of development, the state builds ports and roads, educates an urban work force and protects fledgling industries from foreign competition. Only the state can gather the resources to undertake major projects. Indeed, in the most underdeveloped areas, market mechanisms and private entrepreneurs may not yet exist, or may be dominated by inefficient monopolies. As development progresses, the state is pressed to increase its technical and financial support to firms. Once, the state had protected them against foreign competition. Now, as the firms mature, the state assists them in competing in world markets. Governmental aid is required still again when the country is capable of constructing the expensive and technologically advanced capital-goods industries.[25] Moreover, as the developing nations become more tightly integrated into an increasingly competitive global economy, government involvement in industrial policy intensifies. Proponents of official activism argue coherently that only an aggressive state can hope to overcome the advantages of developed countries' firms, with their historically rooted head start and their access to subsidies from their own governments.

The state and the private sector in industrial and developing countries can work harmoniously and pragmatically to fulfill each other's priorities. Most American businessmen, at least in large firms, understand this. In a survey whose primary respondents were U.S. business leaders, the overwhelming majority favored an active federal role in promoting the "reindustrialization" of the United States.[26] The same survey asked, "Should the U.S. encourage LDCs to rely primarily on private development capital?" Forty-two percent disagreed, and only 14 percent expressed full agreement with such a doctrinaire strategy.[27]

This is not to deny that an inefficient or underfunded public sector can retard private initiative. In recent years, some countries have moved counter to the general trend of rising government intervention. For example, Jamaica, Egypt, Mali, and Sri Lanka have tried to reduce the role of the public sector by decontrolling prices and by selling state-owned firms. Attempts were also made to reduce official subsidies. Yet these reforms aren't necessarily a denial of the effectiveness of all governmental actions on the economy. They are the scrapping of outdated and inefficient interventions. Even in the United States, the role of the government inevitably remains very significant; moreover, it may take on newer, more appropriate forms that are adapted to contemporary circumstances such as official export promotion and energy development.

Sometimes, the objective of budget cutting is not the obvious one —the reduction of governmental activity. The primary intent may be to reverse the incidence of governmental taxes and subsidies; that is, to alter the winners and the losers in the fiscal scramble. The real issue has been income distribution, not the size of government. In the Reagan 1981 budget reform, expenditure reductions hit the poor hardest, while the tax cuts disproportionately benefitted the better-off. Government expenditures as a percentage of GNP actually rose. Escalating defense appropriations substantially offset the slashes in social programs.

Margaret Thatcher and Ronald Reagan notwithstanding, the clear trend in industrial states is toward governments trying to steer the course of their economies' industrial development. The costs and risks associated with rapid technological change often cannot be absorbed by private firms. The complexity and the size of investments now required in some industries argue for an increasing government role. Private enterprise, by itself, may hesitate to risk massive amounts of capital when profits will not be returned for many years. This may especially be true in industries where other governments subsidize competing firms.[28] Moreover, the quickening pace of international competition compels governments to assist their vigorous "sunrise" firms and to soften the impact of foreign competition on contracting "sunset" industries.

"Industrial policy" is a euphemism for the use of government instruments to alter economic structures. Sometimes the policies are planned and consistent, sometimes ad hoc and conflictive. Nonetheless, industrial policies are commonplace in advanced and developing countries. One in-depth study of eight world industries—tobacco, food processing, pharmaceuticals, autos, tractors, tires, electrical machinery, and steel—confirms this trend. It found that "in almost every industry, governments in both home countries and host countries played an important role in shaping industries' development."[29] A separate study calculated that the governments of the United Kingdom, West Germany, France, and Sweden by the mid-1970s were all involved in approximately a quarter or more of total manufacturing investment and research and development. Governmental participation took the form of grants, special loans, loan guarantees, and tax reductions. It included small business assistance, sectoral and regional policies, and export promotion. For example, in West Germany, supposedly a bastion of laissez-faire economics, the Ministry of Economics has assisted sectors in structural decline (coal mining, steel, shipbuilding, and textiles) to rationalize their holdings by preserving only their competitive segments.[30] The Ministry for Research and Technology has the task of actively promoting high-technology, knowledge-intensive industries. This conscious national industrial policy is orchestrated to restructure the economy away from firms that cannot be defended against superior foreign competition and toward world-class industries.

Just as capitalist economies do not meet the orthodox ideal, socialist states no longer blindly reproduce Stalinist centralization, heavy industrialization, and agricultural collectivization. Indeed in theory and increasingly in practice, socialists are experimenting with different mixes of centralization/decentralization and of public/private ownership. From China to Cuba, socialists are discovering the virtues of market mechanisms.

Most Third World countries that call themselves socialist still contain large private sectors. India, Zambia, Somalia, Egypt under Nasser, and Jamaica under Manley have all proclaimed socialism while permitting a substantial, perhaps still dominant, private sector to go on conducting business. The clenched fists and the rhetoric may be Marxist, but the working hands and the politics are often mildly reformist.

Yet, even in countries where the leadership is more seriously socialist in the Marxist tradition, the trend is toward pragmatic experimentation. Outside of Eastern Europe, few governments (even when led by self-defined Marxist parties) now seek to nationalize fully their means of production. In Angola, Algeria, and Nicaragua, for example, important sectors of the economy are in private hands. Moreover, even in states with strong public ownership, there is a definite trend toward locating power in the nationalized firms themselves. The hope is that decentralized decision making will be more efficient. Interestingly, the definition of "efficiency" that socialist managers normally accept approximates the capitalist definition. Efficiency is equated with minimizing costs and maximizing net revenue—in other words, with making a profit.

These tendencies toward decentralization and toward efficiency criteria are the result of several converging trends that are gripping Eastern Europe and many developing countries. First, the dynamics of international competition are establishing a demanding yardstick to measure performance. Second, the stagflation afflicting the global economy since 1974 adds further pressure on governments to give efficiency priority over ideology. Third, those who would benefit from decentralization and efficiency add their personal interests to the pressures for reform emanating from the global economy. Decentralization transfers power from government and party bureaucrats to the managers, technocrats, and skilled workers in firms. Efficiency criteria argue that the latter group ought to be given greater economic incentives; that is, higher salaries, bonuses, and perhaps even access to Westernized consumption styles. Finally, movement toward decentralization of economic decision making dilutes the power of the central bureaucracy and opens space for political relaxation.

Therefore, under these various pressures, many socialist states have been moving not toward communism, but toward the capitalist criteria of efficiency, decentralized decision making, less equal income distribution, and an openness to international trade. While these phenomena seem to be accelerating, they are not brand new. In the late 1940s and early 1950s, Yugoslavia was already experimenting in these directions. In the late 1960s, Hungary began to increase the power of firm managers and opened its economy to foreign trade. By 1980, Hungary was earning half of its export income in the West and was bringing domestic prices into line with world prices. Small-scale private business have also been encouraged to provide services that would be performed inefficiently by larger, more bureaucratic organizations. Today, China, Poland, and, to a lesser extent, Cuba are in the throes of the same impulse toward reform.[31]

In industrialized and developing countries, whether they are market-oriented or statist, nationalized firms are under mounting pressure to be self-financing. Tight government budgets no longer provide these firms with fat subsidies. With financial soundness as the operating guideline, nationalized firms begin behaving like privately owned firms. For example Albin Chalandon, the chief executive of the French state-controlled, oil-based conglomerate, Société-Nationale Elf Aquitaine, candidly admitted: "Elf does business in exactly the same way as a private enterprise and with the same motivations: to make money, to expand, to succeed."[32] It is no longer possible to survive as a sacred cow. Like animals in zoos, minimum levels of exercise and freedom are necessary if these already large enterprises are to experience healthy growth.

When they do grow, these internationally oriented, state-owned companies may also behave like privately owned firms. They may decide to build plants in foreign countries. Their motives will also resemble the motives of private firms: to hurdle tariff barriers that are blocking the entrance of their products; to move closer to raw materials' sources; to sell their technology; or simply to take advantage of opportunities for higher profits. Thus, Elf Aquitaine, which has held investments in such countries as Iran, Angola, and Canada, decided to acquire Texasgulf in the United States. As Elf's chief executive said, "We needed a place where we could make profits and raise funds and send them wherever we wanted to support our operations outside France."[33] The state-owned Petroleos Mexicanos (Pemex) is extending operations throughout the Caribbean, while Petroleos Brazileros (Petrobras) is active in Africa and even in the Middle East. Two Yugoslav companies, Naftaplin and Nafta-Gas, also have foreign holdings, including the oil concession in Angola that is jointly held with Elf and Mobil. Hungarian firms have entered into joint ventures in the U.S. to produce light bulbs and in Cyprus to grow flower bulbs.

Like members of different plant phyla responding to light in the same way, these giant firms have begun behaving similarly under the influences of an emerging—and nourishing—world economic system. Interestingly, neither Marxist nor capitalist ideologues want to recognize this convergence. If public-sector firms are governed by efficiency criteria, they can no longer appear as a panacea for capitalism's ills; but nor are they the metastatic cancers choking off healthy economic growth, as some of capitalism's apologists would have it.

It has been argued that the differences between the supposedly capitalist and the supposedly socialist economies are increasingly a matter of degree: that virtually all economies are idealized points situated along the straight lines of such key variables as centralization/decentralization, public/private sector ownership, and equality of income. It can also be argued that generic differences remain, but whatever the case in theory, convergences are undeniable and all-black/all-white dichotomies no longer correspond to reality. In important respects, we are more like each other than we may care to admit.

The remaining differences are significant enough to affect the relative power and wealth of contending groups and institutions within countries. Local business groups generally wield more clout and can appropriate more wealth in countries where they control a large portion of the economy. But these struggles need not be crucial or even important for hard U.S. economic interests (although, as we saw in chapter 1, they can affect traditional U.S. diplomatic objectives). The widespread tendencies toward openness, decentralization, and inequality are sufficient wedges to provide significant economic opportunities for the United States. From the perspective of U.S. lenders and traders, the differences between the mixed and the more socialized economies are increasingly narrow. All nations want to borrow on international capital markets, attract the talents of U.S. multinationals, and participate in international trade. Fortunately, international finance and trade have been evolving in ways that promise to stitch the many-colored strips of cloth that make up the national economies into the all-embracing cloak of a one-world economy.

The One-World Economy

Whether they are neoliberals, populists, social democrats, or Marxists, most Third-World leaders desperately want to participate in this new international system. They might like to alter it at the margin, or improve their own location within it; they cannot however, overthrow it. It is the only game in town. They are all locked into the one-world economy of integrated financial markets, multinational corporations, and international trade flows.

Neither rightist nationalists nor leftist socialists believe, as some once did, that autarky offers an alternative path to development. Everyone realizes that to rely solely on internal savings would require a prolonged and severe austerity. They also know that efforts to produce domestically all of the necessary goods for consumption and production would be both horrendously inefficient, and for many items, impossible. Their populations are accustomed to consumer goods that would require imported components and technology even if the goods could be produced locally. In fact, autarky is so costly and dislocating that it may even be unsustainable. For the increasing number of LDCs that are food importers, choosing autarky would invite mass starvation. To solve food shortages by "thinning the population" is crazy-quilt logic and any zealots wild enough to try imposing such a harsh regime would face not only internal rebellion, but even external subversion or foreign invasion on humanitarian or ideological grounds.

With its massive population, diversified resources, and backwardness, China offered optimal conditions for autarky. Advances in agriculture and social services were realized during the Stalinist and Maoist periods of self-reliance, but the post-Mao leadership decided that broader advances in labor productivity, industry, science and technology, and national defense demanded an opening to the West.

Premier Zhao Ziyang explicitly called for abandoning self-sufficiency and "advancing boldly" into the world market. Imports have risen rapidly, from $6 billion in 1977 to over $14 billion in 1979. Since 1978, more than $25 billion in credit has been extended to China by official export credit agencies and commercial banks, largely to finance future imports from the industrialized world.[34] China will purchase grain, cotton, steel, power generating equipment, and computer and communications technology in exchange for Chinese textiles, coal, oil, and possibly such metals as titanium, vanadium, and tantalum. Some of this trade will be facilitated by multinational corporations, who are now welcome to establish joint ventures on the Chinese mainland.

Far from desiring autarky, most LDCs would prefer to increase their imports. Their import levels are constrained not by ideological hostility to international trade, but by a very real lack of hard currency. Even Eastern Europe would increase its imports except for its scarcity of foreign exchange. Many LDCs have stretched successfully their capacity to import by borrowing heavily on international capital markets or by borrowing from official lending agencies that finance industrial-country exports.

LDCs do protect certain favored domestic producers against import competition. Assuming, however, that the lack of foreign exchange caps import levels, these trade barriers affect only the composition of imports and not the totals. It is true that during the postwar period many LDCs adopted economic policies that indirectly and inadvertently hampered exports, thereby slowing the growth of import capacity. Over the past decade, however, the pressures of the international economy and of the development process itself have caused many LDCs to dismantle some of these export disincentives, precisely to augment import capacity.

The pressures to improve export performance have been overwhelming. Economic development increases the demand for energy, food and high-technology products much faster than most LDCs can produce them domestically. The rising international prices of these items swell already sizable import bills. When these imports have been purchased on credit, the resulting need to service the external debt makes the foreign-exchange requirements still larger. Caught on this treadmill of ever-rising pressures to augment imports and exports, many LDC economies have increasingly oriented themselves toward international trade—the reverse of an autarkic closure. For some countries, including trade-oriented South Korea, relatively closed India, and socialist Hungary, production devoted to exports grew even more rapidly than GNP in the decade of the Seventies.

LDCs also want to participate more actively in the international capital markets. Most LDCs would borrow even more than they do, if it weren't for the constraints imposed by future debt-service requirements. Even so, many LDCs have been borrowing at a pace that, if maintained, could exceed their means to repay, and the commercial banks or the International Monetary Fund have imposed ceilings on their debt accumulation. Those fortunate enough to have surplus financial resources—from Venezuela to Libya—are pleased to deposit them in the large commercial banks of the West. Nowhere else can deposits so safely earn substantial returns.

Many LDCs have acquired debt service burdens that are eating up 25 percent and more of their export earnings. Nevertheless, none have repudiated these debts recently and those countries who once sinned—the Soviet Union, China, Cuba—are now major borrowers again. In fact, all nations must be concerned with maintaining their international credit ratings for fear of losing access to still higher levels of foreign indebtedness.

Developing countries have also learned to live with multinational corporations. LDCs now recognize that the multinationals offer technology, organizational skills, and information and marketing networks that are domestically unavailable. For example, the president of Mozambique, Samora Machel, told a *Time* correspondent:

> Foreign capital has experience working in socialist countries in Europe, Asia, and Latin America. It will have the opportunity to find out that here, just as in those countries, it will be able to make profits at the same time that it is contributing to the construction of socialism. That is our view in today's world of independence and complementarity.[35]

As the preceding sections have stressed, LDC governments have learned to use their leverage to alter the multinationals' behavior to suit national interests. Brazil, for example, has compelled multinational auto firms to establish local facilities that will produce a growing percentage of their automobiles domestically and then sell more of that production as exports. Mexico is now requiring the auto manufacturers to utilize a specified level of "local content" in their cars and to export enough of the finally assembled products to cover the costs of their imported contents. From China to Nigeria, governments have demanded that multinationals form joint ventures with either the government or with local capitalists.

Some critics of multinationals have argued that MNCs distort income distribution patterns in LDCs by making some workers more productive and by producing luxury items.[36] In some instances, MNC activities may support and even strengthen inequalities. However, their activities in Eastern Europe and elsewhere suggest that MNCs can adapt to societies of more even wealth distribution. If circumstances demanded, they could presumably alter products and production techniques, and make the necessary outlays for research and development and for retooling. After all, many firms in the developed states began producing luxury items for a narrow segment of society and are now delivering consumer goods for the masses. And in many industries today, global competition is forcing a pace of new-product generation that is fiercer than ever.

Other critics have accused MNC subsidiaries of being relatively sluggish in exporting to other Third World countries. Understandably, subsidiaries might not wish to compete with siblings already operating in such markets. In some instances, the subsidiary still might be willing to engage in limited exporting and use its knowledge of global marketing opportunities to achieve export levels above the levels the LDC could gain alternatively. In other cases however, the LDC may decide that only a state-owned or a state-subsidized and nationally owned firm will aggressively promote exports. The trade-oriented Japanese and South Koreans have established many firms on this latter assumption.

Such decisions to support local ownership should not be confused with an intention to opt out of the one-world economy. Quite to the contrary, the objective is usually to increase the nation's participation in international commerce. Indeed, it may be the multinational which is inhibiting market mechanisms in favor of production patterns that benefit the oligopolistic firm. Ironically, in this instance, it is the aggressive LDC state that must overcome the interventions of the oligopolistic MNC to reassert the principle of comparative advantage.

NO OTHER OPTIONS

One obvious reason for the LDCs' intense interest in joining the international economy is the lack of an alternative. Neither autarky, "South-South," or "collective self-reliance" are sufficient replacements. Nations may be able to reduce their dependence on certain imports, but, as China discovered, the very process of development creates demands for other imports. Nations can, to varying degrees, increase their trade with other developing states. Although such trade may be psychologically satisfying, the rules governing economic interchange among LDCs merely reproduce the strictures determining North-South relations. Nor is entrance into the socialist division of labor—the Council for Economic Cooperation (COMECON)—an attractive answer. COMECON markets offer opportunities for trade diversification, but they are not substitutes for the rest of the world. As the next chapter will discuss at greater length, the Soviet Union is leery of paying for "second Cubas"; that is, bankrolling the high costs of socialist transformations. Rather than absorbing new states, COMECON has been increasing its economic contracts with the West and the socialist states of Eastern Europe are also becoming integrated into the one-world system.

Those LDC governments—such as Libya, Angola, Mozambique, Ethiopia, Nicaragua, and Grenada—that have recently adopted an "anti-imperialist" foreign-policy rhetoric have nonetheless continued to concentrate their economic ties with capitalist states. As table 4 vividly shows, neither the radical rhetoric of these states, nor their security ties to the socialist bloc, have prevented them from selling their production to the West, or from remaining dependent upon imports from non-COMECON economies. Those with the requisite creditworthiness are borrowing from international capital markets and are doing business with MNCs. The replacement of political elites or even the transformation of entire state structures within particular Third World nations does not alter the international economy. New elites face the same imperative to participate in the one-world system; they have no other choice.

STRUCTURAL RESTRAINTS

If the developing countries cannot escape the one-world economy, can they, Samson-like, bring it crashing down around them? Can they withhold the vital raw materials that lubricate the Western economies and bring the industrial world to a screeching halt? Can they wreck the international financial system by purposefully defaulting on their debts?

TABLE 4: TRADE PATTERNS OF RADICAL, THIRD WORLD STATES (Percentage of Total Trade With Trading Partners, 1980)

COUNTRY	SOVIET BLOC	INDUSTRIAL COUNTRIES	DEVELOPING COUNTRIES
Algeria	1.9	93.4	4.6
Angola	16.0[1]	53.9	22.9
Ethiopia	7.9	63.8	27.7
Grenada	1.3	55.2	42.3
Iraq	1.3	66.8	31.9
Jamaica	2.1	64.5	32.9
Mozambique	.3	55.7	43.8
Nicaragua	.2	55.5	43.8
South Yemen	1.4	47.3	51.3
Syria	8.4	51.0	39.1

[1]Data available for imports only.

SOURCE: Table based on data from the I.M.F., *Direction of Trade Statistics, 1981.*

Nearly ten years have passed since the OPEC oil embargo. The initial panic that many OPECs would soon crystallize around other critical commodities has proven unwarranted. Other producer cartels have emerged, but none has been able to reproduce OPEC's ability to hold up consumers for ransom. Some cartels (such as those for copper, sugar, bananas, coffee, tin, and bauxite) have failed miserably to stabilize prices at high levels.

The softness of these cartels is due to several structural factors. For example, copper is produced in states—including Chile, Peru, Zambia, Zaire, Australia, Papua-New Guinea, the United States, and the U.S.S.R.—that are geographically dispersed, and culturally and politically divergent. In addition, the handful of multinational corporations that control the refining and marketing stages have been actively developing new sources of copper in Mexico, Australia, Brazil, and Canada. Increased copper production has been keeping pace with demand, which has been sluggish due to the development of substitutes—notably aluminum—and to slow economic growth in the industrial states. As a result, countries have fallen into a pattern of fighting for market shares and of actually trying to increase their own production despite the dangers of generating excess supplies and thereby causing world prices to fall. Copper-producing countries have felt compelled to maintain and even to increase output, despite weak demand, because of their own frail financial positions. Facing chronic balance-of-payments problems, countries such as Peru and Zambia have been in no position to withhold copper exports for long periods in the hopes of higher future revenues. Some state-owned firms have even been forced to sell the metal at a loss, below marginal cost, in order to earn scarce foreign exchange. The factors that have hindered the copper producers—geographic and political dispersion, the development by multinationals of alternative sources of supply and of substitute materials, sluggish demand, and weak country finances—have also created barriers against the emulation of OPEC by other commodity producers.

The effort by Jamaica to raise the prices of bauxite emphasizes the weak positions of many LDC commodity producers.[37] Jamaica was not threatening to withhold bauxite for a political objective, but was merely interested in increasing its income from bauxite, its most important export. In 1974, Jamaica unilaterally increased its export taxes on bauxite by over 600 percent. The immediate result was a sharp increase in the government's income from bauxite, from less than $30 million to over $200 million. At the same time, Prime Minister Michael Manley announced his intention to purchase ownership shares in the subsidiaries of Kaiser, Reynolds, Alcan, Alcoa, and Revere.

Six international firms control the process whereby bauxite is refined into aluminum.[38] The three main phases of production are normally carried out within the same vertically integrated company. By locating the smelters outside of the bauxite-producing country, the multinationals retain control of aluminum production levels and can determine where the necessary bauxite will be mined.

The firms agreed to pay the bauxite levy and were able to pass the added costs onto consumers. Rather than adopt a confrontationist strategy, the multinationals simply cut back production in Jamaica. Jamaica's share of world bauxite fell from 19 percent in 1973 to 13 percent in 1978. Other members of the International Bauxite Association (IBA) were unwilling to raise their taxes as high as Jamaica's, and Brazil, Guinea, and Australia were only too pleased to increase their shares of the world market. Jamaica's income from bauxite remained above the pre-1974 levels, but well below what Manley had dreamed. Eventually, Manley was forced partially to roll back his tax rates and to offer the MNCs other incentives in the hope that they would resume aggressive mining in Jamaica.[39]

The Jamaican experience suggests that the self-interest of competing producing states will often impede effective price collusion. In addition, the tight MNC control of the industry placed production decisions outside of the producing states. Producers like Jamaica can increase their benefits, but the structure of the global market limits their bargaining power. Ultimately, Manley concluded that he would have to take more careful account of international realities and work more harmoniously with the MNCs.

Jamaica was motivated by economic needs. Can other LDCs try to blackmail the United States by withholding strategic materials for political objectives? The Joint Chiefs of Staff believe the answer is yes. In their *Military Posture* statement for 1982, the generals warn that U.S. dependency on imported commodities critical to the U.S. military and industrial base has increased sharply over the last twenty years. For seven crucial commodities, our dependency is 75 percent or more on foreign countries, which "in the foreseeable future (could) deny us our supplies."[40] The joint chiefs vividly demonstrate this dependency with ominous maps showing the countries of origin for bauxite, chromite, cobalt, columbium, tantalum, manganese ore, and nickel. These sources appear far away from a suddenly small and vulnerable United States.

On closer examination, however, the dangers become more chimerical. We have already seen how, in the case of bauxite, overriding factors such as the financial weakness of exporting states and the diversity of suppliers protect U.S. interests. Similarly, the United States imports chromite from such diverse places as the Philippines, Turkey, South Africa, and the Soviet Union; columbium comes primarily from Brazil, Canada, and Thailand; tantalum from Thailand, Canada, Malaysia, and Brazil; manganese from Gabon, Brazil, Australia, and

South Africa. Canada and Norway account for the majority of nickel imports. In the case of each grouping of mineral producers, it is highly unlikely that unfriendly political regimes will come to power simultaneously, and, together, enjoy controlling market shares. It is even less probable that such regimes would be so hostile to the United States and the West that they would attempt to refuse to sell their raw materials for an extended period. A lengthy boycott would devastate their own economies, which are generally much more dependent upon the commodities and the revenues they generate than are the industrial states. Moreover, the embargo could not be leveled against the United States alone, since NATO allies would presumably share their resources with the United States.

This unequal dependence gives the United States a strong hand—made firmer by a factor not mentioned in the joint chief's *Posture Statement:* the reassuring reality of U.S. stockpiles. The United States has stockpiles of chromite equal to approximately five years of consumption requirements; two years of manganese; 1½ years of bauxite; and reserves of tantalum in excess of one year's import needs.[41] These reserves give the United States the leverage to outlast foreign boycotts or negotiate differences with aggrieved foreign governments. The United States has time to alter its sources of supply, to bring on stream domestic production facilities that may be uneconomic at today's prices, and more carefully conserve and recycle existing supplies. The United States could also create commodity-sharing agreements with other importing nations.

Of the seven commodities cited by the joint chiefs, cobalt may present the most serious danger. Deposits are concentrated in Zaire and Zambia. It is not imaginable that Mobutu in Zaire or President Kaunda in Zambia would try to boycott Western consumers, but political instability is possible in the region in the 1980s. Successor governments, once established, could not economically afford to refuse to market cobalt and the associated copper. Copper and cobalt account for the majority of Zaire and Zambia's export revenues, and contribute importantly to their government budgets. The real danger is prolonged *instability* in the mining provinces. Destruction in the mines or disruption of transport links, beyond the control of the authorities, could cut off supplies. The United States does, however, have sufficient stockpiles to cover 2½ years of cobalt consumption needs. Considerable time would exist for a new government to establish control and reopen the mines. An increase in the U.S. cobalt stockpile could guarantee a more comfortable cushion. Eventually, the mining of cobalt nodules on the ocean floors, and technological advances in substitutes based on abundant silicone, could lessen dependence on African suppliers.

The joint chiefs raise the specter of Soviet-controlled regimes in commodity-rich countries purposely depriving the United States of critical materials. To be effective, the Soviets would have to establish control in several countries producing the same commodity. The Soviets would also have to be willing to provide massive financial subsidies to make up for the lost revenues. The question arises: What would the Soviets hope to gain by depriving the United States of a single commodity? U.S. stockpiles, augmented in some cases by resources from such "safe" countries as Canada and Australia, would generally prevent a boycott from having an immediate effect on strategic U.S. industries. Moreover, such a boycott would surely escalate U.S.-Soviet tensions, and the United States would feel free to retaliate in other spheres. A mineral boycott is simply not an efficient political instrument in U.S.-Soviet competition. The Soviets, well aware of LDC sensitivity to being used as pawns in East-West conflicts, have not, in fact, pressured their Third World clients to withhold commodities from world markets.

OPEC, then, has been a special case. Geographical concentration, cultural affinities, common political causes, the crucial importance of the commodity, the absence of near-term substitutes, and the tacit assistance of multinational firms have accounted for the oil cartel's success.[42] Also, the financial depth of the petroleum exporters as a group has given them an unusual ability to forego immediate export earnings in pursuit of longer-term objectives. But these conditions, conducive to a successful cartel, are difficult to reproduce. The image of a future of hydra-headed OPECs, of resource blackmail and even resource wars can inflate rhetoric, making posture-statements and politicians' speeches exciting and even frightening; but the campaign balloons burst once the underlying assumptions are examined.

If the commodity markets are secure, might a frustrated Third World try to wreck the global financial system? For a time in the mid-1970s, the developing countries were proposing a debt moratorium, but the idea was never pushed very seriously. Moreover, it soon became clear that many LDCs were opposed to resolutions that even hinted they were plotting to renege on their debts. Total capital flows, private and public, to the developing world have been growing steadily even after repayments are subtracted. It made no sense to jeopardize these transfers by threatening massive defaults. Those countries most integrated into the commercial capital markets, such as Brazil, Mexico, South Korea, and the Philippines were especially anxious not to endanger their credit ratings in New York and London. Thus, talk of a generalized debt moratorium was quietly dropped from the New International Economic Order agenda. Instead, eyes were focused on institutional mechanisms whereby individual countries might request an orderly debt rescheduling agreeable to creditors.

Individual countries have, from time to time, found themselves facing severe debt burdens in the midst of a national economic crisis when debt servicing has exceeded capital inflows. Even under these circumstances, countries as politically distinct as Poland, Turkey, Zaire, and Nicaragua have chosen to honor their debts, reducing the momentary burden by rescheduling a portion of them. Thus, a carrot/stick methodology has evolved. The system's willingness to postpone payments lessens the temptation to renege and incur the severe costs of defaulting.

Default against the banking system forces a country into paying cash on the barrelhead for imports, an extraordinarily cumbersome and costly way to conduct international trade. Moreover, the banks could attempt to place liens on the country's physical and financial assets and generally disrupt its international economic relations. Access to credit would be suspended for at least the medium term.

This desire to maintain normal international linkages, along with the hope of future credits, compelled the revolutionary government of

Nicaragua to honor the $1.6 billion in debts incurred by the deposed Somoza regime. The leftist Sandinistas assumed the legal obligations of repayment even though the banks had clearly been at fault in lending to Somoza when the Nicaraguan economy and polity were crumbling under the pressures of the 1979 revolution, and even though a sizable proportion of the credits had been pilfered by the Somoza clique. The acceptance of the hated Somozas' international debt by the former guerrilla commandantes was rich in irony: an eloquent demonstration of the overwhelming power of the international economic system.

If the Third World will not purposefully wreck the international system, do they have the wherewithal to restructure it? Can they agree on a common agenda and unite to impose it upon the world? A group of seventy-seven developing nations (the G–77) detailed their New International Economic Order (NIEO) in 1974 in The Declaration and Action Programme adopted by the Sixth Special Session of the United Nations General Assembly. Yet, the NIEO remains largely a paper tiger with paper teeth. Since 1974, it has been reworded, xeroxed, and printed thousands of times, and debated at innumerable international conferences, but with only marginal effect on the actual functioning of the international economy.

Why does the NIEO remain a mirage? Many of the proposals sound fine but are too vague to be implemented. Other proposals are simply utopian. They are unrelated to the real world of the present and near-future international system. Moreover, the long list of proposals does not even represent a lowest common denominator for the G–77. Many proposals, if implemented, would actually be harmful to the interests of some of the developing states. If serious negotiations were ever to begin, the G–77 (whose membership has swollen to 120 countries) would find itself in sharp internal disagreement on key issues. Of course, even if demands were more carefully prepared and more realistic, the members lack the power to impose them upon the unwilling industrialized states. Santa Claus doesn't have to answer the mail.

While the diplomats and bureaucrats representing the G–77 were debating the NIEO among themselves, the global system was undergoing major changes. Most of these changes were not planned by official bodies or governments. Some reforms did, however, reflect sentiments expressed in the G–77's proposals. For example, the industrial states have expanded multilateral aid and long-term export credits, and the International Monetary Fund has established an extended fund facility to help nations adjust more gradually to balance-of-payments problems. These reforms were accepted by the industrial states not because they were afraid of the G–77, but because the industrial states judged that the reforms would strengthen the whole international system. They recognized that capital-short developing nations needed more external credit if they were to be able to continue to import the industrial world's goods while also meeting payments on past debts.

The knife-waving rhetoric aside, most of the NIEO proposals are not threatening to cut the bone out of the existing international system. Instead, they argue for more of the same: more trade; more capital flows; more investment and technology transfer. Some of the proposals, notably those pressing for higher commodity prices and more official development assistance, would transfer resources to the Third World. However, this redistribution would occur within the perimeters of the existing international system.

Portions of the NIEO call for greater official intervention in such areas as commodity prices, food stockpiling, and investment codes. These reforms are less revolutionary than some free-market purists would have us believe. As we have seen, the international economy is already a mix of official and market forces, and many of the NIEO proposals would increase governmental roles only at the margin.

Some of the NIEO proposals, it is true, would affect the global power balance by transferring decision-making power to official bodies, such as the United Nations, where the Third World is influential or even dominant. The industrial states have consistently and successfully parried these thrusts. The incapacity of the G–77 to impose these demands has become obvious even to many of its own members. Their diplomats may continue to make brave speeches, but their governments' actual economic strategies operate on the assumption that the "North-South dialogue" will not significantly alter the world system.

Systemic Faults

Today's world economy is caught in contradictory currents. On the one hand, the pace of technological innovation, industrial competition, and financial flows suggests a creative and expanding system. Growth has been even spectacular in some countries—notably those well endowed in energy resources—and in geo-regions centered around such boom cities as São Paulo, Seoul, and Houston. On the other hand, the statistics that recount the economic health of the entire world are unnerving. Eddies of slow growth, high inflation, monetary instability, and financial imbalance are pervasive and chronic. Growth in non-oil-developing countries had declined from 6 percent in the 1968–72 period to 2.5 percent in 1982. Meanwhile, consumer prices were rising at a staggering rate of 37 percent. The external accounts of the LDCs were especially alarming, as the current-account deficit of the non-oil nations swelled to a record $99 billion. The International Monetary Fund, a traditionally low-keyed and mildly optimistic forecaster, concluded its 1981 *World Economic Outlook* with this gloomy appraisal: "In sum, the picture of the world economy is one of large and widespread imbalances . . . the margin for error is limited, and the stakes are high."[43]

The IMF's *optimistic* scenario for the mid-1980s emphasizes checking inflation at the price of inhibiting growth. Growth rates in the industrial and the non-oil-developing countries, while positive, would remain low. Painful adjustment and austerity measures would continue to dominate the economic news of most countries. Living standards will nearly stagnate in the smaller, less-diversified economies whose raw material export prices have tended to be weak and in the poorer states of Africa and Asia. Some of the more advanced developing countries will fare somewhat better, providing that the industrial states avoid trade protectionism and that the LDCs are able to continue expanding substantially the market shares of their export manufacturers.

The *pessimistic* scenario warns that if the industrial states are unable to control inflation and are then forced to seriously depress their economies, the plight of the Third World will be truly dismal. Per capita growth rates will approach zero and will even turn negative in some countries, despite allowances for continued borrowing. The resulting debt will depress already sluggish exports, making the debt service burdens "critical."[44]

The IMF blames the slowed growth and financial imbalances of the Third World on three principal factors: sluggish economic growth in the major industrial states; the increase in the price of oil; and, more recently, the increase in real interest rates in world financial markets.[45] Another factor can be added to these three: if industrial states, such as Japan, dramatically improve their trade accounts, the trade and current-account deficits of the LDCs will swell still more because of the zero-sum rules of the global balance sheet. If the pie stays the same size, then some can eat more only if others eat less.

The slowed growth rates of the LDCs and the corresponding pressures to reduce their imports are shrinking the potential markets for U.S. goods. LDCs are being forced to devalue their currencies in order to shrink import demand and to shift development strategies away from projects that require imports. The consequent decline in the demand for U.S. exports almost certainly exceeds the losses that might result from trade restrictions imposed for ideological reasons by nationalist and pro-statist regimes. The malfunctionings of the international system with their deleterious effects on LDC growth, and not the Third World's proclivities, are now the greatest constraint on U.S. export opportunities.

Similarly, the danger of default arises less from the anticapitalist instincts of some Third World movements, than from globally induced, balance-of-payments crunches that force LDCs to choose between servicing current foreign debt and maintaining domestic growth. In the 1980s, many LDCs will experience both austerity and increased indebtedness. This tightening noose makes them even more vulnerable to another global economic crisis. It will hardly matter if the crisis is precipitated by further increases in oil prices, by a deep recession in the industrial states, or by some still unforseen shock. The fact is that any constriction of the LDCs' export markets, or any blockage of the

LDCs' access to massive amounts of international capital, would threaten to wreck their economies. Their choices would be bleak, and default might seem the lesser evil. A hanging man isn't likely to be frightened of being beaten tomorrow.

There are no easy solutions, no ninety-day-warranties, for the global crisis. However, elements of a solution are visible. Industrial states must give greater weight to the international ramifications of their national economic policies. Growth rates and monetary conditions in Western Europe and the United States have a tremendous influence on the trade and financial prospects of the developing world. In addition, steps must be taken to stabilize the shaky international financial system.

Several major industrial countries, including the United States, Great Britain and West Germany, have turned the job of inflation-fighting over to their central banks. Restrictive monetary policies have deepened and prolonged the global recession; but tight monetary policies and fears of renewed inflation have kept interest rates from dropping to more normal levels. The United States and other industrial nations with relatively strong balance of payments must try methods for controlling inflation that are less harmful to growth at home and abroad. A reduction, for example, in the United States budget deficit would reduce inflation fears and lessen pressures on financial markets. The political process can decide the preferred mix between tax increases and expenditure cuts. Monetary policy could then be more expansive, providing more plentiful and cheaper credit to businesses and consumers. Concurrently, an incomes policy could provide incentives for firms and unions to tie price and wage increases to cost and productivity trends. As part of a long-term, progrowth strategy, the government itself could become more directly involved in stimulating investment and assisting firms adjust to the ongoing surge in competition from foreign producers. Together, these measures stand a better chance of permanently dampening inflation and interest rates while rekindling growth. These progrowth measures would provide LDCs with more dynamic export markets and less expensive debt.

Renewed global growth may not be enough to stabilize financial markets that have suffered shock after shock. Successive oil price hikes, rapid cycles of global boom and bust, and madly oscillating interest rates, have severely strained the world banking system. Commercial banks will still remain the major source of capital for the Third World in the 1980s. The swollen debt burdens of the developing countries, however, will make the banks more cautious. Official lending institutions must assume greater responsibility for stabilizing the international system. The financial resources of the World Bank and, especially, the International Monetary Fund, must be sharply increased if Third World economies are not to be starved for capital.[46] Furthermore, it may be necessary to create an additional pool of funds to provide a safety net for severe debt crises, and more developing countries should be integrated into the web of emergency credit lines ("swaps") that tie together the central banks of the industrial states. Such official mechanisms can provide a more secure environment for continued commercial bank lending.

To place banking on a still more solid footing, the role of supervisory agencies must be updated and expanded.[47] National regulators have failed to keep apace of the globalization of banking. More timely and thorough information on country debt accumulation is urgently required if debt crises are not to ambush borrowers and lenders alike. Regulatory requirements must be harmonized across borders if banks are not to continue to flee to the most permissive countries. "Lender of last resort" responsibilities must further be clarified, and regulatory agencies need the power to inject capital into failing banks. Regulators also need to consider ways to prevent individual banks from precipitously pulling their money out of a "problem country," thus deepening debt crises and inadvertently endangering their own prospects of being repaid. Regulators might use country exposure rules—now used to set ceilings on loan levels—to prevent banks from suddenly dropping their exposure below a determined floor. More stable financial flows would benefit both borrowers and the financial community.

Finally, since these measures will still be insufficient for some debt-ridden countries, mechanisms need to be established to permit more orderly reschedulings of public and private debts. Existing practices are too cumbersome to accomodate the hundreds of banks now active in international lending, and too rigid for the challenges of the more austere 1980s. Banks should select a permanent steering committee to speed necessary reschedulings, and to police fulfillment of agreements among its member banks. More institutionalized cooperation between the private and public creditors would also help streamline and rationalize the rescheduling process. In addition, rescheduling terms must be flexible and generous enough to allow the debtor country to get back on its feet. As occurs in corporate reorganizations, some debt might be converted into stock-like instruments that would be paid "dividends" only when the country's finances permitted. The long-term interests of both lenders and borrowers would be better served by a rescheduling process that left the debtor with enough resources to resume investment and growth.[48]

The United States ought to concentrate its energies on providing LDCs with an international economic environment that is conducive to their growth and that makes honoring their international commitments more beneficial than burdensome. In such an attractive environment, Third-World leaders will have fewer reasons to disrupt the system. Isolated conflicts would be reduced to mere ripples in the otherwise steady and expanding stream of the international economy.

Conclusion

The economic system is both more complex and less vulnerable to political infection than the alarmists and the confrontationists believe. The system is like the human body, which is a host for countless varieties of microorganisms. It possesses the flexibility to absorb and utilize organisms of striking diversity. At the same time, it is strong and durable enough to bind all but the most irrational regimes.

The world's various national economies are mixtures of public sector and private enterprise. The mix in any one case will vary, and the relationship may be harmonious and stable or tense and uncertain. Still, it is naive to imagine that the balance is going to shift decisively toward the private sector. In some countries, some forms of intervention are being questioned or even dismantled, but new pressures are arising that demand governmental response. The international economy's turbulence—the high costs of energy, the uncertain availability of food, and the heightened competition among industrial products—require difficult and costly adjustments. Governments will be called upon to accelerate some of these adjustments, to slow others, and to reduce the costs of change to damaged groups.

At the same time that new problems are demanding new responses from governments, contrary pressures are rooting out oppressive bureaucracies in favor of decentralized decision-making and market structures. These convergences offer opportunities for increased understanding and tolerance among nations. They should remove the sting from some of this century's poisonous, ideological disputes. Equally important, these convergences, together with the mixed character of the international trading and financial systems, now permit all states to participate in global markets.

Moreover, the factors governing trade and capital flows have evolved in ways that both protect U.S. economic interests and invite the participation of nationalistic developing economies. Developing countries must accept the international system essentially as it is and the pattern of their interactions may not be much affected by changes in local political structures.[49] Although this state of affairs may be a great disappointment to political movements when they discover that their capture of a Third World state does not alter their nation's position in the world economy, it should reassure those who fear disruption of the world system. In fact, the greater threat to the international economic order originates not in the instabilities within developing nations. It arises from the possible mismanagement of the system by its more powerful members.

Many Third World leaders are beginning to acknowledge their relative powerlessness. The pill is not so bitter to swallow, however, given the system's recent evolutions. The flexibility of the multinational firms and the availability of finance capital offer an environment more conducive to economic development and to national freedom.

The active role that governments of industrial and developing nations now play in domestic economics and in international trade is an additional factor supporting the system's pluralism. It should help diminish the paranoia that has been rampant since the advent of the Cold War: the conviction that all large and different fish must be sharks.

If U.S. policymakers had a more realistic and comprehensive vision of international economics, they would be in a better position to advance U.S. economic interests in the Third World and to defend U.S. security objectives. In fact, past failures by the United States to grasp the true dynamics of the global economy has handed the Soviet Union some of its greatest successes. To understand the link between economics and security, we now turn to a discussion of Soviet policies and capabilities in the developing areas.

3 The Soviet Threat

Many senior policymakers show themselves to be unaware of the new mechanisms at work in the world economy, preoccupied as they are with the "geopolitical momentum" of the Soviet Union. During the last decade or so, the argument goes, the Kremlin has aggressively extended its power over Third World states. By orchestrating its military, political, ideological, and (admittedly weak) economic instruments, Moscow has reduced a growing number of developing states to dependent status. Some regimes have willfully converted themselves into Soviet "proxies," while Communist movements have subverted others. The Soviet Union itself has employed threats and even the use of force to subdue still others. Soviet influence has grown in the Third World, while that of the United States and the West has declined. The Soviets are speaking the simple truth when they boast that the "correlation of forces" in the world is moving in their favor. Thus, it seems to matter little that the Western economy is more appealing. The Soviets are gaining ground regardless.

This logic fails on three grounds. First, the evidence it is based on is simply empirically incorrect. A scoreboard of Soviet "gains and losses" would show that, at best, the Soviets have held their own in the Third World over the last ten or twenty years. The importance of several recent Soviet successes has been exaggerated, while their defeats have been ignored. Second, it falsely equates a mere Soviet presence with a domineering political influence. The purchase of Soviet weapons or hydroelectrical machinery does not signal alignment with Moscow. Finally, this erroneous logic underestimates the severe problems that the Soviets have confronted in their Third World diplomacy. It ignores the fact that the Soviets have had grave difficulties in maintaining their grip on erstwhile clients.

Some commentators like to group countries under the dichotomies of "free" or "Communist," pro-U.S." or "pro-Soviet." Even using this crude methodology, the results would suggest that, on balance, the Soviets are not running away with all the gold rings. On the contrary, Soviet "losses"—including China, Indonesia, Egypt, and Somalia—have been at least as significant as the much-publicized Soviet "gains" in Angola, Mozambique, Ethiopia, Vietnam, Laos, Cambodia, and Afghanistan. Also, Soviet influence has arguably declined in such relatively important states as Iraq, India, and Algeria.

One foreign policy research group in Washington counted the countries where a high level of Soviet involvement and presence (but not necessarily control) was accompanied by a close and cooperative relationship with the Soviet Union. The study found that the number of such countries, including Eastern Europe, had risen from seven in 1945 to nineteen by 1980. The number of developing countries, however, has also increased. Thus, the percentage of Soviet-influenced countries in the world started at 9 percent in 1945, rose to a height of about 14 percent in the late 1950s, and then declined to about 12 percent where it has remained for the past ten years.[1] Since many of these Soviet-influenced countries are poor, they account for only about 5 percent of the world's GNP. Before the Sino-Soviet split, the figure had approached 10 percent.

The wrap-up chapter of another comprehensive study of Soviet-Third World relations concurred that "Soviet influence in the Third World remains limited."[2] The study surveyed each region, and found the Soviets facing frustrations and defeats:

> The assessments of Soviet success in Africa differ markedly from the popular view that recent Soviet activism has resulted in a substantial gain for the Soviet Union at the expense of the West.

> At best, the authors view Moscow's accomplishments as mixed. . . . A concerted effort has been made to enlist the Arab states of the Middle East into an 'anti-imperialist' bloc of pro-Soviet states. To date this goal has eluded the Kremlin. . . . Nothing seems to work very well for the U.S.S.R. in Asia, and despite considerable input and energy over the years it has surprisingly little to show for its effort.

The study notes that Latin America has consistently been a low priority for the Soviets and that Cuba (and now perhaps Nicaragua) is their "only success."

One could, of course, create a much longer list of "pro-Soviet" nations. The use of "anti-imperalist" rhetoric, perhaps combined with the purchase of Soviet weaponry, could be grounds for inclusion. Yet, exclusive attention to one or two aspects of a nation's behavior yields a distorted view of the totality. In some allegedly "pro-Soviet" countries (such as India, Algeria, or Nicaragua) Western economic, cultural, and/or diplomatic influence is at least as extensive as the Soviets.

The Soviets, it is true, have developed a wider reach. In the 1950s and 1960s, the Soviets had to stand by while the West sent troops into Suez, Lebanon, the Congo, and the Dominican Republic. By the 1970s, the Soviets were able to stage major sea- and airlifts of military force into distant Angola and Ethiopia. While the Soviet's ocean-going navy still pales in comparison to that of NATO members, Western flotillas no longer enjoy a clear horizon. Even though Soviet overseas economic activity represented a miniscule percentage of global exchange, Soviet technicians and their projects have been popping up in remote regions of Latin America and Africa. The error comes in automatically translating this increased power and presence into a certain ability to control local politics, and to thereby project a threat to the West.

Much has been made of the consolidation of Soviet-backed regimes in Cuba and Vietnam, and the extension of these "proxy" forces into additional countries: notably Cambodia, Angola, Ethiopia, and South Yemen. Yet, these gains have generally occurred in poor, backward countries of marginal inherent value. Nor does the penetration of Cubans or Eastern Europeans into the local security apparatus mean that these Soviet advances are necessarily lasting.

The Soviet Union, it turns out, confronts many of the same stubborn forces that have frustrated the United States when it attempts to manipulate the Third World. Moscow, like Washington, has faced the disappointments of watching friendly regimes collapse. It has learned that liaisons with military governments are often temporary affairs and it has had clients turn toward neutrality or even hostility. The Soviets have also been caught in the quagmire of regional rivalries and have found that the making of new friends entails instant tensions with their ancient enemies. For the Soviets, Communist parties are the equivalent agent of influence that business groups are for the United States; and like their capitalist counterparts, they have proven to be weak, stubborn, and sometimes more of a burden than a benefit. Finally, whereas the West has severe problems in coordinating its economic strength for political purposes, the Soviets do not have the strength at all. The Soviets' lack of hard currency and their low participation in international trade generally leave them without the direct or indirect economic levers that the West enjoys.

Transformations in the global economy, and soft spots in the Soviet economy, are harmful to Soviet ambitions. The diffusion of power in the world is pulling the communist states further and further apart, while nationalism is causing them to clash, sometimes violently. The increasing strength, self-assuredness, and self-awareness of many Third World states render them less controllable by any superpower. As we have noted, recent Soviet gains have tended to come, not in the more important, advanced developing nations, but in the poorer states recently emerging from colonialism or near-feudalism.

As we journey through the maze of Soviet foreign relations, it might be useful to think of the structure of Soviet allies and friends as consisting of a series of five concentric circles. The circles are delineated principally by ideological closeness to Moscow, although security ties can be an important determinant. The inner core consists of members of the Warsaw Pact, Mongolia, Cuba, and Vietnam. These are generally Marxist-Leninist states with close military ties to the Soviet Union. Their relationship to Moscow is, to varying degrees, one of dependency. The second circle is filled by such radical nationalist states as Angola, Mozambique, and Ethiopia. Being neither full-fledged military allies of the Soviet Union, nor developed Marxist states, they sometimes claim themselves to be on a "Marxist-Leninist" path, with the Soviets being their "natural" allies. These radical "anti-imperalists" tend to be economically very underdeveloped and lacking in strong political institutions. The third circle consists of reformist governments, such as Iraq, Algeria, and Egypt under Nasser. Their foreign policies tend to be flexible, and such regimes are easily prone to slide closer to or further away from Moscow. The next circle consists of countries such as India, with whom Moscow shares relations of strategic convenience. Ideological ties are secondary or absent. Finally, in the outermost circle are countries with whom Moscow has issue-specific relations only. The Soviets are interested in Argentine grain and Moroccan phosphate, but are otherwise on the opposite side of most other issues.

As we shall see, governments and countries can hop from one circle to another, or even leap from the outermost circle and escape Moscow's gravitational pull altogether. Nor is ideology always controlling. Geopolitical interests and regional conflicts can drive wedges between Moscow and other socialist or reformist governments. Moreover, ideology itself can be a cause of bitter strife among governments all claiming to be the true Marxists.

Moscow has had great difficulty in developing smooth relations with states in all of these circles. The Soviets seem unable to define formulae that would bring a lasting equilibrium to their foreign relations. As we examine the problems and frustrations that have confronted the Soviets in each of these circles, and note their many concrete failures, we will better be able to place the "Soviet threat" into perspective.

This discussion will avoid the generally inconclusive "theological" debates regarding Soviet motives and concentrate instead on Soviet actions. The Soviets may be driven by ideological fervor or Great Power pride, by fear of encirclement or territorial ambitions, but they will achieve only what their competence permits. Even if the Soviets are engaged in a geopolitical offensive, it is their actual capabilities that will determine the nature of the threat they pose to the Third World and the United States.

Before entering the schemata of the five circles, let us take a brief look at one of the main failings of the Soviet Union, which has soured its relations everywhere: Soviet economics.

Economics: The Soviets' Achilles Heel

Marx had promised that once the forces of production were released from the contradictions inherent in capitalism, wealth would abound. Today, those who still advocate Marxism stress the humanistic or egalitarian strains in Marx. While socialism is not the complete economic disaster generally depicted in the U.S. media, it has failed to prove its vaunted superiority over capitalism as a system for maximizing production.

The Soviet Union itself has been unable to catch up with the industralized West. Despite reasonably steady growth in the postwar years, the Soviet Union remains, in many respects, an underdeveloped country. Roughly half of the population still live in rural areas, and peasant productivity is low. Modern technology is absent from many farms and factories, and the diffusion of new techniques proceeds at a pace typical of developing societies. The prowess evident in military technology is not present elsewhere. Durable consumer goods like stereos, automobiles, and dishwashers are available only in very limited quantities.

The Soviet Union is especially weak in those points of intersection with the international economy—trade and finance. The Soviet system is biased against international exchange. A large economy that has stressed self-sufficiency, the Soviet Union has given little attention to producing for foreign markets. The quality of many Soviet goods is not competitive abroad. Moreover, the rigidity of the five-year plans makes it difficult to take advantage of new trade opportunities as they arise. The nonconvertibility of the ruble into hard currency further divides the Soviet economy from the rest of the world. Moscow cannot readily invest abroad. The Soviet Union plays virtually no role in the international financial system (except as a modest borrower and, perhaps, as ultimate guarantor of the debts of Eastern Europe).

Soviet trade, such as it is, is slanted toward the industrialized states. We have the technology—and the grain—that the Soviets seek. Of the $61 billion in the total of Soviet imports and exports in 1980, 72 percent was with the developed world. Only $16 billion in goods were exchanged with the Third World. This accounted for a mere 2 percent of total LDC trade.[3]

The Soviets have a visible presence in some large development projects in the Third World; for example, in Indian steel mills, Guinean bauxite mines, and Brazilian hydroelectric dams. But these projects pale into insignificance compared to the thousands of subsidiaries and joint ventures of Western firms active in the Third World. And, in developing-country markets, the Moscow Narodny Bank cannot match the activities of even one of the large Western banks.

Nor can Soviet economic assistance compare to that of the West. The Soviets are absent from the International Monetary Fund—the linchpin of the world financial system—and from the World Bank and the regional development banks. Moscow's bilateral aid commitments have amounted to less than $1 billion for most years, while the industrial West provided $18 billion in bilateral loans and grants in 1980.[4] A penurious 0.1 percent of GNP, Soviet aid has amounted to a mere 5 percent of the world's official development aid, and the Soviet share is declining. Facing declining growth rates in the 1980s, and constant demands for more consumer goods and military hardware, the Soviet regime is unlikely to make foreign aid a high priority. Soviet aid is also concentrated in a small number of countries mostly located relatively near to the southern rim of the Soviet homeland. The more distant Latin American (Cuba excepted), Black African, and Pacific nations have received small portions of an already skimpy foreign aid budget.

Soviet aid programs lack the flexibility and breadth of the West's. Soviet aid is generally tied to Soviet products, and often to machinery, which takes years to arrive. Disbursements have been painfully slow.

Of some $18 billion in commitments made over the last 25 years, only $8 billion has actually been spent.[5] The record of Eastern European donors is even worse, with actual drawings equaling only about one-third of promised assistance. Nor are Soviet funds always well spent. Moscow concentrates on large, showcase projects of the sort that the West largely discarded a decade ago as "white elephants." As the CIA concluded in a 1979 report to Congress, "Moscow has never been able to compete with the West, either in the size or kind of economic aid programs it has offered."[6]

Earlier Soviet dreams of drawing the developing countries into a socialist system have been erased by these stark realities. Moscow cannot possibly hope to offer an alternative economic bloc competitive with the West. Red Square may still be surrounded with slogans proclaiming the inevitable triumph of socialism worldwide, but Soviet economic policy in the Third World has already surrendered to Western superiority. Some Soviet scholars may cling to old pretensions, but most have abandoned the Stalinist notion of "two world economies," as the socialist economies themselves are becoming engulfed by the one-world capitalist system.[7]

The model the Soviets now trumpet to Third World leftists is closer to the "New Economic Policy" (NEP) of the 1920s than to Stalinist centralism and autarky. In speaking of Third World development options, the Soviet scholar Kiva Maidanik told me at his prestigious Institute for the World Economy and International Relations, "The Bolsheviks had originally intended the NEP to last for twenty years or more." Unfortunately, the Soviet experiment with market mechanisms and openness to foreign technology and capital was aborted by circumstances now considered peculiar to the Russian case. The Soviets today advise Third World regimes to observe efficiency criteria, to recognize that private enterprise can play a "positive" role, and to negotiate with Western multinationals. The opening of Eastern Europe to Western trade, technology, and finance is the relevant contemporary example.

Soviet economists chastise advocates of "self-reliance" as being naive, extremist, adventurist—even Maoist.[8] The Soviets look with disdain on governments that would try to reinvent the wheel—and that would want to undertake their experiments at Soviet expense. Facing tighter budgets at home, the Soviets are not interested in subsidizing social transformations abroad. As I was told repeatedly by Soviet specialists in Third World affairs during a visit to Moscow in 1981, the Soviet Union wants to avoid having to foot the bill for costly "second Cubas." Progressive Third World states are urged to remain integrated into the global capitalist network. Moscow will verbally support efforts by developing nations to make the international system more equal—words and votes at the U.N. cost it nothing—but Moscow does not urge the system's subversion or replacement. Anatoli Gromyko, Director of the African Institute of the Soviet Academy of Sciences, has frankly stated that the "liquidation of dependency of individual countries has become possible without their leaving the world capitalist system."[9]

The Soviets have resisted pressures for more economic aid and trade from radical Third World states. Moscow has disappointed friendly governments, such as Allende in Chile and Manley in Jamaica, that were struggling desperately against "counter-revolutionary forces."[10] Repeated pilgrimages to Moscow by representatives of these left-leaning (third circle) regimes were told to look to the West for economic resources. Second-circle governments, more solidly in power and ideologically closer to the Soviets, such as Mengistu in Ethiopia and the MPLA in Angola, have found that their offers of solidarity are not enough to squeeze hard currency out of Bolsheviks. Nor is the signing of a Treaty of Mutual Friendship and Cooperation a guarantee that real resources will soon be forthcoming.

Moscow has urged radical states to maintain their prerevolutionary trading ties. As we saw in chapter 2, radical states are by necessity following this advice. Moscow has even discouraged some countries from seeking admission to COMECON, the Eastern European Common Market. The Soviets evidently feel that the economic burden of granting trade preferences would exceed the diplomatic benefits.

Soviet economic relations have increasingly taken on a more narrowly "national interest" cast. Trade patterns are established more to meet the needs of the Soviet economy than for ideological or political objectives. Those who view every Soviet trade deal as merely a front operation for broader Soviet geostrategic plans are having increasing difficulty explaining Soviet behavior. For example, in Latin America, rather than seeking trading ties with Nicaragua or Jamaica under Manley, the Soviet Union has concentrated its economic agents in Brazil and Argentina. More relevant to Moscow than the conservative tinge of these nations' regimes is their possession of grain, soya, and other foodstuffs. In Africa in the late 1970s, rather than aiming economic aid at politically promising southern Africa, Moscow dedicated the lion's share of its aid to mine Moroccan phosphate to be shipped to the USSR for use in fertilizers. The Soviets may hope to gain some diplomatic presence from these commercial ties with conservative states but do not hope to gain exclusive rights to these resources, much less subvert the governments or incorporate the economies into an alternative socialist system.

These trends in Soviet economic capabilities, philosophy, and behavior are making Moscow a less attractive patron to Third World states. The Soviet Union offers no solution to the ballooning and chronic balance-of-payments deficits facing the developing nations. Soviet behavior with Allende and Manley suggests that Moscow would rather allow some friendly regimes to fall than to risk substantial economic resources. The disillusionment of regimes in Egypt, the Sudan, and Iraq with the Soviet Union was partly the result of their discovering that friendship with the Soviets was economically unrewarding; each has, to varying degrees, moved diplomatically away from Moscow. Moscow's inability to incorporate self-proclaimed Marxist regimes such as Angola, Mozambique, and Ethiopia into a socialist economic system will inevitably weaken Moscow's ability to dictate their foreign policies.

The inability of COMECON to fulfill all the needs of the economies of even the favored inner circle of Eastern European states has propelled them to increase their trading and financial links with the West. COMECON's economic weaknesses, and the opening to Western ideas, has unleashed powerful centrifugal forces in Eastern Europe.

The upheavals in Poland have been the most dramatic sign of the region's economic troubles. Poland gambled that a sudden infusion of Western technology and capital would dramatically boost development—and lost. Hungary, with over 50 percent of its trade with the West, has boldly applied for membership to the International Monetary Fund.

The upkeep of the Red Army occupation forces and rising economic subsidies have greatly increased the costs to the Soviet Union of maintaining its sphere of influence in Eastern Europe. Moscow will make these payments because Eastern Europe constitutes a vital buffer zone against NATO forces, and because it cannot risk the collapse of socialist regimes on its doorstep. In more distant areas of the world, a Kremlin besieged by competing demands for scarce economic resources is likely to continue to judge that the costs of most potential client states exceed the probable benefits. The Western economy will remain the only option open to the Third World.

Soviet Foreign Relations: The Five Circles

THE INNER CIRCLE

Marxist-Leninist governments have proven to be among the most difficult for Moscow to handle. The advent of socialism has not, as the earlier Marxists believed, led to an end of interstate rivalries. Quite the opposite: ideological disputes have added another dimension to traditional, nationalist rivalries. Moreover, the Soviet Union has been unable to escape the syndrome of resentments that arise from unequal relations between states of vastly disparate size and wealth.

Soviet relations have so openly deteriorated with former allies or satellites that, today, the Soviet Union is flanked by hostile or untrustworthy Communist states and populations. China, North Korea, Romania, Albania, and Yugoslavia have all asserted their national interests against those of the homeland of the first socialist revolution. In those states that have remained more conformist—Bulgaria, East Germany,

Czechoslovakia, and Poland—the populations are restless and heavy-handed repression has been required to maintain the domination of pro-Soviet regimes.

Marxist-Leninist parties that come to power through armed struggle are especially prone to reaffirm their independence. The indigenous leadership can rely on their domestic base in a confrontation with the Kremlin, and their armed followers, experienced in guerrilla warfare, give the Soviets pause. Despite massive Soviet economic and technical assistance to China in the 1950s, Mao split with Khrushchev. A decade earlier, Tito, the leader of the "partisans" in their bloody battles against the Nazis, had defied Stalin and pulled Yugoslavia away from the Soviet bloc.

Romania and Albania have also successfully pursued foreign policies independent of Moscow. The Romanian leader, Nicolae Ceausescu, has deviated from the Kremlin line by maintaining close relations with Israel, denouncing the Soviet invasions of Czechoslovakia and Afghanistan, and by criticizing military alliances and spending in the East as well as in the West. Romania, like Yugoslavia and Albania, has refused to accept Moscow's conception of regional economic planning, and over half of Romania's trade is now with the West and the Third World. The ruler of Albania, Enver Hoxha, went even further, and moved his country into an alliance with Moscow's archenemy, Peking, that lasted until Hoxha decided that Mao's heirs had succumbed to "revisionism." That countries so near to the Soviet Union and the reach of the Red Army have been able to defy the Kremlin is suggestive of the difficulties that Moscow is having in controlling Communist governments.

Vietnam, together with Cuba, may be the Soviet Union's closest ally outside of Eastern Europe. The Soviets have been willing to extend military and economic aid to the tune of some $2.5 to $3 million a day.[11] This crucial infusion, together with the military umbrella that the Soviet Union extends over Vietnam in its battles with China, has been sufficient inducement to gain Hanoi's loyalty. Immediately after the civil war, Vietnam sought membership in the IMF, the World Bank, and the Asian Development Bank, proclaimed its interest in attracting foreign investment, and limited its participation in COMECON to observer status. Western credits, however, were not forthcoming in sufficient amounts to spur reconstruction of Vietnam's war-devastated economy. In particular, the U.S. Congress restricted bilateral aid, and sought to discourage multilateral donors as well. Only the Soviets were willing to come across with large-scale assistance. Most importantly, as relations deteriorated with China, the Vietnamese became increasingly reliant on Soviet military support. Facing hostile relations with Peking and Washington, now united in their strategic alliance, Hanoi had nowhere else to turn but toward Moscow. When China, with apparent U.S. agreement, decided to support the Pol Pot insurgents against the Vietnamese-backed government in Cambodia, in order to "raise the costs to Soviet intervention by proxy," the alliance between the Soviet Union and Vietnam was further solidified.

The Vietnamese-Soviet alliance, however, is only as solid as the current international alignments that forged the relationship in the first place. An improvement in Vietnamese-Chinese relations, in Soviet-Chinese relations, or a change in U.S. policy, would create a new array of forces and induce a reexamination of policy in Hanoi. Even within the existing international environment, strains in the Soviet-Vietnamese relationship are visible.[12] The Vietnamese complain about the level and quality of Soviet economic aid. As people, Russians and Vietnamese do not mix easily. Indicative of their distrust for their benefactors, the Vietnamese restrict the legal movements of Soviet advisers, and require that Soviet naval vessels go through lengthy procedures before they can enter Vietnamese waters. Moreover, there is a natural competition between Moscow and Hanoi for influence in Cambodia and Laos. There are also different priorities. For Hanoi, Indochina is of primary importance, where it is of secondary interest to the Soviet Union and therefore dispensable should other opportunities arise in the region or in East-West bargaining. But most of all, Soviet influence in Vietnam is threatened over the long run by the demonstrably fierce Vietnamese nationalism. The Soviets must know that they are riding the back of a tiger, and could well be jilted as the French and Americans were before them. Once economic reconstruction is complete, and if Hanoi can reduce tensions with Peking, Vietnam may well look to a more balanced set of foreign alignments.

Vietnam's future relations with the Soviet Union may be foreshadowed by those between the Soviet Union and North Korea. The Soviets placed Kim Il Sung, the president of North Korea and secretary general of the Korean Workers party, into office, defended his regime during the Korean War, and continue to provide economic and military aid against a U.S.-supplied South Korea. Nevertheless, Kim, too, has dared to deviate from the Kremlin line. The disillusioned Soviets find Kim's cult of personality distasteful, disagree with some of his domestic policies, and consider him ungrateful, cantankerous, and potentially reckless.[13] Moscow has been irritated more than once by Kim's periodic tilts toward Peking, which Kim uses to maintain leverage against Moscow. Kim's denunciation of the Soviet-backed Vietnamese invasion of Cambodia and his recognition of the Chinese-backed Pol Pot faction signal another swing toward China. In Third World meetings, the North Koreans encourage smaller states to resist pressures from the big powers. Kim himself has not allowed a Soviet military base on Korean soil, and has refused to join COMECON. He has sought to increase his room for maneuver by diverting some 40 percent of North Korea's trade toward non-Communist markets. In sum, North Korea may serve as a buffer state for the Soviet Union, as Kim prevents hostile powers from approaching the huge Soviet base at Vladivostok, but North Korea is far from being a compliant satellite.

RADICAL NATIONALIST REGIMES

Like the heat generated from the collision of tightly-packed molecules, the inner core of Communist states is glowing red hot from internal friction. The relations between Moscow and the next circle of states —the radical nationalist regimes—are less intense. The countries are more distant, and ideological ties are less tight. Tensions are nevertheless bubbling just beneath the surface. Ethiopia illustrates the problems that Moscow has in dealing with radical states in the Third World.

The Ethiopian revolution caught both superpowers by surprise.[14] The United States was stranded on the sidelines as its long-term and reliable ally, Emperor Haile Selassie, was swept from power. Despite $250 million in military aid and decades of training programs, the U.S. military lacked good contacts at the middle and lower levels of the officer corps—where the revolution was being made. According to U.S. officials in the country at the time, neither the U.S. Ambassador nor the CIA station had either good information or an understanding of events. For too long, they had been attached to the emperor and his entourage, and had allowed themselved to be lulled into a false sense of the regime's security.

The revolution was rapid and radical. The emperor had systematically eliminated moderate alternatives to his autocracy. In the resulting political vacuum, power fell into the hands of those able to seize the initiative. A relatively obscure colonel, Mengistu Haile-Mariam, managed to eliminate his rivals and gain dominance in the governing junta, which named itself the Provisional Military Administrative Council, or Derg. The Derg, in quick succession, nationalized the major banks, insurance companies, and key industries. It proclaimed a sweeping land reform that simply decreed that all land was state property and was to be redistributed to those who tilled it. The Derg then nationalized all urban land and rental properties. Grassroot peasant and urban associations were created to administer local affairs.

The military seizure of power and the reform proclamations came before the Soviet Union played a significant role in Ethiopia.[15] The regimes' leaders assumed power with little political experience or sophistication, and they issued the key reforms before Marxism-Leninism was their official ideology. The military officers would only later enter into an alliance with a student-based Marxist group; this marriage ended quickly with the army bloodying the students in a bitter and unequal confrontation.

How did the Soviets enter Ethiopia? Soviet penetration of Ethiopia followed a path that, by now, is familiar to readers of this book. The Derg feared U.S. reactions to their revolution: we had been close to the emperor for so long. The Derg correctly anticipated that the United

States would disapprove of some of their economic reforms, particularly the nationalizations; the United States and the World Bank suspended aid in part because of the nationalizations of foreign firms.[16] Washington also restricted arms shipments and even refused to deliver some arms that had been paid for. The United States singled out Ethiopia as a human-rights violator. While violations certainly were occurring, the Derg undoubtedly felt that U.S. sanctions were politically motivated; Washington had not condemned Haile Selassie after his government callously failed to respond to a severe drought that brought death to some one hundred thousand Ethiopian peasants in 1973–74.

Washington turned hostile just as Addis Ababa's traditional enemies decided to take advantage of the political turmoil in the capital to press their long-held secessionist aspirations. The guerrillas in the northern province of Eritrea launched a full-scale offensive. Loss of Eritrea would deprive Ethiopia of access to the Red Sea. Simultaneously, neighboring Somalia was preparing an offensive in the Ogaden, the southeastern corner of Ethiopia, to annex the desert region into a "Greater Somalia." Faced with secessionist wars on two fronts, and armed uprisings by hostile political factions at home, the Derg required massive armaments for its very survival. Only the Soviet Union was willing to provide arms quickly and in volume. Some $2 billion in Eastern-bloc weapons and thirteen to fifteen thousand Cubans enabled the Derg to turn back the Somali invasion and to contain, if not completely crush, the Eritrean rebels. The Derg also managed to assert its authority against domestic challengers.

Thus Soviet arms, once again, gained Moscow a friend in the Third World. But will this friendship endure? Should the threats to Ethiopian unity dissipate so that the need for external military aid decreases, the knot that binds Addis Ababa to Moscow could unravel. Already, it is possible to distinguish emerging tensions in the spheres of economics, politics, and culture, which will become more prominent if Ethiopia's security environment is normalized.

The roughly $85 million in annual Soviet economic aid and credits have been only a fraction of Soviet military shipments.[17] Moreover, work has been slow to begin on the Soviet's few large development projects, including a hydroelectric dam and a cement plant.[18] The Ethiopians and Soviets have reportedly quarrelled over the price of Soviet oil and repayment terms for the Soviet military equipment acquired since 1977. As Ethiopian economic officials begin to turn their attention from the redistribution of existing land and resources toward the objective of generating new wealth, the need for foreign exchange will become more salient. Stirrings in this direction were evident in Mengistu's overtures to several Western European governments; facing a deteriorating external account in late 1981, he suggested a willingness to adopt more pragmatic economic policies and underlined his desire to receive more Western aid and investment. An early positive response came from French Foreign Minister Claude Cheysson, who, at the end of his visit to Addis Ababa in early 1982, pledged to extend financial aid.

Whether the West will offer sufficient finance to counter the Soviet military presence remains to be seen. The old chicken-and-egg adage is apt: some Western nations hesitate to extend credits to a pro-Soviet, Marxist state, but Ethiopia may need financial inducement to become nonaligned.

Soviet-Ethiopian relations are also strained because of political differences. The Soviets have been urging Mengistu to form a Marxist-Leninist party. He has preferred to rely instead on less disciplined grassroots organizations and his army. Mengistu and the military undoubtedly fear that a well-organized political party would pose a threat to their power. In the Third World, military governments have generally avoided creating strong civilian parties that might challenge their own political hegemony.

The Soviets view a Marxist-Leninist party as their best avenue for long-term access and influence. Their emphasis on the formation of a party implicitly reveals lack of confidence in the loyalty of the Ethiopian armed forces to the Soviet alliance. Sensing this, the wary Ethiopian soldiers do not want to create a Trojan horse.

Efforts to build a large Marxist party will encounter the same obstacles in Ethiopia as in other, poorer countries of the Third World.

Many values of Ethiopian Christianity are antithetical to Marxism, and tribal beliefs and loyalties are deeply rooted. The social class that the Soviets consider most appropriate for "scientific socialism," the urban proletariat, is tiny in a country that is still 90 percent rural. In the dying years of the emperor and in the early revolutionary period, Marxism was attractive primarily to students, especially those studying abroad.

Soviet purposes are further endangered by Ethiopian pride and culture. The sizeable Soviet presence, including over two thousand military advisers, is an irritant to Ethiopia's fierce nationalism. Ethiopia is the only African country to have escaped colonization. Ethiopian rulers have sought to use, in their turn, the Portuguese, French, British, and Americans—and now the Russians—to help them hold their country together or enlarge it. The discarding of an ally no longer needed is firmly embedded in Ethiopian diplomacy. Hints that at least some Ethiopians were already thinking along these lines were evident in a comment made by a government official to an Ethiopian friend: "If the Russians cannot provide economic aid, and send us third-rate advisers, and if their real intent is to rule over us, then to hell with them."

Nor do the Russians mix well with Ethiopians at the personal level. Mengistu dismissed a Soviet ambassador whom he reportedly considered abrupt and condescending. Merchants in Addis Ababa have refused to sell their merchandise to Soviet advisers, and some Ethiopians have refused to allow their children to play with Soviet youngsters. The Cubans typically enjoy a better rapport with their hosts; nevertheless, the strains in personal relations between the Russians and the Ethiopians will be more telling in determining Ethiopia's ultimate foreign alignment.

Soviet influence is dependent upon the Derg—a regime whose stability is far from certain. Mengistu himself seized power by physically eliminating rivals and could fall victim to the same techniques. While the overall popularity of the regime is hard to gauge, the Derg is deeply hated by many Ethiopians, conservative and radical. These dissidents associate the Soviets with the Derg's bloody repression. Should the Derg fall, the Soviets would almost certainly lose as well.

A change in Ethiopian foreign policies could come as a result of a new power struggle, or could emerge from within the current regime. But will the Ethiopians be able to free themselves from the grip of the Soviet and Cuban security advisers? The precedent of the successful Egyptian ouster of Soviet troops is suggestive, although the Soviets and Cubans have more deeply penetrated the Ethiopian security apparatus, and have been more central to the survival of the regime. There is not yet enough experience with this new dimension in Soviet diplomacy to judge its import definitively. It would seem, however, that a Soviet position grounded in its penetration of local security forces would be inherently unstable. If the regime's weak domestic political base keeps it dependent on a large Soviet or Cuban military presence, it is by definition an unreliable client. Such a government is also likely to be economically and diplomatically costly. Its repressive nature will reflect badly on the Soviet Union, just as U.S. involvement with local police forces in Latin America and elsewhere in the 1960s tarnished the U.S. image and compromised the U.S. relationship with successor governments. On the other hand, if the regime consolidates its domestic hold —presumably the Soviet objective—then it will no longer need foreign military advisers. In this case, while the Soviets might have cultivated some influence within the regime, they will probably discover that their leverage is as limited as U.S. military advisory groups found theirs to be in the past. This issue, however, is likely to remain academic until Ethiopia's external security improves. Fighting has eased in the Ogaden, but the threat from Somalia remains and the Eritrean nationalists continue to occupy troops of the central authority.

Angola and Mozambique are sometimes cited, along with Ethiopia, as a new brand of Communist government that will remain loyal to Moscow. Yet, the Soviets themselves appear to be hedging their bets in southern Africa. Soviet ideologues have been careful not to bestow the medallion of Marxism-Leninism on the MPLA or Frelimo. The substitute label, "socialist-oriented," has a distinctly ambiguous and condescending tinge. Having been burnt so often in Africa, the Soviets want to limit their exposure. After all, scientific socialism (that is, Marxism, Soviet-style) cannot readily be reproduced in backward regions. And armed movements that gained their national independence and power primarily through their own resources (unlike those Eastern European governments who rode to power on the back of the Red Army) are notoriously unreliable allies. Moscow has not been very generous with economic aid, nor has it offered its African friends membership in COMECON. Reciprocating this restraint, Angola and Mozambique have continued to trade primarily outside of COMECON, and both regimes have denied military bases to the Soviet Union, although the Soviet navy does have access to Angolan ports.

The MPLA and Frelimo require military assistance to defend their countries against repeated incursions of the South African armed forces, and to ward off externally assisted domestic challenges. Should they consolidate their power and reach a *modus vivendi* with Pretoria, their need for Soviet security assistance would diminish. They would then be free to follow the well-trodden path away from Moscow toward a genuine nonalignment.

The sentiments of many Africans—including, undoubtedly, many in the MPLA and Frelimo—were summed up by Nigeria's head of state, General Olusegun Obasanjo, in his speech to the Khartoum summit of the Organization of African Unity (OAU) in July 1978:

"To the Soviets and their friends I should like to say that, having been invited to Africa in order to assist in the liberation struggle and the consolidation of national independence, they should not overstay their welcome. Africa is not about to throw off one colonial yoke for another."

Mindful of this conditional welcome, Cuba may be forced to withdraw its troops from Angola once South Africa agrees to honor Angola's sovereignty, perhaps in the context of granting independence to Namibia. Frelimo consciously avoided becoming so dependent upon Soviet or Cuban troops in the first place.

REFORMIST GOVERNMENTS

Moscow has not limited its partners to self-declared Marxist regimes. The Soviets have been willing to waltz with reformist regimes dominated by military institutions or civilian strongmen: as well as with ruling social democratic alliances. Yet, relations with regimes in the third and fourth circles have been especially frustrating for the Soviets.

The Soviets have had to stand helplessly on the sidelines as many of these friends were ousted from power by domestic rivals. Sometimes the Soviets had recognized from the beginning that the chosen friend was less than stable, but the actual overthrow was still jolting. On other occasions, the Soviets were genuinely surprised by the adverse turn of events.

Stalin, like John Foster Dulles, took the position that Third World countries had to choose between the communist and capitalist blocs. Stalin viewed most postcolonial governments in Africa and Asia as nothing more than convenient Western clients masking continuing imperialist domination. Khrushchev, however, believed that decolonization had revolutionary implications and praised nonalignment as a break from Western tutelage. Moscow devised the formula of "revolutionary national democracy" to describe such regimes as Nasser in Egypt, Nkrumah in Ghana, and Sukarno in Indonesia. (More recently, variants have been sighted in Peru under Velasco Alvarado [1968–75] and Forbes Burnham in Guyana.) Such governments were clearly not Marxist or even truly socialist in Moscow's eyes (although they often claimed to be). Soviet scholars revived an old Leninist category—the "non-capitalist path to development"—to describe their policies in favorable, if guarded, tones. Such countries might be able to jump from underdevelopment to socialism without passing through a mature capitalist stage. The exact content of this stage, and the precise nature of the transition, was never clearly articulated. The whole idea seems to contradict basic Marxist tenets, and smacks strongly of sophistry in the service of foreign policy. In the end, Stalin has been proven partially correct. Many of these "noncapitalist" regimes proved untenable. Those that have survived have often been transformed from within beyond recognition, or have simply proven to be unreliable allies.

As the 1960s closed, virtually all of the leading revolutionary democrats were no longer in office. The regime of General Kassem in Iraq was removed in 1963. Ben Bella in Algeria and Sukarno in

Indonesia were ousted in 1965. Nkrumah was deposed by a military coup in February 1966. Modibo Keita, the Marxist-oriented head of Mali, was overthrown in November 1968.[19] The fact that Ben Bella, Nkrumah, and Keita had all received the Lenin Peace Prize made their demises especially embarrassing for Moscow.

What had happened? These regimes were supposed to be the leading wave in an oceanic surge toward socialism. Instead, they proved to be highly vulnerable and ephemeral phenomena. Soviet scholars now offer several explanations for the failures of their theories and the collapse of old friends. Soviet propaganda draws attention to Western imperialist machinations, but specialists at the Institute for African Studies in Moscow admitted to me that internal factors have generally been primary.[20] The path toward socialism in Third World nations has been strewn with more obstacles than anticipated in the heady days of decolonization.

In the least-developed countries, the Soviets now recognize, the national democrats inherited a woefully inadequate state apparatus, desperately short of trained technocrats and managers. In Africa especially, exoduses of expatriates and weak colonial systems of higher education left countries short of capable administrators. Of those that did not flee, many still objected to socialist discipline. White-collar bureaucrats are exceedingly good at passive resistance, to the great frustration of central planners. Without an efficient, organized, and motivated government, it is hardly possible to realize the essential task and promise of socialism: the productive planning of the economy. Even worse, government officials, for all their socialist rhetoric, often indulged in personal corruption. Especially in Africa and the Middle East, bureaucrats siphoned off government revenues to their relatives, who invested in private enterprise for the benefit of all family members. The bureaucrat became bourgeoisified.

Revolutionary democratic parties were plagued by structural weaknesses. They typically lacked the tight organization and discipline admired by the heirs to Lenin. The deficient Third World parties were neither able to mobilize the masses swiftly nor implement official policies promptly. The party intelligentsia were susceptible to romantic notions of "African" and "Arab" socialism. From the Soviets' perspective, these were often rationalizations for "petty bourgeois reformism," or impractical "utopianism" based upon notions of traditional village life that bore no relation to contemporary conditions.[21] The party leadership was also vulnerable to corruption. They typically held government positions and came to aspire to life styles of privilege and comfort. Better educated, lifted into official status, and heading stagnant political organizations, the party leadership tended to lose touch with the masses. Personalistic leaders like Nkrumah were especially susceptible to becoming estranged from any organic ties to the populace. Perched on tall trees with hollow trunks, such regimes could be cut down with surprising ease.

From the perspective of the more radical Soviet analysts, the error was to be found in the tendency of the revolutionary vanguard leadership to move too far ahead of the masses. The leadership—whether educated in London, Paris, or Moscow—was filled with Western aspirations that alienated them from their more traditional followers. Once in power, the party elite tended to become too preoccupied with administration to concentrate on building a strong political base.

Soviet analysts blamed some setbacks on the "backwardness" of the local population "still under the sway of tribalism."[22] Mired in traditional religious superstitions and ethnic and tribal mythologies, the masses could not assimilate the more advanced ideas of socialism; class relations were too "immature." According to their analyses, the peasantry was especially prone to vacillation and betrayal. Only the working class is a consistent and dedicated fighter for socialism; but, alas, the proletariat is woefully underdeveloped in many Third World nations. As for the local bourgeoisie, while it might support national democratic alliances momentarily, they too were prone to switch positions and side with reactionary forces if given the opportunity.

Together, these factors are more than sufficient to explain the collapse of revolutionary democratic experiments. Governments became increasingly isolated in the face of economic inefficiencies, widespread corruption, the bourgeoisification of a portion of the ruling party, and the passivity of the masses. The Soviets apply these explanations, with varying degrees of emphasis, to such apparently different failures as Ghana, Indonesia, and Peru.

Most "revolutionary democrats" owed their power to military coups or the domination, by force, of opposing political parties. The Soviets, however, while inherently suspicious of "bourgeois" elections on the Anglo-Saxon model, have on occasion pinned their hopes on "progressive" Third World regimes that arrived in power through the ballot box. Both Salvador Allende and Michael Manley received warm praise from the Soviet leadership and were viewed as opportunities for the advance of Soviet and Cuban influence in the Western Hemisphere. Both governments fell—Allende by the sword, Manley by the ballot—while the Soviets looked on helplessly.

The Allende experiment aroused considerable attention in Moscow, as it did throughout much of the world. At stake, for the Soviets, was one of the oldest and strongest communist parties in the Third World. Moreover, Chile's reputation for mature politics made it a potential model for the more advanced developing countries and even for such Western European countries as France, Italy, and Greece. Soviet scholars agree that Allende's defeat was a grievous blow, although they divide over the reasons for Allende's demise.[23] Some argue that the more radical elements in Allende's camp fatally alienated the middle class and provoked the military. Others hold the opposite: only a bolder thrust against the centers of opposition power could have preempted the counterrevolution. For most Soviet analysts, the Allende disaster reaffirmed their skepticism that it is possible to build socialism within the context of "bourgeois legality."

Increasingly disillusioned with "revolutionary democrats," whether they stand at the head of armies, one-party states, or bourgeois democracies, Moscow seems to be drawing back toward a narrower preference for more traditional Marxist-Leninist parties. In Ethiopia and Nicaragua, for example, the Soviets have been urging the ruling governments to construct disciplined parties controlled by trained, Communist cadres. When several Sandinista leaders visited Moscow shortly after their triumph in search of assistance, the Soviets reportedly asked them if their party was Marxist-Leninist. When they were unable to respond in the affirmative, the Soviets instructed them to deal with the Bulgarians. This insult was no doubt intended to impress upon the Sandinistas that Moscow would not trust them as a reliable ally until they had constructed a serious party.

BETRAYAL BY OLD FRIENDS

For a superpower to have an ally overthrown may be humiliating, but betrayal is even more unkind. The United States has frequently been disappointed by governments drifting toward nonalignment and a willingness to favor the Soviets on particular issues, but rarely have once-friendly regimes jumped wholeheartedly to embrace Moscow. A change of government is usually a prerequisite for the Soviets to receive an open invitation. The Soviets, however, have been subject to wholesale expulsion by reformist regimes, of the type found in the third and fourth circles. When regimes decided that the Soviets had outlived their usefulness, they simply discarded them like so many outworn suits.

One of the starkest cases of a Third World state selfishly using the Soviet Union and then coldly ejecting it is the Egyptian-Soviet relationship. President Gamal Abdel Nasser was rebuffed in his request for military and economic aid by the United States; only the Soviets could provide him with the materiel he needed. Strongly anti-Communist and Arabist, Nasser had no ideological attachment to Moscow. But Moscow could serve his purposes by negating the military superiority that Israel enjoyed because of U.S. backing. The Soviets not only provided Egypt with over twenty thousand military "advisers" but made Egypt a favored recipient of scarce Soviet economic aid and helped construct the "showcase" Aswan Dam. High-level diplomatic ties were also very visible.

The Soviets were eager to make a substantial investment in Egypt to gain influence in an important North African nation. At the same time, Moscow sought to limit its direct military exposure, fearing that an exaggerated Soviet involvement could jeopardize U.S.-Soviet relations, as well as drag the Soviet Union into the Middle East disputes more deeply than seemed wise. Moscow was especially anxious to avoid placing its own troops in combat.

Nasser became obsessed with avenging the Arabs' humiliating defeat of 1967 in the six-day Israeli blitzkrieg. He consistently pressured the Soviets to increase their military commitment. Finally, in January 1970, as Israeli planes were hitting targets deep inside Egypt, Nasser flew to Moscow to obtain advanced Soviet anti-aircraft missiles and the necessary trained Soviet crews. Mohamed Heikal, Nasser's confidant, recorded that Brezhnev immediately noted that this increased Soviet military presence would have serious international implications. Nasser responded: "Why is it the Americans can always escalate their support whereas we sometimes behave as if we were scared. . . . As far as I can see, you are not prepared to help us in the same way that America helps Isreal. This means that there is only one course open to me: I shall go back to Egypt and tell the people the truth. I shall tell them that the time has come for me to step down and hand over to a pro-American president."[24] Heikal reports that Nasser's words "electrified" the room. Presented with this ultimatum by a supposed client, Brezhnev huddled with his Politburo and military officers and promptly capitulated.

As Heikal explains it, Nasser was intent upon sucking in the Soviets:

> [After the 1967 defeat] Nasser saw that the two superpowers were edging toward a detente and he could sense that the Johnson Administration was unsympathetic toward the Arabs in general and toward him in particular. He was therefore determined to get the Soviet Union as deeply involved in the Middle East problem as he could. He wanted them to feel that his defeat had been their defeat, and to make them take the lead in diplomatic efforts to overcome the disastrous legacy . . . [He felt that] the Soviet Union would be obliged to give him the material help of which he was in need. His whole aim was to lift the Middle East dispute from the local to the international level.[25]

Nasser's protege, Anwar el-Sadat, publicly described his decision to break with Moscow as a reassertion of Egyptian independence.[26] In fact, he expelled the twenty thousand Soviet soldiers and advisers because Brezhnev was unwilling to increase the Soviet military presence in Egypt at the pace Sadat felt was necessary or to risk another Middle Eastern conflagration.[27]

Sadat did not break completely with Moscow when he expelled their soldiers, because he wanted to continue to receive equipment for use in his planned attack on Israel. The Soviets proved sufficiently willing to swallow their pride, and continued to supply equipment until the 1973 Yom Kippur War. Once Egypt attacked, Prime Minister Kosygin flew to Cairo and stayed for four days in a show of solidarity, hoping no doubt to regain favor.

Having squeezed enough weapons out of the Soviets to obtain his military objectives, Sadat felt that the Soviets had served their purpose. His remaining needs were diplomatic and economic, and only the United States could help him. Only the United States possessed the leverage over Israel to make possible a peace satisfactory to Egypt. Only the United States could provide the massive economic aid that the ailing Egyptian economy required. Sadat proceeded to tear up the Soviet-Egyptian Treaty of Friendship that he himself had initialed and to cancel some $7 billion in debts owed Moscow.

The Soviets were "deeply annoyed and hurt"[28] by their loss of Egypt. The very military triumph that their arms had made possible set the stage for their dismissal. Sadat preferred to gamble that the other superpower would be more useful in meeting the new set of Egyptian needs.

The loss of Soviet influence could also at least partially be attributed to the sort of internal developments responsible for Soviet undoings in other countries. Certainly the politico-bureaucratic circles around Sadat had lost the revolutionary mystique of Nasser and were more interested in personal wealth and copying Western consumption styles. Trade liberalization and U.S. economic aid had permitted an orgy of imports of designer jeans, stereo equipment, and other luxury goods. To provide work incentives and stimulate efficiency, growing inequalities of income and wealth were allowed. Whatever the economic justification, the political effect was to further distance the elites from the masses.

Soviet officials and advisers were not particularly well liked by many Egyptians. As Heikal reports, "The Soviets were sometimes extremely tactless. . . . and presumptous."[29] Sadat himself told Brezhnev: "You look on us as though we were a backward country."[30] The large numbers of Soviet advisers increased the frequency and intensity of these irritations and offended Egyptian pride.

One can, therefore, point to four reasons for the Soviet loss of Egypt: the bourgeoisification of the Egyptian politico-military-bureaucratic elite; the clash of Soviet and Arab cultures; Egyptian and Soviet differences regarding the risks of escalating regional warfare; and the West's superior economic resources and, at least for the moment, more useful diplomatic position. These domestic and international factors have, in various combinations, jeopardized Soviet ties throughout the Third World.

The Sudan presents a similar case where a leader expelled the Soviets once their usefulness to him had declined. The Soviets extended substantial military aid to President Gaafar Mohammed al-Nimeiry, a self-proclaimed socialist, which he used to contain a rebellion in his southern provinces. Once Nimeiry reached a compromise with the rebels in 1972, his need for Soviet military aid was diminished. Nimeiry felt safe in gradually diminishing the Soviet presence, until, in 1977, he expelled the last Soviet military advisers.

Nimeiry had two other reasons for breaking with Moscow. Following Sadat, Nimeiry was turning increasingly to the West, and to conservative Saudi Arabia and Kuwait, for economic aid. Also, Nimeiry had collided with the Moscow-backed Sudanese Communist Party (SCP). In early 1971 Nimeiry moved to reduce Communist influence, despite their having supported and even participated in his regime. In a countermove, the Communists took part in a coup attempt. After foiling the uprising, Nimeiry harshly retaliated against the SCP and blamed Moscow for backing the aborted coup.

The Sudan and Egypt, once considered by Moscow to be "progressive, anti-imperialist" governments, have become among the most anti-Soviet spokesmen in the Arab world. Their chorus is joined by nearby Somalia, another former Soviet friend. President Siad Barre expelled a significant Soviet military presence in 1977, when Moscow chose to give aid to his enemy, Ethiopia.

As an extensive Brookings Institution study of Soviet military diplomacy concludes, erstwhile Third World friends of the Soviets repeatedly demand, "What have you done for me lately?" The study notes that the status of the U.S.S.R. "typically has not been of imperial overlord but of guest worker."[31] Guest workers are allowed only temporary visa status and may be asked to depart when changing conditions render them superfluous or harmful. Thus, when the Soviets have hesitated to meet the latest set of demands, or when they meet the demands so well as to remove the need, the host government feels justified in revoking their passes. The host government may choose to rely on its own resources, or switch to alternative sources of supply.

Iraq is another country that has turned away from an earlier alliance with the Soviets. The Soviet-Iraqi friendship, which seemed so solid to many observers in the early 1970s, can now be seen to have rested on several transitory elements.[32] The U.S. intervention in Lebanon in 1958 was, in part, a response to revolution in Iraq, and the rise to power of the radical nationalist Baaths. Since then, Iraq has feared U.S. intervention in the region. When Iraq nationalized the holdings of British and American oil companies in the early 1970s, its fear of retaliation was heightened. The Iraqis, who were already dependent upon the Soviets for military equipment, looked to Moscow for technical assistance in running the oil fields and in marketing oil. The Iraqis also needed Soviet equipment to counter a rebellion of Iraqi Kurds, which had the support of the Shah of Iran and the CIA. Moreover, Iraq sought weapons to strengthen its posture in its more direct quarrels with Iran over access to the Persian Gulf and several of its strategically located islands.

Beginning in the mid-1970s, events began to dilute Iraqi dependencies on the Soviet Union. The jump in world oil prices and tightness in supplies freed Iraq from its reliance on Soviet economic and technical aid. The Western oil companies, having become more flexible in dealing with nationalist regimes, and more dependent upon major sources of supply in a tight market, were willing to help find, pump, and market Iraqi oil. Literally flooded with hard currency, the Iraqis revealed their true preferences for Western products, and for dealing with Western banks, where they would deposit $25 billion by the end of 1980. Iraq offered its oil for Western technology, and sought government-to-government barter contracts. Japan, for example, agreed to pay for its oil with power stations, refineries, and petrochemical plants; by 1979, Iraq was importing twice as much from Japan alone as from the entire Eastern bloc. The Italians exchanged a fruit and lifestock farm complex for petroleum. The French agreed to provide a nuclear power reactor (the one bombed by Israel in 1981), an iron and steel plant, and Mirage jet fighters. Iraq has used its petrodollars to diversify its source of military supply, and the Soviet share of Iraq's military imports fell from 95 percent in 1972 to 63 percent in 1979. In addition to France, Iraq has turned to Italy, Yugoslavia, Portugal, and Brazil for weapons.

At the same time as oil wealth was allowing Iraq to stand on its own feet, the regional conflicts that had stimulated Iraq to turn to Moscow were resolved, at least temporarily. In 1975, Iraq and Iran signed an agreement apparently settling their main dispute over access to the Persian Gulf, and Iran agreed to drop its support of the Kurds. The Iraqi army proceeded quickly to crush the demoralized Kurds.

Meanwhile, as old economic and security ties were loosening, fresh areas of friction were emerging between Baghdad and Moscow. The ruling Baath party represents that particular blend of Arab nationalism, egalitarianism, and moderate socialism that is fervently opposed to "internationalist" (that is, pro-Soviet) communism. The pro-Soviet Iraq Communist party had been supporting the "progressive, anti-imperialist" Baath government, but this did not prevent President Saddam Hussein from turning on them in 1978–79. Ignoring Moscow's pleas, he executed several dozen Communist organizers, driving the leadership into exile and the party underground. He denounced the Communists as "a rotten, atheistic, yellow storm that has plagued Iraq."

Iraq, oil-rich and enjoying relative political stability, has aspired to preeminence in the Middle East—hence, its attack on Iran in 1981. Trumpeting Arab nationalism, Iraq has championed an Arabian Persian

Gulf free from superpower—and Iranian—control. Consequently, Hussein has denounced the American Rapid Deployment Force, as well as the Soviet intervention in Afghanistan. Iraq has also supported efforts to reduce Soviet influence in the Yemens, and has denounced Soviet aid to the Ethiopians because of Addis Ababa's repression of the Eritrean Moslems. At the same time, Iraq has moved closer to anti-Soviet Saudi Arabia, partly with the intention of wooing them gradually away from Washington. Iraqi relations have also deteriorated with Syria, whose own ruling Baath party is a natural rival for Hussein's brand of Arab socialism. The war with Iran has interrupted Iraq's drive for regional power, but it seems unlikely that the general direction of Iraq's other foreign policies will be reversed.

The shifting alliances and conflicts in the turbulent Middle East could give the Soviets future opportunities to sell arms to Baghdad and to try to regain influence, but a return to the earlier closeness and dependency seems unlikely. Iraq has become strong and self-confident enough to feel comfortable with nonalignment. In addition, while Iraq is more profoundly egalitarian than Egypt was, even under Nasser, the Iraqi leadership is nevertheless undergoing the kind of materialist transformation that invites closer ties to the West. As the *Wall Street Journal* has noticed:

> [Iraq's] is a convulsive transformation accompanied by dictatorial political methods and by strident Arab-nationalist rhetoric that sounds threatening to Western ears. But the rhetoric shouldn't obscure the fact that Iraq, probably more than any other Mideast nation except Israel, is embracing Western values and technology. As a result, many analysts believe that Iraq is evolving into an advanced, secular society—with a car in every garage, a television set in every living room, universal education, and chic French fashions for emancipated Iraqi women. Such a society should eventually become congenial to the West.[33]

The Baath government has always pursued a mixed economy, albeit with strong state intervention. But, as the business-oriented London publication, *The Economist,* reported with satisfaction, collective farms are being dismantled and the value of production in the private commercial and light industrial sectors has been expanding rapidly. In short, Iraq is being integrated into the one-world economy. The Iraq case strongly suggests that, once external threats have been reduced and/or access to non-Soviet weaponry is secured, and Western economic ties are strengthened, a country's diplomacy is likely to move toward nonalignment, if not anti-Sovietism.

If the Soviets are displaced when a country becomes wealthy, Moscow can also lose influence in the reverse case; namely, when a country faces economic bankruptcy. When the Peruvian military seized power in 1968 and nationalized American firms, including oil holdings, Washington suspended arms sales. The Peruvian generals then turned to Moscow, who proceeded to deliver some $1 billion in military hardware. Some Peruvian officials may have been preparing to avenge their country's defeat at the hands of Chile on the hundredth anniversary of the 1879 War of the Pacific. But if the Soviets hoped that the "progressive, anti-imperialist" Peruvians were on the road to a pro-Soviet socialism, they were very mistaken. Moscow was never able to translate its arms sales into significant political influence. As a State Department official who was director of the office covering Peru told me, "Peru gave the Soviets more headaches than anything else." The Peruvian revolution soon ran out of steam and began to move rightward. The generals also gave up whatever dreams they may have nourished about renewing their old fight with Chile. Finally, a severe balance of payments crisis forced the regime to impose austerity in 1977–78, and to search desperately for foreign exchange. The only available sources were the Western banks and official lending agencies. As economic factors became dominant, and tensions with Chile eased, the Soviet military presence became a mere sideshow.

Guyana is another case where a once "progressive, anti-imperialist" government finds that Moscow is of no use during an economic crisis. Having experienced declining economic fortunes throughout the 1970s, Guyana turned in 1980 to the World Bank and the IMF to alleviate its balance of payments squeeze and to finance ambitious development programs. Guyana's foreign policy rhetoric took on a more moderate tone, and relations with Havana cooled.

The precarious balance of payments positions of many oil-importing developing countries in the 1980s make Peru and Guyana important lessons. With its meager economic assistance program and limited trading interests, the Soviets will have increasing difficulty in consolidating openings created by arms sales, regional tensions or even ideological affinities. As noted earlier, several of the same processes that worked against Soviet influence in Peru and Guyana can be divined in their early stages in Ethiopia, now one of Moscow's strongest and most avowedly radical of allies.

MARRIAGES OF CONVENIENCE

India exemplifies Soviet relations with an important Third World state in the fourth of the five concentric circles that define Soviet foreign policy. Soviet-Indian relations are based essentially on a geopolitical convergence of interests. Since independence, India has not undergone a social revolution, and is still governed by the political party that inherited the country from the British. India maintains a Westminster parliamentary system and a mixed economy of the sort favored by the British Labor party. Yet, India has been a good friend of the Soviet Union for some time. This bond, in some measure, is a response to the historic U.S. tilt toward Pakistan and, more recently, toward China. India and Pakistan have fought three wars since the countries were partitioned at independence, and India and China, natural geopolitical rivals, clashed in 1962 over disputed borders. With the United States standing first behind Pakistan and, later, China, India has inclined toward "the enemy of its enemies" for succor. This was especially true in the decade following the 1965 Indian-Pakistani war over Kashmir and the Rann Kutch, when Western countries embargoed armed sales to New Delhi. The Indians shifted dramatically to the Soviet Union, and all three of the Indian military services became equipped with Soviet arms.

Some observers and U.S. government officials have considered

India to be "a Soviet lap-dog tamely tagging after its master and yelping on call."[34] New Delhi has, for example, sided with Moscow on the Vietnam War and Hanoi's invasion of Cambodia, and failed to condemn firmly the Soviet invasions of Czechoslovakia and Afghanistan. But a closer look reveals that, if the Indians are a Soviet creature, that creature is straining at the leash and its master has suffered many bites.

Even during the years of relatively high Indian reliance on the Soviet Union, the alleged client failed to follow the lead of its patron in votes recorded in the U.N. General Assembly approximately half of the time.[35] Not only has New Delhi been willing to set its own course in global fora, but Indian governments have also defied Soviet directions on regional matters. The Indians have resisted repeated Soviet calls for an "Asian collective security system." Brezhnev himself expounded the virtues of this proposal before the Indian parliament in November 1973, and the subsequent Indian silence could only be interpreted as a striking setback for Soviet diplomacy. At the same time as New Delhi has slipped out from under this proposed Soviet security umbrella, it has implicitly criticized the Soviet naval presence in neighboring waters. New Delhi has proposed that the Indian Ocean be made a "zone of peace" free from all superpower militaries, and has denied a Soviet request for bases on Indian territory. The exclusion of both Soviet and American bases and armadas from the Indian Ocean would leave the waves clear for Indian frigates. India's rejection of a Soviet-led Asian security alliance, and advocacy of an Indian Ocean free from East-West conflict, are both rebukes to Soviet ambitions as well as assertions of India's own national security interests.

In the same spirit of independence, India has sought to lessen its reliance on Soviet military equipment by constructing an indigenous arms industry. Arms manufacturing in India employs two hundred fifty thousand workers and can produce a wide variety of weapons including jet fighters. Moreover, when the Western arms embargo was lifted in 1975, India hastened to diversify its external sources of supply by purchasing in France and Great Britain.

The Indians have tended to treat Soviet military interventions once undertaken as *faits accomplis,* and have preferred not to irritate Moscow with strong condemnations. The Indians have, however, sought to place some distance between themselves and the Soviet action. For example, following the entrance of eighty thousand Soviet troops into Afghanistan, Prime Minister Indira Gandhi issued a carefully hedged statement: "I am strongly against any interference. But in Afghanistan, the Soviet interference is not one-sided. Other interferences were going on there." By slapping China and the United States for encouraging the Afghan insurgents fighting the communist regime, Mrs. Gandhi managed to criticize all the superpowers, while forcefully condemning none of them. Privately, she urged the Soviets to negotiate a withdrawal.

The Soviet Union has not been able to win over the "hearts and minds" of the Indians. A survey of Indian government officials, journalists, and businessmen concluded that, despite the heavy Soviet investment in propaganda, "attitudes toward the Soviet system and ideology are hostile and suspicious."[36] While the Moscow-oriented Communist party has strength in some states, it is the weaker of India's two Communist parties, and has little prospects of taking power in the central government.

There are strong trends suggesting that Soviet influence in India may decline further in the future. In the past, India has been a favored recipient of Soviet aid, although the bulk of India's economic ties remained outside the Soviet bloc. More recently, as the Indian economy progresses, dissatisfaction with Soviet technology is voiced with increasing frequency. For example, the Indians have elected to replace Soviet with West German designs for large-scale power generators. Italian pharmaceutical technology is replacing Soviet antibiotics, and Western oil firms are edging out Soviet and Rumanian ones. Altogether, the Soviet share of the Indian market for imported machinery and equipment fell from about three-fourths in 1968 to under one-quarter by 1977. This trend toward Western technology is also visible in weaponry, most notably in the Indian decision to purchase a large number of sophisticated French Mirage 2000s.

The Indian economy has experienced considerable state intervention within a "mixed economy" framework. The Soviets have, nevertheless, given up early hopes for a genuinely socialist India. As one U.S. expert has written, the Soviets probably recognize that "such a development may create more problems than it would solve."[37] A socialist India would place strong and expensive demands on the Soviet economy, and an attempt to impose a more centralized and egalitarian economy on India would destabilize the entire subcontinent and create additional tensions near the Soviet Union's southern perimeter. In any case, India has gradually been shifting in the opposite direction, toward somewhat greater reliance on market mechanisms and efficiency criteria. In 1981 India signed a loan agreement worth over $5 billion with the International Monetary Fund, the guardian of Western liberal economic thought. India had to agree at least not to increase state intervention in the economy, while promising to offer profitable incentives to private investors.

The friendship with the Soviet Union will continue to serve Indian interests within the existing context of security ties in Asia. Relations with China, however, have shown some signs of improving, and negotiations were opened in 1981 on the disputed border areas. The Soviets are undoubtedly deeply concerned that an Indian-Chinese rapprochement would lessen Indian reliance on them. The apparent improvement in relations between India and Pakistan in 1982 could also allow New Delhi more room for diplomatic maneuver.

As experts on Indian affairs have argued, there are certain parallels between Indian and Soviet objectives that some mistake for Indian subservience.[38] India does, it is true, take Soviet interests into account in drawing its own foreign policy positions. But India has deviated from the Soviet line in the past, and diverging interests suggest that India will do so with increasing frequency in the future. The parallels with the U.S.-Brazilian relationship (see chapter 1) are striking. Like Brazil, as India moves to maximize its own room for maneuver vis-à-vis the superpowers, seeks diversified and nonpoliticized trade and access to the best technology, and develops its own military capabilities, it will design an increasingly subtle and personalized foreign policy.

Communist Parties

The large majority of Third World states, having very weak, if any, ties to the Soviet Union, lie outside the fifth circle. The Kremlin may still hope to influence some of these countries through traditional diplomacy. Like the United States, however, the Soviet Union does not limit itself to state-to-state relations in its efforts to alter the Third World. In conservative states, as well as in some non-Communist reformist ones, the Kremlin may seek to influence events through the instrumentality of local Communist parties. In the Third World, as in Western Europe, loyal Communist parties can articulate the Soviet perspective on international affairs, and can otherwise pressure their own governments to adopt policies more in line with Soviet wishes.

While sometimes useful to Moscow, local Communist parties have proven at least as disappointing and unreliable to the Soviet Union as businessmen have been for the United States. Many Communist parties have, of course, broken with the socialist homeland. In Western Europe, this splintering has taken the form of "eurocommunism." The Italian and other European Communist parties are designing a future independent from Moscow. Moscow's influence over Asian Communist parties has, with few exceptions, diminished as well. Victory for the Filipino, Malaysian, or Burmese Communists would probably benefit China more than the Soviet Union. Moscow is simply no longer the unchallenged source of inspiration for Communists and must now compete with other power centers and ideologies. Moreover, many Third World leftists are willing to voice their own nationalist concerns; they have noticed that the positions of the Communist party of the Soviet Union tend, with great regularity, to mirror the national interests of the Soviet state.

As previously noted, Communist parties have often been more a burden than a benefit for Soviet foreign policy. This anomaly is due to three phenomena normally overlooked by observers, especially those who see a powerful and dangerous international Communist movement cleverly manipulated from Moscow. First, Soviet efforts to maintain good relations with non-Communist governments have been hampered by the local presence of a pro-Soviet Communist party. Second, when the Soviet Union has given priority to state-to-state relations to the detriment of local Communist or national liberation movements, the progressive image of the Soviet Union has suffered. Finally, Communist parties in power that become unstable present Moscow with the unpleasant alternatives of either escalating its support even to the point of military intervention, or else facing at least the appearance of impotence and defeat.

Despite rhetoric about its selfless regard for socialist principles and revolution, much of Soviet foreign policy consists of the more normal state-to-state relations that one would expect of an established Great Power. Yet local Communist parties represent a constant, if often dormant, threat to the local status quo. Governments thus threatened are forever looking over their shoulders with suspicion at the Soviet Union, fearing a doublecross. When the local party increases the tempo of its hostility, the local government may hold Moscow responsible, if only for propaganda purposes. For example, the deterioration in relations between the Iraqi and Indian governments and their local Communist parties in the late 1970s and early 1980s adversely affected Soviet relations with those governments. In the more extreme case of the Sudan, a failed coup attempt by a group of Communists in 1971 against the then pro-Soviet government of Nimeiry triggered a sharp decline in Soviet influence. Nimeiry rejected Moscow's protestations of noninvolvement in the aborted coup, and swung away from Moscow toward Egypt, Saudi Arabia, and the West.

The Soviet Union has often tried to resolve this dilemma simply by betraying local Communists on the altar of state-to-state relations and the Soviet national interest. As early as the 1920's, the Soviet Union gave military support to the Kuomintang, who was willing to deal with the young, isolated Bolshevik regime. These Chinese nationalists proceeded violently to repress the Chinese Communists. In the 1930s, Stalin restrained his support to the Communists in the Spanish civil war. He gave priority to not antagonizing France and Great Britain, whose friendship he deemed more essential for Russian interests.

Moscow has sometimes directed local parties to participate in governments friendly to the Soviet Union, even when such governments have been anti-Communist. The local parties typically splinter, and that fraction that joins the government as a minority partner is subject to sudden ouster from the ruling coalition. Once dismissed, the Communists may face intense repression. Soviet silence during these purges has spoken loudly for Moscow's diplomatic priorities.

The Soviets could rationalize their support for such anti-Communist governments as Egypt under Nasser, Iraq under the Baaths, and Libya under Qaddafi on the ground that these were "progressive, nationalist" regimes. More difficult to explain has been Soviet support for the military dictatorship in Argentina and for Idi Amin in Uganda. The Argentine junta was willing to sell wheat to the Soviets, and Idi Amin may have seemed to be one avenue of influence against Chinese penetration of East Africa. Murdered Argentine and Ugandan Communists could take little solace.

These zigzags and betrayals have tarnished the image that the Soviets would like to project of a comradely, idealistic foreign policy. A nation that so frequently has placed the interests of Soviet diplomacy over those of the local party is just another superpower. Chinese barbs, that Russia is engaged in "social imperialism," have a sharper and sharper sting.

The gravest dilemma, however, that local Communists can present to Moscow occurs when a Communist government is on the verge of being toppled. The myth is widespread in the United States that once Communist parties come to power, their "totalitarian grip" can never be shaken. Historically, Communist parties that have entered into governing coalitions, far from devouring their allies, have often themselves been turned upon and ousted. This occurred, for example, in Chile and in several Western European countries in the early days of the Cold War, and on numerous occasions in the Middle East in the 1960s and 1970s. Their "bourgeois" allies may use them for a time to help control the labor movement or gain parliamentary votes, only to discard them when priorities change.

Even when Communist parties claim a monopoly on power, they are not immune to political decomposition and dissent. Were it not for the presence of the Red Army, Communist parties may well have been removed from power in Eastern Europe on several occasions. Internal party discipline can disintegrate, as may have been occurring in Czechoslovakia in 1968, or alternative centers of power can spring up, as Solidarity demonstrated in Poland in 1981. These challenges to orthodox Communist hegemony in Eastern Europe arose even after the regimes had had a generation to solidify their hold. The near defeat of the Communist party government in Afghanistan in 1979 is especially relevant for the Third World, where Communist parties will often need to struggle over an extended period to consolidate their revolution. Only the Red Army saved the Afghan Communists from being slaughtered at the hands of a popular, anti-Communist insurrection. One lesson of Afghanistan is that not even the presence of a Marxist-Leninist party is a guarantee of stability for the Soviet Union.

The Soviet Communist party, the author was told in Moscow, felt a moral duty to rescue the Afghan party from a bloodbath. This obligation held even though the local party had refused to heed Soviet counsel and had pursued policies too radical for the population. The stubborn Afghan Communists had brought the house down on themselves, but Moscow felt impelled, for moral as well as geopolitical reasons, to intervene. The costs to Soviet diplomacy in the Third World and in East-West relations have been great.

The economic defects of Communist regimes, such as in Cuba and Poland, have also been expensive for the Soviets. Soviet subsidies to Cuba have been estimated at some $3 billion annually. The Soviets may have plundered Eastern Europe in the immediate aftermath of World War II, but more recently Eastern Europe has been extracting subsidies from the Soviets, equal to roughly $20 billion in 1980, according to some estimates.[39] The Soviets, for example, have been supplying oil at prices well below world market levels. Now, Moscow is even being compelled to pick up a portion of the tab for the massive Western debts incurred by some Eastern Europe states. The costs of political control are mounting.

Fortunately, perhaps, for the Soviet Union, most Communist parties are a long way from power. Far from advancing toward the declared goals of smashing the bourgeois state and building socialism, Communist parties are generally stagnant or in retreat. In many Third World countries, Communist parties are weaker today than they were a decade ago. Some large parties that once seemed promising—in Indonesia, Chile, Uruguay—have been badly beaten.

Why this rollback of the forces who claim to have history on their side? The reasons, as we have seen, are deeply rooted in the histories, cultures, and economies of the Third World. An international, proletarian ideology, Marxism clashes with more narrow-minded ethnic and tribal loyalties. Moslems, Hindus, and Christians all tend to view Marxism as atheistic, and efforts to blend these religions with Marxism have generally occurred outside of the orthodox pro-Soviet parties. The Soviet variety of Marxism, which emphasizes the urban worker and views the peasant as backward and best controlled by the forced collectivization of land, goes over poorly among peasants, who still make up the largest single group in many developing nations. The urban proletariat remains too small in most countries to gain and maintain power on its own. In many cases, government repression has taken a heavy toll among Communist cadres.

The Left in many Third World nations has fractured into hotly competing parties. The traditional debates among Western socialists are replicated in Asia, Africa, and Latin America, and have the same tendency to splinter leftists over issues which, to outsiders, seem obscure and scholastic. The wars among disputing factions certainly benefit the "reactionaries and fascists." Moscow itself is partially responsible for these fractures, since its tendency to brand those who disagree with the current orthodoxy as "adventurists" or worse is mimicked by Moscow's local loyalists. Moscow's dispute with Peking added another issue over which Third World Communists felt obliged to argue and divide. Those factions that sided with Peking, or otherwise took a more "leftist" position, often became fiercely anti-Soviet and denounced local loyalists for being bureaucratic, overly cautious, sectarian, authoritarian—in short, for being faithful reproductions of their mentors in Moscow.

Most of the successful revolutions in the Third World have not been led by pro-Soviet Communist parties. Some—as in Ethiopia and Libya—were spearheaded by military officers. Several—as in Algeria, Angola, and Nicaragua—were led by broad-based "national liberation forces," which may have professed a socialist ideology but were not constituted as pro-Soviet Marxist-Leninist parties. Indeed, the Sandinistas in Nicaragua, and ZANU (led by Robert Mugabe) in Zimbabwe, had opposed pro-Soviet parties. In Iran, it was more the fundamentalist clergy than the pro-Soviet Tudehs that brought down the Shah. China and Vietnam are examples of those relatively rare cases where self-proclaimed Communist parties have, indeed, won. Once in power, a governing party may transform itself into a pro-Soviet Communist party—as occurred in Cuba—but that is more a testament to the governing and coercive capacities of a disciplined party apparatus than to the ability of orthodox Communists to make revolutions.

The dreams of the early Bolsheviks, that revolutionary parties would sweep to power in Europe and Asia (Latin American and Africa were beyond their purview) lie buried with them under the Kremlin wall. Moreover, the Communist movement today is fragmented beyond repair, and many parties are intensely hostile toward the Soviet Union. Most parties are too weak to matter, and others absorb more energies and resources of the Soviet Union than they can be worth. It is not an overstatement to say that Communist parties have become a recurrent headache for Soviet foreign policy.

The Military

Marxists traditionally viewed militaries as instruments of the oppressive ruling class that controlled the state apparatus. The officer corps, at least, was an enemy that insurgent Communists had to liquidate or neutralize. With the poor showing of Communist parties, however, Moscow reexamined its options. Recognizing that the military had become a central political force in many Third World countries, Soviet analysts convinced themselves that militaries could play "progressive, nationalist" roles. Events in the late 1960s and early 1970s seemed to support this view, when military coups installed reformist or leftist leaders in Iraq, Congo-Brazzaville, Peru, Somalia, Dahomey (Benin), Libya, and Ethiopia. In the late 1970s, the Soviets also uncovered "progressive elements" within the Argentine military who were willing to sell them grain. New recruits were thus added for the third, fourth, and fifth circles, as seen from the Kremlin.

If the Soviets were not forewarned by their ideology, events have certainly demonstrated that the loyalty and reliability of Third World militaries is no more certain for Moscow than for Washington. In some cases, the more pro-Soviet officers have been ousted. For example, Moscow's friend in Congo-Brazzaville, President Marien Ngouabi, was assassinated in 1977, and his former military colleagues proceeded to resume relations with the United States and to opt "for an open approach to Western countries for aid and investment."[40] In other instances, as we have seen, once-friendly soldiers have shifted gears and tossed the Soviets out. A Soviet scholar explained this capriciousness by noting that, whereas Third World armies may be capable of playing a progressive role in the early stages of struggle against colonialism or a backward landed oligarchy, before the revolution advances too far, "conservative tendencies nearly always become apparent." The army then "strives to preserve its privileges" and "opposes radical changes."[41] In other words, Third World armies may sometimes be mildly reformist, but rarely are they truly radical. Even then, their nationalism, or their regional security needs, may place them in opposition to Soviet policies.

The Soviets have not been immune to the temptation to place their chips on rightist, even blatantly anti-Communist governments. Apparent geopolitical advantage has taken precedence over ideological sentiments. Opportunistic entrance into this game, of course, exposes the Soviets to the same risks faced by the United States when it relies on conservative Third World regimes. While the Shah was not a Soviet ally, Moscow had established a *modus vivendi* with the Pahlavi dynasty, and had restrained the Iranian Communist party, the Tudeh, in its opposition. As a result of its understandings with the Shah and the secondary role played by the Tudeh in the revolution, the Shah's fall left a nervous Moscow without strong influence in Teheran. The Soviets were also willing to enter into a security relationship with Idi Amin. His defeat at the hands of the Tanzanian army—with its long friendship to China—must have been especially galling to Moscow.

The Soviets have relied heavily on arms sales to cement ties with Third World military regimes. Yet, as an exhaustive study of arms transfers to developing countries recently concluded, "Whatever leverage the shipment of arms provides, Moscow's experience confirms that it is not guaranteed to be lasting."[42] Third World officers can conclude that shifting security requirements, alternative offers, or simple dissatisfaction with Soviet aid warrant a policy reversal. The transfer of $1.2 billion in arms to Indonesia did not inhibit Sukarno from shifting to a pro-Chinese foreign policy. The Soviets were ordered out of Egypt, even though they had seventeen thousand military personnel there and had reorganized the Egyptian forces in Soviet style. Siad Barre ousted the Soviets from the prized base at Berbera facing the Indian Ocean, and the Somali president offered use of the facilities to the United States. Large-scale weapons shipments to Peru failed to increase significantly Soviet influence. Nor have arms transfers to Iraq, India, or Algeria transformed these nations into pliant allies. Arms sales may be good business for both superpowers, but in the modern world of shifting alliances, the provision of armies no longer forges bonds of fealty.

Local Rivalries

By joining the influence game in the Third World, the Soviets inevitably encounter some of the traps that have waylaid the United States. The Kremlin has discovered that it is not only capitalist nations who are prone to misstep; the webwork of crisscrossing politics in the Third World has ensnared the Soviets more than once.

For example, Soviet efforts to expand their influence in the Horn of Africa came up against the region's deep-seated nationalist and ethnic rivalries. The Soviets had established a close relationship with the "socialist-oriented" government of Siad Barre in Somalia. The Ethiopian revolution next door seemed to offer an unexpected opportunity to enlarge the Soviet presence in the Horn. Moscow recognized that Ethiopia and Somalia harbored historic resentments but hoped that these could be settled peacefully. Both Soviet President Podgorny and Fidel Castro attempted on-the-spot mediations and proposed a sort of socialist Red Sea federation. Under the umbrella of a regional Pax Sovietica, ideological affinities would overcome Somalia's fervent desire to annex the Ethiopian province of Ogaden (inhabited by ethnic Somalis) and would erase Addis Ababa's imperial legacy. But the peace missions failed, and Somalia proceeded to invade the Ogaden. Siad Barre expelled the Soviets, who were supplying Ethiopia with an increasing quantity of weapons and advisers. The Soviets thus lost the choice naval base at Berbera, and the harbor facilities that Ethiopia has since granted the Soviets are of less value.

The Soviets have repeatedly found themselves unable to control the ambitions of their clients. Third World states have used Soviet weapons in the pursuit of nationalist objectives not always consonant with Soviet interests. In this regard, Ethiopia has been almost as troublesome as Somalia. Mengistu neglected Moscow's advice that he negotiate a political solution to the Eritrean rebellion. Addis Ababa has preferred to try to repress the Eritrean Moslems' struggle for greater local autonomy. Despite its preference for a peaceful compromise, Moscow has been identified with Addis Ababa's military strategy. Moscow's relations have consequently suffered with those Moslem states, including Iraq, who sympathize with the Eritreans.

The Middle East, where internecine rivalries are so intense, has been hazardous territory for Soviet diplomacy. Despite Syrian dependence on Soviet weaponry, Moscow was unable to dissuade Damascus from intervening in Lebanon in 1976 against the leftist Palestinians. Again, Syria's national interest outweighed ideology—and the Soviet preference. Nor could Moscow have been happy when another purchaser of Soviet weaponry, Iraq, attacked Iran in 1981. Moscow had gradually been trying to warm up its cool relations with the fundamentalist mullahs.

Such problems are not confined to the Middle East. Fearing that the unruly Kim Il Sung might attack South Korea, the Soviets have refused to provide him with sufficient offensive capabilities. North Korean aggression against the South would upset Soviet relations throughout Asia and provoke a confrontation with the United States.

When a pro-Soviet regime plays an aggressive game in its own region, neighboring states can react by banding together in self-defense and by seeking outside aid. Just as an activist U.S. policy can push some states into the arms of the Soviets, so have the Soviets and their allies frightened states into appealing to the U.S. or some other offsetting force. The Soviets may be pleased that Vietnam has extended into Cambodia, but the costs of Hanoi's aggressiveness have been high for Soviet diplomacy. The Association of East Asian Nations (ASEAN), including Thailand, Singapore, Hong Kong, Indonesia, and Malaysia, have consequently welcomed a greater American and Japanese—and even to some degree, Chinese—presence. Despite ASEAN's qualms about the ultimate ambitions of these nations, they are seen as a useful counterweight to a Soviet-backed, militaristic Vietnam. Its strident overstatement notwithstanding, the *Peking Review* hit upon an important truth when it editorialized: "[The Soviet Union] thinks it has scored a major gain in having Vietnam as its stooge for the pursuit of hegemony in Asia. But, contrary to its wish, this actually serves to show up the atrocious features of the Soviet expansionists. This also has opened the eyes of the people of Southeast Asia, the whole of Asia and the rest of the world and has thus promoted the growth of an international united front against [Soviet] hegemonism."[43]

Similarly, the activist Cuban policy in Central America and the Caribbean has alarmed Venezuela and the more conservative Caribbean islands. The result has been to grant the United States somewhat greater leeway in establishing a counterpresence.

To date, superpower clashes in Third World theaters have not exceeded manageable levels of intensity. The danger remains that such competition could lead to direct confrontation between the United States and the Soviet Union, and uncontrollably escalate into a full-scale nuclear holocaust. The superpowers could be dragged toward a confrontation by Third World clients run amok. Country A, supported by the Soviets, might unexpectedly invade pro-U.S. Country B. The resulting infusion of American arms and advisers enables Country B to turn the tide, and the regime in Country A begins to totter. The Kremlin is then faced with the dilemma of intervening to save its local friend, or admit defeat at the hands of a U.S.-backed "proxy." A decision to intervene would find the United States and the Soviets staring at each other across borders in some distant Third World region. Perhaps the superpowers would be able to restrain their clients and negotiate a peace. But the worry is that the complex whirl of competing pressures would cause events to spin out of control.

Conclusion

The Soviet Union is not without resources and the will to use them. A massive, centralized state in the heart of the Eurasian landmass, the Soviet Union can directly bring its power to bear along an arc extending from the Baltic Sea through central Europe and southwest Asia to East Asia and the North Pacific. More recently, the Soviets have developed the capabilities to project their influence into more distant regions of the Third World. Certainly, the Soviet Union is a global power, and will remain so for at least the remainder of the twentieth century.

Nevertheless, the vision of the Soviet Union standing at the center of a tightly knit and relentlessly expanding empire is clearly erroneous. Moscow's relations with other Communist states are frayed from years of bickering over matters of ideology and the widespread rejection of Moscow as the natural Rome for all Communists. The ties between the Soviet Union and non-Communist Third World states, including radical regimes, are generally much less solid than official communiques of friendship might suggest. The Soviets have been able to develop and maintain true, if uneasy, relations of clientage only where the Red Army is stationed (Eastern Europe), or where a Third World state, caught in an extremely hostile environment, is desperately dependent on Soviet military support (Cuba, Vietnam). Elsewhere, Soviet relations tend to be tenuous and reversible.

The inability of the Soviet Union to forge lasting ties is explained in considerable measure by its lack of organic links to institutions, political parties, or social classes within Third World nations. Military establishments tend to be too nationalist or conservative to be attracted to overbearing and ideological Russians. The permanent bureaucracy in Third World states is also imbued with a sense of national interest. Moreover, the bureaucrats' elitist tendencies, consumerism, and interest in economic modernization and technology make them elusive targets for the Soviets. Private businessmen, while willing perhaps to engage in profitable deals with COMECON, prefer of course to direct most of their activities toward the much larger and more dynamic markets of the West. The Soviets themselves distrust the petty bourgeoisie and the peasantry, finding them to be too opportunistic or reactionary. Even Communist parties are often unreliable. They may reflect local prejudices, and too often they adopt a pro-Chinese or some other anti-Soviet line. In any case, they are generally too weak to matter.

Given the chronic difficulty the Soviets have in constructing organic ties with Third World societies, it is no surprise that the alliances they are able to form at the top—with heads of state—can prove ephemeral. A change in leadership, a shift in local political alignments, or a local geopolitical disturbance can upset years of persistent Soviet diplomacy.

The dynamics of a country's economy can also unravel Soviet designs. When a one-time Soviet friend becomes wealthy, as happened to Iraq and Algeria, it suddenly possesses the wherewithal to pursue more independent policies. But the converse does not hold: a descent into poverty does not necessarily result in new opportunities for Soviet influence. As the cases of Peru and Guyana illustrate, governments whose economies are contracting may become more susceptible to the temptations of the West.

The Soviet Union lacks the instruments with which to build a permanent and solid structure of alliances. Ideologically, its gray authoritarianism, compromised by national self-interest, is of declining appeal in most of the Third World. Economically, the Soviet Union is facing mounting pressures at home and within Eastern Europe. Moreover, its timid entry into the world economy has left the Soviet Union without the tools that are most relevant to the Third World's major concern—economic development. Moscow has become increasingly dependent upon military transfers to gain influence. But weapons can convey great influence only so long as the recipient country feels threatened by a third party, or is without an alternative supplier.

Moscow's congenital inability to form lasting ties suggests that countries that today profess great admiration and friendship may tomorrow travel the well-worn path toward nonalignment or anti-Sovietism. Marxist governments may argue with Moscow over ideological doctrine or national interest: as China, Yugoslavia, Albania, and, to a lesser degree, North Korea, have already done. Third World nationals may find that the Soviet Union is unwilling to meet their needs as they see them or may take unwelcome positions in regional disputes: as Egypt and Somalia have learned. For example, should the Soviets succeed in increasing their influence in Iran, Iraq—Iran's rival for primacy in the Persian Gulf—may feel betrayed and decide to seek other allies. Elsewhere, the Soviets may overplay their hand, demanding more control than local leaders feel comfortable bequeathing to foreigners. Revolutionary elites may be displaced or they may mature, as occurred in Egypt and Algeria. One or more of such sources of friction are already visible in Soviet relations with several of its closest friends, including Ethiopia, Angola, and, to some degree, Vietnam. The Soviet or Cuban military presence in these countries is unlikely to prove permanent or to outweigh these other centrifugal forces in the long run.

Even regimes relatively close to and dependent on the Soviet Union have hesitated to provide the Soviets with military bases. Angola, Mozambique, and Vietnam have denied permanent basing rights, and have been willing to provide only limited access to airfields and naval facilities. Moreover, as Sadat dramatically demonstrated, basing rights are of uncertain duration.

The more advanced developing countries that have had close relations with the Soviet Union are outgrowing them. Just as Brazil now plots a diplomacy more independent of the United States, so are Iraq and India, wealthier and increasingly self-confident, likely to seek more balanced international relations.

THE COSTS OF EMPIRE

It is not coincidental that Soviet gains have been concentrated in the poorer, more underdeveloped countries. Infusions of relatively small amounts of external resources can make a difference, especially when the recipient country is further weakened by internal strife. But if such countries are easier to influence, the tangible returns may be hard to measure. In hard military and economic terms, what have the Soviets really gained from their expanded influence in Africa?[44]

Vietnam and Cuba have been more valuable allies. But they have also been much more costly. Economic aid to these two militarized societies ballooned in the late 1970s and early 1980s. The aid often took the form of price subsidies as the market value of oil rose and sugar fell. At the same time, Soviet loans and subsidies to Eastern Europe skyrocketed as the Soviets felt compelled to keep their Warsaw Pact allies solvent. While the extent of Soviet aid can only be estimated, the annual costs of the inner-core states of Eastern Europe plus those of close Third World allies like Vietnam and Cuba may reach $30 billion.[45]

The Kremlin badly miscalculated the costs of intervention in Afghanistan. I was told in Moscow by a source with access to high party officials that the government initially believed that they could win a quick victory against the Afghan insurgents. Even so, had the economic crises in Eastern Europe been apparent before the collapse of the Amin regime in Kabul, the Soviets may have been less willing to intervene massively.

The mounting costs of control, coming on top of domestic economic strains, must be raising questions in Moscow. When are firm alliances worth the economic expense? If the economic burden could be reduced, should less structured relations be sought? Most certainly, the Soviets will think twice before committing themselves to additional, expensive clients. "No more Vietnams" is a refrain as relevant for the Soviet Union as it is for the United States. Neither superpower can easily afford the expense of funding costly Third World conflicts and their aftermath.

SOVIET SETBACKS

Apparent Soviet gains may prove to incur more costs than benefits. What seem to be victories may turn out to be destructive drains of scarce resources. At the same time, and judging by more traditional, geopolitical criteria, the Soviets have suffered many "losses."

Soviet setbacks have most often been the result of the Soviets' own errors and weaknesses, or the outcome of dynamics inherent to the particular bilateral relationship. The United States has generally not been the primary cause for the Soviet reversal, although the United States may have been a beneficiary. The splits among Communist states are internecine quarrels, and the United States has sometimes hardly been aware of their intensity until well after the fact. Strains in relations with such states as Somalia, Iraq, and India have more often been the result of regional dynamics, or the clash between Soviet interests and those of the Third World country, than of U.S. diplomacy. Some countries have simply outgrown Soviet tutelage.[46]

While the United States has generally not been the prime cause of Soviet troubles in the Third World, U.S. willingness to exploit differences as they surface can be important if radical regimes are to be weaned away from Mother Russia. Alternative offers of financial or military support, from the United States or other capable states, can be essential if a government is to reduce its dependency on the Soviet Union. Prompt Western assistance, for example, was crucial in allowing Tito to resist Stalin's attempt to pressure Yugoslavia back into line. In contrast, the U.S. refusal to offer alternatives to Vietnam, Cuba, and Angola has surely lessened their ability to maneuver away from Moscow.

If the United States has generally not been behind Soviet defeats, U.S. mistakes have contributed importantly to Soviet successes. Opportunities have arisen for the Soviets in countries where the United States or other Western powers have, for too long, helped prop up highly coercive or outmoded regimes. In Iran and Ethiopia, for example, the regimes were widely perceived as being repressive, rigid, and under the influence of the U.S. embassy. In Indochina, southern Africa, and Nicaragua, the United States or the Western European powers became deeply identified with colonial or semicolonial regimes that refused to adapt to changing circumstances and were finally blown away in revolutionary upheavals. The resulting revolutions gave the Soviets opportunities to increase their influence. Only, however, where the U.S. has remained unremittingly hostile to the new regime have the Soviets been able to retain control over an extended period. Cuba and Vietnam are the exceptions that prove the rule.

The next chapter will discuss more fully how an aggressive or rigid U.S. policy can needlessly create opportunities for Soviet diplomacy.

4 *Avoidable Costs*

An essential task of foreign policymakers is to define what constitutes threats to the national interest. How serious are these threats, and how likely are they to materialize? In designing overall foreign policy, perceptions of threat heavily influence the choice of strategies and the allocation of human and material resources.

Many of the problems facing U.S. policy in the Third World are a result of incorrectly assessing threats. Some perceived threats, while real, have been exaggerated, while others should not be interpreted as threats at all. Tragically, the misidentification of threats has often resulted in costly and even counterproductive policies. Other U.S. interests have needlessly been sacrificed in order to deter or attack a threat that was either imaginary or exaggerated out of proportion. In some cases, U.S. missteps have brought about the very calamity that policymakers were striving so intensely to avoid. In other instances, what were perceived as threats could actually have been transformed by an astute diplomacy into advantages.

The miscalculation of threats results from a faulty or incomplete understanding of recent trends in the Third World. Some policymakers worry that important Third World political movements may jeopardize the stability of the international economy. As chapter 2 argued, these fears exaggerate the leverage of developing countries, mistakenly identify rhetoric with actual intentions, and implicitly assume that Third World leaders will behave irrationally. Another, even more persistent concern, has been the fear of Soviet expansion. As we have seen, while this concern is valid, the Soviet Union has been stymied by many of the same stubborn forces that have frustrated the United States when it attempts to manipulate the Third World.

Underlying the fear that the Soviet Union will be able to exploit the decline of U.S. influence is the assumption that there is no separate ground. Third World countries are allegedly too weak to stand on their own, even in mutually supportive regional alliances. In a bipolar world, the argument runs, peripheral states are inevitably drawn toward one of the two fountainheads of power. In reality, however, the case is increasingly otherwise: Third World states have both the interest and the ability to resist being the pawns of either superpower.

Exaggerated Threats

An exaggerated sense of threat (and, sometimes, the need to extract resources from Congress) has led successive administrations to claim that U.S. "credibility" worldwide depended on honoring commitments to particular Third World regimes. The inherent importance of these countries to the United States was vastly inflated. Administrations, underrating the individuality of developing countries, have tended to amplify the danger that disturbances in one country would spill over into neighboring states and even beyond. Some Americans, moreover, fear that ideological waves originating in developing countries might wash onto our own shores. Finally, as we shall see, the view of the world as a "zero-sum" game—where decline of U.S. influence results inevitably in a Soviet gain—has added to a profound distrust of the ultimate intentions of all leftist movements. Even if such political groups appear, for the moment, to be keeping their distance from Moscow, the presupposition is that they will ultimately seek the Kremlin's protective embrace.

DILUTING OUR CREDIBILITY

The United States naturally wants to deter others from infringing upon its vital interests. For our warnings to be credible, nations must fear that we will act, and that we possess the means for effectively doing so. We thereby place a shield around our vital interests, and lessen the risk of actual conflict.

However, if we commit ourselves vociferously to defending less important interests, we risk confusing our adversaries and allies, as well as ourselves. In the event that secondary interests are actually threatened, we may decide to limit the resources we are willing to devote to their defense. We may even sacrifice them on behalf of more salient interests. Yet, a failure to vigorously defend declared interests would damage our credibility. Eventually, nations may doubt, and even we may doubt, our willingness to defend genuinely vital interests. We risk a loss of confidence if all interests are treated as though they were equally vital.

When a secondary interest to which we have previously made a strong commitment is challenged, some will contend that we must respond; our credibility is at stake. Even when this argument prevails, it will be increasingly hard to sustain. As we saw in chapter 1, the United States is having ever greater difficulty in imposing its will around the world. The costs of such attempts rise, and success is not guaranteed. In times of slow economic growth and budget cuts, Americans are less likely to want to pay the price.

Vietnam was the classic case of abusing the credibility doctrine. Indochina was elevated to the level of an overridingly vital interest. American presidents warned that the credibility of all of our commitments worldwide would be jeopardized if we failed to prevail. As Lyndon Johnson stated with characteristic flare, the alternative to standing by our commitments in Indochina was,

> to throw in the towel . . . and pull our defenses back to San Francisco . . . [the United States] would say to the world . . . that we don't live up to our treaties and don't stand by our friends.[1]

Writing in 1969, George Ball, who had served as a high-level State Department official under Kennedy and Johnson, warned against the self-defeating nature of overstating commitments:

> Not only is it factually dubious to exaggerate the dangers that may flow from the inability to achieve our overblown objectives [in Vietnam], but it involves the risk of undercutting our own authority. . . . if we continually emphasize that a North Vietnamese encroachment would be a worldshaking catastrophe, we may well find ourselves in a self-fulfilling prophecy.[2]

In the aftermath of Vietnam, some observers thought that the United States should more carefully and narrowly define its commitments. Dr. Kissinger was supposedly among these advocates. Indeed, neoconservatives have attacked Kissinger and ex-President Nixon for allegedly abandoning the doctrine of universal or global containment. Nixon, writes Norman Podhoretz, editor of *Commentary Magazine,* "who once denounced containment as 'cowardly,' and would in the past have been expected to abandon it if at all in favor of a more aggressive stance, moved instead in the opposite direction—toward withdrawal, retrenchment, disengagement."[3] Nonetheless, in Chile, Angola, and Indochina, Kissinger behaved as though our interests were still universal and nonhierarchical. In each case, although important, tangible U.S. interests were not clearly at stake, Kissinger felt the urge to act.

Kissinger has argued intensely that U.S. credibility suffered when we failed to respond forcefully to the introduction of Cuban troops into Angola in 1975. In this case, the "credibility" being tested was not based on a commitment to a regime, since the Portuguese had just withdrawn, and the closest thing to a government in the capital, Luanda, was the MPLA, whom the Cubans were supporting. Rather, Kissinger's invocation of "credibility" centered around the perceived requirement that the United States respond to this—and any other—example of Cuban/Soviet expansionism in the Third World.

The Republic of South Africa, however, had already intervened militarily on behalf of UNITA and the FNLA, the two guerrilla groups that were already receiving covert assistance from the CIA. By accepting South African aid, the anti-MPLA forces were discredited among Black Africans. Additionally, the United States and Western Europe were widely criticized for not halting the South African invasion, and even for sponsoring it. The Cubans were accepted by many Africans as having "intervened as a consequence of failure of Western policies and on behalf of legitimate African interest."[4]

Nor was Kissinger's proposal sustainable in the United States; fearing an open-ended commitment in a non-strategic zone, Congress effectively handcuffed him. The Clark Amendment prohibited covert military programs in Angola. Having declared U.S. credibility to be at stake in Angola and then being unable to act, the Ford administration lost face. Swinging wildly, it gave itself a black eye.

The Angola episode is important because it illustrates a central flaw in the undifferentiated commitments of the global containment strategy. The strategy ignores or glosses over the complex diplomatic, regional, and moral issues that cut across conflicts in the Third World. Third World flashpoints are often not governable by simple formulae of us versus them, democracy versus communism, the West versus the East. It isn't enough to make nations or governments our allies only because they are enemies of our enemies. Such "allies" may turn out to be on the "wrong side"—a side we would not have chosen on the merits—of some of these complex issues.

When Alexander Haig elevated El Salvador to a vital interest, and proclaimed loudly that the United States would do "whatever is necessary" to prevail there, he probably felt he had a firmer grounding in public opinion than Kissinger enjoyed on Angola. Nevertheless, adverse congressional and public reaction checked the administration from undertaking a truly rapid and massive escalation; the advice of NATO allies, and the limited absorptive capacity of the Salvadoran armed forces, also pushed policy toward a material commitment less than Haig's expansive words might have suggested. History has yet to reveal whether our restrained involvement will be sufficient to honor Haig's pledge.

PUBLIC OPINION: THE UNCERTAIN ELEMENT

The American public is an ever-present danger to an administration that abuses the concept of credibility, or that indulges in a prolonged identification with an authoritarian, unstable government. Whether naive or not, many Americans believe that U.S. foreign policy ought not to contradict deeply held moral principles—at least not too blatantly. Yet, too many of our foreign friends utilize instruments of domestic terror that Americans find repugnant. When such a regime is subject to serious and extended challenge, the American public becomes all to familiar with each incident of torture. Whether it is the tiger cages of Vietnam or the assassination of nuns and villagers in El Salvador and Guatemala, public and congressional pressures for U.S. withdrawal will mount.[5]

The attempt by the neoconservatives to construct a new morality by distinguishing between "authoritarian" and "totalitarian" does not seem to have taken hold. Jeane Kirkpatrick, Reagan's ambassador to the United Nations, has argued that friendly "authoritarian" states might be distasteful, but they are more pro-U.S., less repressive, and more open to gradual reform than the likely alternative—communist "totalitarianism." Therefore, we are morally justified to support them.[6]

This "lesser-of-two-evils" doctrine would paralyze the United States into supporting unstable, status quo regimes. Kirkpatrick has not convinced the U.S. Catholic Church, whose bishops have spoken out strongly against the Reagan administration's military assistance to the succession of bloody Salvadoran governments. The administration initially relied heavily on geopolitical arguments (the Soviet/Cuban threat) to defend its commitment in El Salvador. When domestic opponents seized the moral high ground, however, the administration altered its rhetoric: rather than label the government of El Salvador "moderately authoritarian," the administration described it as a democratic (if imperfect) regime seeking sincerely to improve its human rights performance. Liberal U.S. opinion, however, was skeptical that the change in rhetoric reflected a significant shift in the substance of administration policy or in the reality inside El Salvador.

Many Americans remain deeply fearful of entanglement in Third World "quagmires." Neoconservatives inveigh against this "Vietnam syndrome," but have not been able to exorcise the anxieties that lie behind it. Kissinger's failure to take this public attitude into account in formulating his policy toward Angola proved to be a fatal error. The Reagan administration's bellicose rhetoric on El Salvador aroused public apprehension regarding military involvement in underdeveloped countries. Another administration learned that it is perilous to announce foreign commitments in the absence of a broad, public consensus.

Commitments are normally extended to defend the security of a nation, but American commitments have often implicitly been transferred to a particular ruler, and the "threat" becomes his own people. Meeting this commitment to a ruler has then become, in the minds and hearts of U.S. officials, a matter of honor. Yet, should Americans feel guilty when a foreign potentate is overthrown by his own subjects?

More generally, "honor" has to be placed in context. When genuine national interests are threatened, a nation's self-respect may require their defense. Vital U.S. interests, however, are rarely so fragile as to depend on the survival of a particular regime. One of the ironies of recent American diplomacy is that policymakers who pride themselves on their realism and toughness display such touching sentimentality toward longstanding foreign friends. In American culture, the bonds of friendship should transcend either partner's self-interests. It is a grave mistake to transpose this ideal of personal relations into the realm of international relations. International politics is a matter of interests, and interests inevitably shift with time. Our "honorable" overseas associates normally understand this, and they would be quick to abandon us if their shifting interests so required. As Charles de Gaulle said, "A state worthy of the name has no friends, only interests."

DOMINOES

U.S. policy-makers have persistently feared that our failure unequivocally to support tottering autocrats and kings will produce a chain reaction. One after another, pro-U.S. governments will fall, while those that manage to survive will become neutral or even join in a bandwagon rush to seek shelter under the Soviet tent. The world system will collapse, and the United States will find itself alone and surrounded by hostile states.

This extended version of the well-known "domino" theory is not without insight. Successful coups or revolutions in one country will send reverberations into neighboring states. Those who are out of power will be heartened, while those in power may be frightened or demoralized. Socialists in Europe were excited after the Bolshevik revolution, just as South American leftists were aroused when Salvador Allende was elected president of Chile. Individual symptoms do not make a contagion, however. Conservatives were able to regroup and the perceived threat was contained in Europe and rolled back in South America.

Other factors were at work. The history and internal political structures in Peru and Argentina were very different from those in Chile. Even had Allende survived, it is now clear that the indigenous conservatives in neighboring Peru and Argentina had more than enough resiliency to overpower their domestic challengers. In Europe, the Spartacists and other radical left movements were easily crushed.

Where countries display a greater commonality, the possibilities for dramatic spillover are greater. Thus, Laos and Cambodia were subject to revolutionary dynamics in a widening Indochina revolution (although it must be granted that Western resistance contributed to the sweep and profundity of the upheavals). The many parallels between Nicaragua, El Salvador, and Guatemala intensify the impact of the Sandinista revolution in Central America. However, Costa Rica, which borders Nicaragua on the south, has a different past and a more democratic political tradition and will be less easily destabilized.

How does U.S. policy toward one country affect the psychological dynamics of political struggles in other countries? Conceivably, an opposition that perceives wavering U.S. support for their government could become emboldened. Certainly centrists in Nicaragua took heart when the Carter administration symbolically disassociated itself from the Chilean strongman, Augusto Pinochet. By the same token, ruling regimes could become demoralized; but it is difficult to measure such indirect, psychological influences, and it would be a mistake to exaggerate them. Despite Nicaragua's geographic and historical closeness to the United States, the Sandinista rebellion had a dynamic that was independent of the Carter human rights policy.

The presence of so many factors in a revolutionary or prerevolutionary situation renders uncertain any hypothesis regarding the impact of potential actions of a foreign power. In the wonderland of hypothesis, one can, moreover, imagine the opposite effect: a regime that felt less secure about its external prop might decide to coopt dissent before it fully blossomed. By removing its hand from the tiller, the United States could allow states to adjust to prevailing winds and currents and find their own, more stable, heading.

Ultimately, other questions have to be answered. If a regime is so inherently weak and unpopular that the mere perception of a possible U.S. withdrawal of support is fatal, is it an appropriate ally? Isn't dependency upon such a regime a dangerously weak link in any regional or global strategy? Would a less decisive U.S. posture be more moral and more prudent?

Policy has to be judged by its effects. A U.S. policy that successfully stabilizes a government, either moderating or defeating an aggressive revolution, may indeed calm a region. However, a tactic that fails to win quickly can perversely amplify regional tensions. The prolonged U.S. involvement in Indochina contributed to the destabilization of Cambodia. The Reagan administration's campaign against the Sandinistas risks the stability of the fledgling democracy in neighboring Honduras.

Of course, some argue that the United States ought to remain blindly loyal to friends because of Soviet opportunism. Not once, however, has a regime that was once heavily reliant upon the United States feared abandonment and firmly allied itself with the Soviet Union. Many anti-Communist regimes are too politically conservative to become the ally of a socialist superpower, and the Soviets generally would be too cautious to accept such an offer. The danger of doublecross is so great. A regime disillusioned with the United States might, however, seek to diversify its foreign relations to include ties with Western Europe and other developing states, as well as with the Soviet Union. Adopting such a nonaligned posture, as Argentina has done, should not be confused with becoming a Soviet client. Since a genuinely nonaligned, self-confident nation deprives the Soviet Union of control over its resources and power, nonalignment should generally be seen as an advantage, not a threat, to U.S. interests.

IDEOLOGY

Americans like to think of themselves as a pragmatic and nonideological people. However, we also see ourselves as evangelists with a mission to perform in the world. The Third World often feels pressure from the United States to copy its ideas and institutions. Because we are wealthy, strong, and stable, we view the wisdom and virtue of our ideas as self-evident. Other nations, however, may wish to reproduce the fruits of our technology without reproducing our culture and our political and economic institutions.

Many American conservatives equate efficiency with private enterprise and the unguided free market, and urge developing countries to adopt these principles. President Reagan explicitly called on developing countries to place their faith in "the magic of the marketplace." His administration has sought to impose these precepts by urging the International Monetary Fund, the World Bank, and U.S. AID to condition their loans on countries adopting such "self help" measures. American liberals are often just as insistent on the universal appeal of multiparty democracy. While overlooking the authoritarian rules of many Third World friends, Democratic administrations prefer competitive party politics and a system of checks and balances. Democrats sometimes place less rhetorical emphasis on private enterprise, but they also tend to assume that a strong private sector is a prerequisite for liberal democracy.

United States foreign policy, to be sure, has lost some of the ideological fervor of the 1950s and early 1960s. Even then, the State Department was often willing to overlook the absence of democracy or a free market, provided that the government in question was adequately anti-Soviet. Nevertheless, ideology remains an active element in many U.S. policies, especially in Latin America and the Caribbean. Today, congressional debates still ring with ideological incantations.

The desire to promulgate one's own values is hardly unique to Americans. Nevertheless, at this particular juncture in history, missionary zeal can produce more problems for American foreign policy than converts to Americanism. Sharpened ideology creates conflict. It introduces friction between the United States and governments that already disagree with the United States on principle. It also can exacerbate political tensions within societies where the United States has some influence. For example, when the mix between private and public sector activity is elevated to an ideological issue, passion replaces pragmatism. Local businessmen may decide to fight for their "freedom," only to disturb a delicate social balance previously struck between business, labor, and government.

Chapter 2 discussed at length the more complex public and private sector mixtures that characterize the world economy. Shifts in both directions are occurring, usually at the margin, and these often for reasons that are little connected to ideology—and even less so to American preferences. By making the degree of private enterprise a guideline for U.S. support, the United States needlessly, and generally uselessly, raises tensions between and within countries.

Laissez-faire economies were more characteristic of nineteenth-century models of European industrialization than contemporary Third World development. Nor has the number of liberal democracies been multiplying. While there have been some cross-currents, the tide since World War II in the Third World runs in the opposite direction. Immediately after decolonization, many formerly French and British-ruled nations in Africa had parliamentary systems. Today, most are one-party states or military dictatorships.

Chapter 2 argued that U.S. economic interests are not hothouse flowers dependent upon the climate control of laissez-faire economics.

Mixed, and even state-directed, economies can grow alongside the U.S. economic system. The United States can maintain its own predominately private-enterprise system within a world of nations with more centrally administered economies.

Americans have also feared that their democracy cannot be unique and survive. All high school students learn that Woodrow Wilson fought to make American democracy safe by defending democracy in Europe. More recently, Alexander Haig said, "We are fully conscious of our historic role in the defense of freedom, wherever it may be. . . . Our objective remains simple and compelling: a world hospitable to our society and our ideals."[7]

Yet, the United States has lived comfortably with authoritarian regimes in many countries to the South. Neighboring Mexico is ruled by a single, coercive political party that emerged after a bloody revolution earlier in this century. Much of Central America has been subject to military hegemony at least since the 1930s. Few Americans are aware of these nearby political systems, and they are even less informed about political systems in Africa or Asia. Moreover, the condescension many Americans feel toward the Third World further reduces the impact of events there. The collapse of democracies in Western Europe would clearly have a greater psychological impact in the United States, but the United States is in a way too provincial to be much affected by the Third World's political choices.

Suppose many Third World countries chose, not right-wing authoritarianism, but some version of Marxism. Would that threaten U.S. political institutions? If these nations entered into military alliances with the Soviet Union, the defense of the United States would, no doubt, be complicated. But how would American political values be altered? Would Americans be swept in a headlong rush toward Marxism? That is unlikely. Alternatively, in a self-fulfilling prophecy, might Americans be so frightened at the threat to democracy that they would abandon the Bill of Rights? While perhaps more probable than the first reaction, this flight-from-freedom scenario seems unduly pessimistic.

The political isolation of the United States is, in this sense, a blessing. Political transformations in developing countries are unlikely to transform American political values or institutions. The United States need not wage a holy war to preserve its values in the Third World for them to be safe at home. And, if the United States reduced the ideological content of its foreign policy, the world would be made safer for the United States and for citizens of other countries as well. A policy that tolerated diversity would reaffirm our own democratic values, while serving to deflate global tensions.

At the same time, the United States neither can nor should completely divorce its foreign policy from all moral issues. As Kissinger discovered, Americans will not be satisfied with a foreign policy limited to balance-of-power politics, or to a callous materialism. On behalf of our own humanity and because ideas do play a role in East-West competition, the United States should defend basic human rights.

If the United States condemns governments that systematically torture and kill their citizens, the criticism may widely be accepted as legitimate. Most governments are signatories to such documents as the United Nations Universal Declaration of Human Rights. These documents condemn the flagrant abuse of the "rights of the person"; that is, arbitrary arrest and physical maltreatment and murder. Such rights can be considered "universal." Moreover, international observers such as Amnesty International and the Inter-American Commission on Human Rights can provide generally reliable and quantifiable reports on the presence or absence of government-organized violations of basic rights. However, when the United States carries its "torch of liberty" quickly past questions of basic human rights to those of particular forms of government, it is not only overreaching; it risks igniting uncontrollable fires.

INDEPENDENT NATIONALISM

When the United States exaggerates threats, it may see only dangers where opportunities lie. For example, in his memoirs, *The White House Years,* Henry Kissinger argues at great length that the election of Salvador Allende in Chile posed a serious threat to the United States. His staff warned him:

> An entrenched Allende Government would create considerable political and psychological losses to the U.S.:
> a) Hemispheric cohesion would be threatened;
> b) A source of anti-U.S. policy would be consolidated in the hemisphere;
> c) U.S. prestige and influence would be set back with a corresponding boost for the USSR and Marxism.[8]

Kissinger cites U.S. Ambassador Edward Korry that cooperating with Allende would be a "practical impossibility" because Allende was likely to undertake "specific actions including nationalization of U.S. industries, recognition of Cuba, North Vietnam, etc."

Whether Chile might have become "another Cuba"—a Marxist-Leninist state closely aligned with the Soviet Union—will never be known. Had Allende survived, it is at least possible that Chile would have taken a different path. The orthodox Chilean Communist Party probably would have had difficulty dominating both the popular Christian Democrats and the anti-Soviet Socialists (Allende's own party). Moreover, the Soviet Union was hesitant to integrate Chile into COMECON; indeed, the Soviet ambassador in Santiago reportedly told his staff that Chile would not be a "second Cuba."[9] Moscow was not prepared to subsidize heavily another Latin revolution. Chile could well have evolved into an independent, nationalist country. The state sector of its economy, traditionally strong, would have expanded; but Chile would have remained integrated into the international system and in need of Western financial assistance.

From Kissinger's perspective—with its emphasis on U.S. prestige, its vision of Latin America as a U.S. sphere of influence, and its "zero-sum" assumption that any decline in U.S. influence is a gain for the Soviets—even this more moderate Chile might have seemed a threat. Indeed, it might have been more dangerous than an orthodox Marxist state, precisely because of its wider appeal.

Rather than define any Latin socialism as a *prima facie* threat, the United States might have received Allende's election as an opportunity to permit the development of a leftist alternative to the Cuban model. Chile's relatively high level of political development and its outstanding pool of intellectual talent provided the potential for designing an innovative political system. Just as the Yugoslav example is an inspiration for some European leftists, so a nonaligned Chile could have been an alternative model for Latin Americans.

In this context, an Allendista Chile could have been an advantageous asset in an anti-Soviet strategy. Instead, Allende's overthrow not only destroyed Chilean democracy, tarnished the U.S. image, and drove many Latin leftists toward insurrectionary politics, but it also left Cuba as the only state that Latin leftists could readily turn to for aid. One of the costs of Kissinger's Chile policy was paid when the Sandinistas decided that Cuba, alone, was a reliable source of security assistance.

Making Problems Worse

Advocates of reassertionism generally share a set of propositions about how a great nation should exercise its power. Borrowing from military jargon, the world is divided into "friendlies" and "enemies," with marginal political forces falling into gray, neutral areas. A Great Power's first task is to define clearly who its friends and enemies really are. Forces friendly to the United States should gain from their allegiance and receive praise and support. Hostile forces, on the other hand, should pay a price for their defiance.

Henry Kissinger put it most succinctly: "The United States must show that it is capable of rewarding a friend or penalizing an opponent. It must be made clear . . . that our allies benefit from association with us and our enemies suffer. It is a simple-minded proposition perhaps, but for a great power it is the prerequisite, indeed the definition of an effective foreign policy."[10]

Cases can, of course, arise when a Third World government threatens U.S. interests. It may be physically threatening a peaceful neighbor and U.S. associate. It may be systematically murdering its own citizens. In such instances, the United States can legitimately respond, and other nations are also likely to be aroused. But more often, U.S. hostility has been directed at targets whose threat to U.S. interests was exaggerated or very hypothetical. U.S. objections have often been confined to the ideology and rhetoric of the regime, or to its treatment of particular U.S. investments. Alternatively, we may have judged that the direction of events was ominous; we acted to preclude the realization of a "worst-case" scenario.

If they are carefully modulated, U.S. pressures can sometimes alter specific policies of Third World states. If instruments are well chosen, and objectives limited, governments may be willing to modify their behavior. During the Carter administration, for example, the United States successfully leveraged modest amounts of economic or military transfers in return for gradual improvements in human rights practices. The United States has frequently traded certain favors for countries' votes in the United Nations. Indeed, much of diplomacy involves attempts by one state to frame incentives to induce another state to alter its behavior on particular issues.

If the U.S. is careless in applying pressure, however, or makes demands that a regime interprets as threatening its very existence, a hostile response is more likely. Indeed, if the U.S. is too aggressive, it may find itself worse off than if it had ignored the distasteful regime entirely. The target nation's domestic and international behavior may move in the opposite direction from Washington's intentions. Waving the banner of "anti-imperialism," the target regime can rally nationalist sentiment, while invoking "national security" as a convenient excuse for muzzling remaining dissent. Antiregime elements—including those more palatable to Washington—are placed in "no-win" positions. If they remain quiet, the government triumphs by default. If they object, they are accused of aligning with foreign interests, even of being CIA agents. U.S. hostility thus undermines those very political forces it is intended to support. At the same time that it provides the target regime with an opportunity to strengthen itself domestically, it also justifies increased spending on armaments. The suppliers may well be states less friendly to the United States, making future changes in policy even less likely.

One of the little noted achievements of the Carter administration was that it began dissipating fears of U.S. hostility among Third World nationalists. Many Third World leaders momentarily questioned their assumption that Washington styled itself sheriff of a counterrevolutionary posse. Admittedly, this shift in attitude was more often evident in private conversations, and not always reflected in publicized international forums like the United Nations and the Non-Aligned Movement, where rhetoric is the daily bread. Also, the Carter administration did not diffuse some issues, such as the Palestinian question, that receive an inordinate amount of attention in public meetings dominated by Third World countries.

The Carter administration was not in office long enough to expunge fully certain deeply engraved symbols, but memories were fading. One consequence of the Reagan administration's rhetoric has been to revive images from an unhappy past. The United States and the Third World are being forced to reenact parts in an old plot. If Washington insists on assuming the caricature of the reactionary imperialist, Third World leaders are perfectly capable of playing their assigned roles as well.

CREATING ENEMIES

A bellicose U.S. posture too often plays into the hands of our real or imagined opponents. Leaders of small states that incur our ire are immediately thrust upon the world's stage. They become "Davids" valiantly struggling against "Goliath": receiving standing ovations at the United Nations and other international forums. When Allende denounced ITT, and when the Sandinista leader Daniel Ortega recited the litany of U.S. interventions in Nicaragua, the applause was loud and long.

More modest spectacles, too, are vaulted to international notoriety, sometimes directly as the result of our own measures. For example, Maurice Bishop, head of the New Jewel movement on the tiny island of Grenada—population 110,000—sought to increase his stature at home and in the Caribbean through constant denunciation of U.S. "destabilization" plans. Simply ignoring Bishop, the Carter administration could have left him shadow boxing. Unfortunately, the Carter administration had drifted into more traditional behavior in 1979–80. The U.S. pointedly demanded that Grenada not establish security ties with Cuba, repeatedly denounced its human rights practices (with notably greater fervor and frequency than in the case of equally repressive but less provoking governments), refused to accept the credentials of Grenada's choice for ambassador to Washington, and generally tried to isolate Grenada from its Caribbean neighbors. Bishop's importance was inflated and he gained some justification for his enlarging of Grenada's militia.

In jostling with Grenada, the Carter administration reverted to the hybrid logic that sparing the rod spoiled the apples in the barrel. If Bishop went unpunished, other movements and governments in the Caribbean might follow his example. Yet, the United States seemingly lacked the leverage to chasten tiny Grenada. The New Jewel's conservative fiscal policies made the government less vulnerable to external financial pressures and more creditworthy. Other aid donors were unwilling to follow the U.S. lead, and Canada and Venezuela actually authorized additional development aid. Grenada's neighbors, while generally friendly to the United States, resisted U.S. efforts to isolate Grenada diplomatically. And Bishop's Cuban-armed militia was more than adequate for taming any domestic dissent.

The unsuccessful attempt to hang a scarecrow impressed no one. Still, the New Jewel movement's politics did not inspire emulation by neighboring governments or populations. Steeped in the parliamentary tradition, most of Grenada's other English-speaking neighbors had little interest in moving toward a one-party state. The United States did not need to lecture them, or to convince them of the "costs" of such a course.

To the extent that images and ideas matter, playing the bully does not serve U.S. interests in the struggle for influence in the Third World. An aggressive U.S. policy leaves the Third World uncertain as to who is the primary enemy. In its efforts to build a "strategic alliance" among Persian Gulf states against the Soviet Union, the Reagan administration found, much to its annoyance, that the local states did not share the same enemies list as Washington. Yes, the Soviets were a potential danger, but so was Israel, and the injection of U.S. troops into the area raised questions regarding U.S. intentions. Most Persian Gulf leaders dislike Libya's Colonel Qadaffi, but when U.S. warships entered waters claimed by Libya in the Gulf of Sidra and shot down two Libyan planes, six conservative Persian Gulf states denounced America's "cowboy" tactics. Qadaffi's image at home and in the Arab world was at least momentarily inflated. Again, the U.S.-led "Bright Star" military exercises, including paratrooper drops and amphibious assaults, were designed to impress the region, but mainly aroused Arab anxieties.

A number of these problems are inherent in being a global, military giant. Some nations will always be suspicious of U.S. motives, and wary of our power. Affirmations of U.S. will, and even displays of force, are useful when our case is certain and our genuine interests clearly involved. For example, the establishment of a Soviet military base in Nicaragua, even if not a strategic threat, would still warrant a strong response; other Latin nations might even support the physical destruction of the Soviet military intrusion. A working of America's "will," however, when it amounts to an empty exercise in pride, is dangerous to successful policy. A strategy serving to impress the gods and ourselves of our greatness may only succeed in arousing the furies against us.

GENERATING INSECURITY

Third World regimes are like any other: when they are attacked, survival is the first priority. Their population and their resources are mobilized for national defense. Economic growth is sacrificed for immediate security.

When hostile U.S. policies drive Third World regimes to elevate security over economics, America negates its major strength. Many nations, including the Soviet Union, can supply the instruments of national security. The United States also has trade, technology, and finance at its disposal. When Washington forces a regime to choose between guns and butter, we risk dealing away our best suit. When our threats to a regime's security become life-threatening, we risk the whole game.

As suggested in the previous chapter, the ability of the Soviets to make or consolidate inroads has often been aided by ill-conceived U.S. policies. The United States too often backs regimes that have lost popular support. Washington also finds it difficult to establish relations with revolutionary governments. In the aftermath of the Indochina war, the Vietnamese Communists seemed to be seeking more diversified and balanced foreign relations. Although their diplomacy was clumsy and beset by internal squabbles over how best to approach the West, the Vietnamese appeared anxious to avoid dependency on the Soviet Union and to gain access to Western finance and technology. But mutual misunderstandings and distrust, and a simmering U.S. hostility fed by Vietnamese demands for war reparations, dashed hopes of a nonaligned Vietnam. Hanoi felt it had no choice but to turn to Moscow.

Aggressive actions by regimes friendly to the United States can also aid the Soviets. South Africa's invasion of Angola in 1975, like Israeli policies in the Middle East, have created openings for the Soviets to provide security assistance to the other side. Similarly, meddling by a regional power in the affairs of smaller states can be destabilizing and provide opportunities for Soviet expansion. It has been argued that the Shah of Iran's intervention in the internal affairs of Afghanistan disturbed a delicately balanced political system. By encouraging the repression of leftists, the Shah contributed to the polarization of Afghan politics.[11]

But aren't some Third World radicals inherently anti-American and pro-Soviet? Don't they use the charge of American aggression as a pretext for a Soviet alliance?

Third World radicals and religious fundamentalists may reject those aspects of American culture that they view as capitalist, bourgeois, or decadent. In the arena of international affairs, however, judgments on other nations' cultures need not preclude the establishment of normal and even close relations. The French, after all, dislike many aspects of German and American culture; and northern and southern

Europeans view each other with a mixture of mirth and contempt. Yet these distinct cultures not only maintain good diplomatic relations but are joined in a military alliance.

Cultural clashes do not preclude economic interchange. As we saw in chapter 2, "anticapitalist" sentiments no longer drive Third World leaders, whether Marxist or Moslem, to reject economic ties with the West. Moreover, now that the international economy is a mix of capitalism and socialism, of private and public sector activities, ideological labels are less compelling.

What can drive Third World leaders to oppose the United States is the memory of past U.S. interventions and the fear of their repetition. These fears are not always an irrational "paranoia," as U.N. Ambassador Jeane Kirkpatrick suggested when the Sandinistas charged the U.S. with aggressive designs. They are sometimes a reasoned response to history and to an actual or apparent policy of hostility in Washington. John B. Oakes, former senior editor of the *New York Times,* criticized "The Haig-Reagan model of the 'Big Stick' in Central America," and explained:

> For 20 years, the United States Marines were stationed in Nicaragua nominally to preserve law and order, actually to preserve conservative governments. It was the United States Marines who campaigned against the rebel 'bandit' Augusto Sandino, the same Sandino whose name is today the symbol both of independence from the United States and of resistance to the abominable Somoza dictatorship for which our intervention had paved the way.
>
> Sandino, who was subsequently murdered by orders of the first Somoza, died nearly 50 years ago, but his memory is not lost on Central Americans and on Nicaraguans in particular. Perhaps if General Haig were a little more mindful of this history, he would be less surprised by the present Sandinist Government's suspicion of the United States.[12]

Some opportunistic Third World leaders will try to use a rhetoric of anti-Americanism to strengthen their domestic base. If the United States has intervened in recent memory, such demogogues have a better opportunity to succeed. But it requires another step before this rhetorical anti-Americanism goes beyond nonalignment to become pro-Sovietism.

The Soviet state is not the shining beacon that it was in the 1920s. For most Third World radicals, Andropov and his aging colleagues are about as glamorous—and revolutionary—as American corporate executives. Nevertheless, there are sometimes elements within a regime that are genuinely pro-Soviet. Such factions may hope to gain power through Soviet aid and influence. But these pro-Soviet elements are unlikely to prevail against the forces of nationalism and international economics unless they receive inadvertent assistance from outside. Aggression by neighboring states or by the United States amplifies the voice of pro-Soviet groups within their own government. As the need for Soviet aid becomes more compelling and urgent, the wisdom of those who advocate it becomes self-evident. The United States cannot guarantee that pro-Soviet forces will lose, but we can greatly increase the probability that they will prevail.

The heated debate over whether Fidel Castro intended from the beginning to secure an alliance with the Soviet Union is inconclusive. Castro may have anticipated a hostile U.S. reaction to his economic nationalism. He may also have reasoned that anti-Yanki slogans would help him consolidate his popularity. Nevertheless, had there not been a long history of U.S. intervention in Cuba, and had the Eisenhower administration not reacted so predictably, Castro would not have been ably to rally as much support around his anti-Yanki banner. He may not have received the justification—in the eyes of the Cuban public and within his regime—to invite in the Soviet Union. The debate over Castro's intentions is less relevant for future U.S. policy than the generally ignored fact that past U.S. policy made a pro-Soviet strategy logical, and the policy of the moment made it politically feasible. The United States will often be unable to know a leader's intentions. U.S. policy makers can, however, try to create an environment making it more difficult to realize any hostile plans.

DESTABILIZATION

The United States has succeeded in overturning some regimes who opposed U.S. policies. Too often it has been a Pyrrhic victory. It is not coincidental that it is in countries where CIA covert operations were most successful that the United States today faces some of its most difficult problems. In Iran, Guatemala, and Zaire (where the United States helped defeat, if not assassinate Patrice Lumumba, and install Mobutu), the subsequent conservative regimes have been unable to build stable, healthy societies. Perhaps the interruption by external force of social processes created a disequilibrium. Perhaps the regimes continued to rely more on the outside support that installed them than on building internal legitimacy, while some opposition elements were radicalized. In Iran and in Guatemala, the legacy of violence and resentments are such that the United States would probably have profited by not intervening. The price of the intervention in the former Belgium Congo, yet to be paid, is likely to be high.

Destabilizing a nation is like dropping a stone in a pond. The impact is greatest among the vanquished, who will harbor deep resentments and fears. Eventually, however, ripples will reach distant observers, who will also draw conclusions about the nature of U.S. foreign policy. The United States, for example, successfully sponsored the overthrow of the reformist government of Guatemalan President Jacobo Arbenz in 1954.[13] Ernesto "Che" Guevara, who witnessed the coup, was not the only Latin American to conclude that the United States would violently oppose reform in the Caribbean basin. Guevara decided that only armed struggle could liquidate reactionary regimes and strengthen revolutionary forces to resist eventual American aggression. Guevara and Castro gave priority to building the Cuban Revolution's security forces and militia. The United States paid for its Guatemalan success at the Bay of Pigs.

The Nixon administration helped Allende's opponents come to power in 1973. The CIA-assisted destabilization campaign was studied in great detail by many Latins, their efforts aided by the revelations of the U.S. Senate Intelligence Committee.[14] When the New Jewel movement seized power on the Caribbean island of Grenada in 1979, its leaders moved consciously and rapidly to assure that they would not share Allende's fate. The opposition press, for example, had played a key role in building the psychological atmosphere conducive to a coup in Chile; the New Jewel movement sharply restricted the media. Similarly, in Nicaragua, the Sandinistas decreed that newspapers could not print alarmist reports that could cause panic buying—as the opposition media, with CIA help, had done in Chile. PSYOPS (psychological operations) worked in Chile, but in the longer run, it convinced Latin leaders that the United States would encourage the abuse of rights of free speech and association to stimulate violent rebellions against their governments. The "lessons" of Chile have taught the "virtues" of limiting democracy, while giving some justification to those who would restrict opposition activities. (Ironically, covert destabilization programs have had little success in closed, Communist controlled states). Indeed, the New Jewel movement was such a good student that the Reagan administration reportedly decided against trying to destabilize the regime, precisely because of that preparedness. "We simply lacked sufficient confidence that covert action would succeed," a policy-level administration official said privately in 1982.

The American public has also learned some "lessons" from past CIA successes and adventures. Some citizens believe that covert actions discredit basic American values at home and abroad, while others fear that they are eventually, if not immediately, counterproductive. People have learned to spot the CIA's *modus operandi.* In this atmosphere of mutual suspicion, leaks from disgruntled CIA personnel are more likely to occur, and the press is more willing to publish them.

When covert-action plans are publicized, those that the CIA intended to harm may be strengthened, while those receiving assistance are placed in jeopardy. In March 1982, the press informed Americans that the CIA was undertaking covert actions against Nicaragua.[15] The Sandinistas wrapped themselves in the banner of nationalism, and many in the opposition felt compelled to denounce the United States and to muzzle their criticisms of the Sandinistas. The Sandinistas were able, in effect, to blackmail them by threatening to label them CIA agents. Free speech became an admission of guilt.

THE POLITICIZATION OF ECONOMICS

A foreign policy bent on humbling, squeezing, or unseating governments looks for methods of punishment. With the declining utility of military force, economic weapons become more attractive. In its first two years, the Reagan administration repeatedly contemplated using trade and private finance to force foreign governments to comply with U.S. objectives. Technology and trade credits to the Soviet Union were restricted. European firms were penalized for supplying the pipeline being built to transport natural gas from Siberia to Western Europe. Libyan oil exports were embargoed. Nicaraguan access to foreign capital was reduced. Moreover, access to the trade and investment incentives offered in the administration's Caribbean Basin Initiative were confined to those countries fulfilling certain political criteria: Cuba, Nicaragua, and Grenada were to be excluded. Finally, the administration considered, but rejected, declaring Polish debts in default.

Viewed historically, the use of economic levers against the Soviet Union was hardly new. The Reagan administration's policy of reducing economic linkages with Moscow was basically a return to the status quo before détente. But the increasing willingness to use economic coercion against Third World states suggested that, even in less vital relationships, the administration valued perceived security objectives more than economic interests.

Bilateral aid programs are political by their very nature. Every administration uses official aid to advance its policies, whether it be Nixon on behalf of private U.S. investors or Carter on behalf of human rights. The Reagan administration, however, repeatedly sought to distort *private* trade and investment flows. Firms and banks were asked, or ordered, to follow official policy rather than private profitability.

The postwar economic system depends on insulating private trading and finance systems from political warfare. Economic warfare violates the rules or spirit of a series of international and regional agreements. Thus, one objective of the General Agreement on Trade and Tariffs (GATT) was to minimize commercial discrimination against states on political grounds. The charter of the Organization of

American States declares definitively that "no state may use or encourage the use of coercive measures of an economic or political character in order to force the sovereign will of another state and obtain from it advantages of any kind."

These rules were designed to protect weaker states and to preserve an open and stable international economy. The concrete experience of the interwar years taught that economic warfare increased international tensions and threatened the economic system itself. If one state used economic instruments for coercive purposes, other states might follow, and the escalation of punitive measures could deflate the whole international system. Countries and businessmen would begin to lose confidence that contracts would be honored and that markets would remain open. At the least, nations would look inward and away from international commerce. At worst, the entire system could collapse in a gradual contraction or in a sudden panic.

The international financial system is especially susceptible to disruption by transforming commercial credit into an instrument of national coercion or destabilization. The financial system is a "confidence" game that depends upon all parties meeting their obligations. If one or more parties is prevented from doing so because of government intervention, confidence can quickly erode. Everyone is warned that borrowers and bankers, however well intentioned, may arbitrarily be forced to break the rules of the game. Banker-client relations, which depend so heavily upon good will and trust, are subject to sudden intervention by third parties. Indeed, governments may compel their nations' banks to drive a foreign client to the brink of bankruptcy, with the explicit intention of forcing nonpayment.

Shortly after U.S. diplomats were taken hostage in Iran in November 1979, the United States froze some $12 billion in Iranian financial assets deposited in U.S. banks and their overseas branches. The freeze followed an Iranian threat to default on the "Shah's debts" and to withdraw Iran's dollar deposits from U.S. banks. While some U.S. banks that held large volumes of Iranian deposits and liabilities felt better protected by the freeze, many members of the financial community were upset at Washington's interference with contractual obligations. Robert Carswell, who was the second-ranking official in the U.S. Treasury Department at the time, recorded that central bankers were particularly unhappy, since they "traditionally have taken the view that the intrusion of political considerations into the international financial and banking system would ultimately destroy the system—and in this they may well be correct."[16]

Bankers in New York, London, and Frankfurt were further alarmed by reports in early 1982 that the Reagan administration was going to attempt once again to use the financial system for punitive purposes. This time the target was the martial law government in Poland and its Soviet backers. Secretary of Defense Casper Weinberger was reportedly arguing that the U.S. government ought purposefully to declare Poland in default in order to trigger the "cross default" clauses in loan documents. When the U.S. government began attaching other Polish assets, there would be a mad scramble among Poland's official and private creditors to declare their loans in default and to attempt to collect. Assuming that Poland would not and could not pay, the more exposed banks would suffer severe losses and face possible bankruptcy.

The international financial system would have to absorb two shocks with unforeseeable consequences. Future creditors would know that we endangered worldwide financial stability to accomplish the perceived security interest of "hurting" the Soviets. The whole financial credit system could shrink as creditor institutions and some borrowing nations moved to limit their vulnerability to future U.S. actions. More directly, important financial institutions in Western Europe would have wantonly been placed in jeopardy for political reasons. This could endanger the welfare of our major allies and place a serious strain on NATO. Moreover, if major Western financial institutions begin to fail, a tidal wave of financial and industrial defaults could occur. Fortunately, more responsible advice prevailed, and the banks and the Polish government continued to try to arrange a businesslike settlement of a difficult financial situation.

The use of economic instruments as negative sanctions is appealing to a government that feels it must act and finds itself short of other tools. This compulsion, however, is partly the result of living the delusion that the U.S. can and ought to control events around the world. If we could rid ourselves of that misconception, we might feel less compelled to undertake potentially costly and destructive sanctions. Doing "something" doesn't mean doing "anything."

One can argue that Iran and the Soviet Union are special cases and justify special risks: Iran, because of the hostage seizure, and the Soviet Union because it is our principal adversary and the other great power. Moreover, Iranian deposits in U.S. banks were substantial, and Iran's interest in recovering them probably contributed to the decision to release the hostages. Even so, the deepening tendency to use economic sanctions is clear and disturbing. Such policies ignore the potential cumulative effect on the international economic system. They also mistakenly emphasize immediate political objectives by disregarding the longer-term benefits of maintaining and strengthening economic ties. Third World governments, if given the opportunity, will integrate their economies into the international financial system. This integration eventually tends to moderate their foreign policies.

Imposing economic sanctions, moreover, can boomerang. Even if the sanctions fail to bite, the targeted government is likely to diversify its economic relations away from the United States to prevent future attempts at economic blackmail. The general population will bitterly resent U.S. actions. Their government can exploit this ill-feeling to consolidate power. If the sanctions succeed in exacting costs, the danger is real that the besieged regime will turn to the Soviets or to Soviet allies for aid. It may even minimize its international commerce altogether. Developing nations, too, can be driven to give priority to security at the expense of economics. So, even when the U.S. successfully exercises its power to punish, future U.S. influence shrinks.

From a purely practical point of view, economic sanctions usually fail. One major study found that, of twenty-two cases investigated, decisive success was achieved only in four cases, whereas thirteen attempts were clear failures.[17] Sanctions are difficult to enforce. The U.S. government itself controls few resources, and may have difficulty in peacetime in marshaling the resources of the U.S. private sector. Moreover, the entire U.S. economy accounts for a declining share of world output. On top of all this, it is also relatively easy to circumvent boycotts. For example, Iran was able to meet its most critical import needs by purchasing on world markets through hard-to-trace middlemen.

Economic sanctions sometimes work. The U.S. government orchestrated a credit squeeze against the government of Salvador Allende that contributed to his downfall. A boycott against Ugandan coffee weakened Idi Amin. Both of these cases, however, point out a hidden danger in sanctions: overthrowing a government is not the same as controlling subsequent events. Although Ugandans were certainly relieved to be rid of Amin, violence and disorder have continued. While many Chileans welcomed the coup against Allende, they did not anticipate prolonged and harsh military rule. Moreover, it should be noted that the credit squeeze against Allende occurred in the early 1970s, when the U.S. banking system was less exposed overseas and less fragile than it will be in the 1980s. Today, alternative sources of finance in Western Europe, the Middle East, and Japan are available to Third World borrowers.

The United States must choose. It cannot be a reliable member of the international economic community if it arbitrarily exerts political pressures against foreign governments by disrupting their links to that same community. In a few cases, the political cause may be overriding. But in the long run, both our economic and security interests will be better served by preserving the international economy—the backbone of U.S. strength.

THE STIGMA OF IDENTIFICATION

When policymakers draw coarse distinctions between hostile and friendly states, their behavior is likely to be equally blunt. Unfriendly governments will receive the palpable wrath of the United States, while accomodating regimes will be handsomely and publicly rewarded.

Americans generally like to display their affections. We bestow gifts and attention upon foreign leaders to demonstrate our friendship. We also believe that our generosity strengthens its recipients. Our dollars and fighter-bombers are intended to increase a foreign leader's esteem among his local supporters and to intimidate his enemies, domestic and foreign. The United States hopes thereby to make all of the potential dominoes in the region more secure.

Ironically, Washington's embrace may be as deadly as the Midas touch. The more a leader gleams in our eyes, the more the popular imagination may be convinced that it is Washington that is really calling the shots. Much of the Third World overrates the United States's ability to control events, just as we do. The Iranian revolution of 1979–80 had many roots, of which the history of U.S. diplomacy is not the only one. Still, the highly visible U.S. presence in Iran ironically contributed to the Shah's demise. The Shah's frequent and highly publicized visits to the United States, and senior U.S. officials' visits to Teheran, replete with florid toasts of mutual loyalty and friendship, aroused suspicions among Iranians that the Shah was not ruling in the interests of Iran. The large U.S. embassy, and the frequent socializing among U.S. diplomats, businessmen, and soldiers and the upper-crust of the Shah's regime, confirmed the Shah's image as an American hireling. Bani-Sadr, who served briefly as president after the Shah's ouster, summed up a common feeling when he claimed that "the [American] embassy was the real center of power in Iran."

The large-scale arms transfers, instead of cowing opposition, aroused it. It soon appeared that the Shah's first priority was protecting the strategic interests of the United States in the Persian Gulf, not expanding his own economy and securing the welfare of his own people. As one formerly pro-Shah Iranian union leader complained, "The United States Government, by frightening the Iranian people with the spectres of their neighbors, by selling us used weapons at exorbitant prices, has poured billions of rials into the pockets of U.S. military cartels."[18] Iranians were first baffled, then infuriated, by multibillion dollar defense budgets when so many Iranians were still poverty-stricken. Only the United States, and a clique of nouveau riche bureaucrats, soldiers, and businessmen around the Shah, seemed to benefit visibly from the sales of massive amounts of sophisticated weaponry.

If an overly public American embrace can be smothering, a regime can fashion its own noose by responding too warmly. Naturally, U.S. diplomats are pleased when a friend expresses public appreciation. We Americans like the reassurance of knowing that we are loved. Anwar Sadat responded to our aid and praise with an equally warm devotion. Partly for this reason, his death was not mourned deeply in Egypt. As a U.S. observer present at the time of the assassination noted:

> Most important, intense popular feelings have been directed . . . against the Egyptian president who took in the America's Shah; who offered military facilities to the U.S.; who did not protest American shelving of the West Bank/Palestinian issue; . . . Sadat seemed, to Egyptians, almost pathetically eager to proclaim his loyalty to his U.S. ally . . . most [Egyptians] also felt that Sadat had compromised Egypt's independence and dignity; that he had made Egypt a toady of the United States.[19]

Although the United States government cannot be blamed for the death of Sadat, an indiscreet courtship served neither partner.

Now the Reagan administration is wooing the Saudis. Fortunately, the Saudis have drawn the correct conclusions from the fate of Sadat and the Shah and are trying to keep some distance. Although they have purchased U.S.-made AWACS (sophisticated radar planes), they have limited the U.S. military presence in Saudi Arabia. The Saudis have emphasized that the AWACS purchase is a cash deal and that they do not share our security objectives. Israel, the Saudis insist, not the Soviet Union, remains their primary enemy.

The Saudis also have expressed their independence on other occasions. They rebuffed a proposal by Secretary of Defense Casper Weinberger that the U.S. help construct a regional arms industry and support the Gulf Cooperation Council (which groups five smaller Persian Gulf nations behind Saudi Arabia).[20] Additionally, the Saudis refused to participate in the "Bright Star" paratrooper exercises that the U.S. military carried out in the region in 1981. They have avoided public association with the Rapid Deployment Force (RDF), refusing to grant bases for U.S. equipment or troops. The Saudis are constructing an infrastructure of military facilities that U.S. forces could use in an emergency, but are doing so quietly. The House of Saud knows that too close an association with the United States would be harmful at a time when U.S. military exercises and the publicity over the RDF are stirring up anti-American feelings in the Middle East. The Saudis also fear that a highly visible U.S. military presence could be a magnet drawing more Soviet forces into the area.

The Saudis' caution has not been appreciated by enough policy makers. The Saudis were especially dismayed when President Reagan issued his corollary to the "Carter Doctrine" (which had extended a U.S. security umbrella over the Middle East). Reagan, in an apparently off-the-cuff remark at a press conference, said: "Saudi Arabia we will not permit to be an Iran."[21] The following dialogue ensued:

> Question: Mr. President, you said a few minutes ago that you would not allow—you would not permit—what happened in Iran several years ago to happen in Saudi Arabia. How would you prevent that? Would you take military intervention, if that was necessary, to prevent it?
>
> Answer: I'm not going to talk about the specifics of how we would do it, except to say that in Iran I think the United States has to take some responsibility for what happened there—with some very short-sighted policies and let a situation come to a boiling point, but there was no need to do that. [In Saudi Arabia] there's no way that we could stand by and see that taken over by anyone that would shut off that oil.

Although the president undoubtedly wished to reassure the Saudis and warn their enemies, he misspoke. By assigning them the status of a client state, he was cutting away at an essential Saudi need—the appearance of independence. Reagan was playing the role of the boy who cries "The emperor has no clothes!" Although the cloak of legitimacy is sheer, it affords more protection than the thickest armor.

Under certain circumstances, visible U.S. support is productive. If a local government is clearly independent, and derives its strength and authority from its domestic roots, expressions of U.S. sympathy and concrete shipments of economic aid and modest military hardware can be beneficial. The danger begins when the U.S. presence is so great as to dwarf the government's autonomy. Alarm bells should ring when the ruler begins to depend more on external backing than on a firm domestic base. When he begins to tie his policies to U.S. interests rather than what is widely perceived as the national interest, he is tempting fate. If U.S. diplomacy is not sufficiently agile, we will go down with him.

Unfortunately, our emotional identification with particular rulers reduces our ability to adjust to changing circumstances within countries. His fears become our fears; his enemies, our enemies. He asks us not to associate with opposition elements and may even make this a litmus test of our loyalty to his regime. We are asked to rely upon his intelligence services for information on his opponents, and upon his personal interpretation of their strength, motives, and objectives. Once we have chosen to limit our personal contacts with the society outside the regime's gates, we lose the basis for evaluating the regime's self-interested assessments. Having identified our welfare with his, we make his enemies our own.

The stage is then set for an all too familiar denouement. The U.S. embassy is caught by surprise at the sudden groundswell of organized unrest. Policymakers oscillate between branding the opposition as "Pol Pots" (as the U.S. ambassador did in El Salvador in 1980), and desperately rushing to make last-minute contacts with an unknown and suspicious opposition leadership.

Sometimes we will remain firm, more out of loyalty than good sense. When we finally change strategies, choosing to fashion an "acceptable" alternative, it is like trying to switch jockeys in the final stretch of the race. We abandon our old associate only after it is obvious to virtually everyone that he cannot win. By then, the "moderate" alternatives that suddenly seem "acceptable" are also unable to finish first. Events have radicalized expectations, and the country has moved beyond the "moderates."

Paradoxically, blind U.S. support may be a factor in producing upheavals. If the ruler becomes convinced that his external support can substitute for domestic consent, he may arrogantly and needlessly alienate his people. He may fail to notice gathering dissent and refuse to compromise while compromise is possible. Both Somoza and the Shah ignored or taunted the opposition; by the time they sought to negotiate, their regimes were beyond saving.

The close identification of the United States with a particular regime can become a self-fulfilling prophecy. When the old regime falls, factions that have come to see the United States as the enemy come to power. Not only do the new rulers harbor deep resentments; they often assume that the United States remains actively hostile. Thus, Bani-Sadr told Americans, "Your government has not yet given up the idea of ruling Iran. . . . Within the country and its marches [*sic*] your government's hand is implicated in bloody incidents."[22] Similarly, Rafael Cordova Rivas, a member of the ruling junta in postrevolutionary Nicaragua, complained after a visit of three U.S. congressmen, "the mind of U.S. politicians cannot get used to seeing in Nicaragua a free, sovereign, independent and autonomous country, regardless of how small it is. . . . We cannot accept anything which is not done with dignity and honor in this country."[23]

In such postrevolutionary situations, the new leadership will be hypersensitive to any U.S. pressure. Jealous of their sovereignty, they may be unable to engage in the normal give-and-take of international diplomacy. They will appear strident, stubborn, and unrealistic. With a U.S. government equally full of regrets, guilt, and suspicions, mutual dislike and hostilities will be hard to avoid.

Superpowers and Lesser States

Many errors in American foreign policy result from the application, in the modern setting, of traditional conceptions of the relationship between large powers and lesser states. Policymakers often act as though the strong can bolster the weak through overt identification with them.

But the reality is more complex. Domestic psychological reactions in both the sending and receiving country, the dynamics of regional rivalries, and the possible response of other powers can sometimes yield perverse results.

Similarly, large states that attempt to bring weak governments to heel through direct pressures may only strengthen their enemies. Moral constraints, among others, generally prohibit the use of massive military force. Efforts at diplomatic coercion may only congeal the target nation's population around nationalist leaders. Rather than driving a wedge between the Third World state and the Soviet Union, U.S. hostility pulls them together.

The dualist world view, that divides states purely into good guys and bad guys, contributes to the polarization of nations. Ultimately, such a working model will be frustrated by the many contrary forces loose in the world. An alternative strategy, as outlined in the next chapter, would view the diffusion of power as a potential centerpiece of a modernized diplomacy capable of limiting Soviet expansionism with less stress and strain; the United States would be moving with the tide, not against it.

American foreign policymakers typically recognize that military, economic, and diplomatic instruments can each be useful in select settings. The Reagan administration, however, in its budgetary allocations and strategic thinking, has placed unusual confidence in the utility of military power. Yet, as we shall see, an exaggerated emphasis on military spending misreads the contemporary sources of power, and misweighs the relative utility of the instruments of influence.

Military Spending

The same drive that leads us to try to shape events in the Third World leads to excessive military spending. If the United States is to restore the confidence of friendly rulers and deter their adversaries, it must be able to project military power freely and widely around the globe. Military intervention will sometimes be necessary to maintain loosely extended commitments, and to stymie takeovers by hostile movements.

These tasks go well beyond the two essential objectives of U.S. military power: to deter a Soviet nuclear strike against the United States and to inhibit a Soviet invasion of Western Europe. This defense against our main military rival responds to geopolitics rather than to a desire to enhance national prestige or political ideology.

In the immediate aftermath of World War II, some observers argued for a strategy centered exclusively on containing Soviet military power. Realist writer Walter Lippmann, for example, believed that the Eurasian landmass was the real prize, and that it would be a grave mistake to squander resources on less strategically significant zones. He warned that efforts to build anti-Soviet coalitions in the Third World, and to defend friends and attack enemies there, would be a costly and "impossibly difficult" task:

> It would require, however much the real name for it were disavowed, continual and complicated intervention by the United States in the affairs of all the members of the coalition which we were proposing to organize, to protect, to lead and to use. Our diplomatic agents abroad would have to have an almost unerring capacity to judge correctly and quickly which men and which parties were reliable containers. Here at home Congress and the people would have to stand ready to back their judgments as to who should be nominated, who should be subsidized, who should be whitewashed, who should be seen through rose-colored spectacles, who should be made our clients and our allies.[24]

Contrary to Lippmann's advice, the United States adopted a strategy of global containment. The spread of Soviet influence virtually anywhere in the Third World came to be seen as a strategic threat. Moreover, the United States sought to contain not only Soviet military power but Marxist ideas, and to expand U.S. influence throughout the Third World. Consistent with a global containment strategy, the United States has maintained divisions well equipped for fighting in theaters peripheral to what would be considered decisive U.S.-Soviet combat zones. Forces optimized for intervention in the Third World could still be used directly against the Soviet Union, but they are not ideally suited for that purpose. Such intervention forces have the identifiable attributes of being highly mobile and lightly armed.[25] Since we know where the Soviet armies are and where they are most likely to go, defending forces can be prepositioned in advance. While the United States needs some mobile forces to counter possible Soviet thrusts, it has traditionally possessed more mobile forces than likely anti-Soviet contingencies required. Similarly, whereas light infantry and other unarmored forces may in some circumstances be useful against Soviet divisions, they are better suited for operations against thinly armed Third World units.

Current military plans call for a substantial enhancement of what is already a formidable intervention force. The military services are massively procuring additional sealift and airlift capabilities. New aircraft carriers, battleships capable of shore bombardment, and "forcible-entry" amphibious assault ships will be added to U.S. forces configured for operating in Third World theaters.

Experts differ on whether this buildup of mobile forces is necessary to cripple a direct Soviet military assault on the Persian Gulf, the one Third World arena now widely considered to be of strategic importance. Some analysts argue that, with relatively minor reforms, and with more prepositioning of equipment in Western Europe, on ships, and in places like Diego Garcia island, the United States already possesses sufficient forces for the task.[26] The advantages that geographic proximity confers on the Soviets could be outweighed by the rugged terrain, the difficulty the Soviets will have acting with the element of surprise, and by the existence of many "choke points" where exposed Soviet forces could be smashed.

A Soviet invasion of the Persian Gulf is, in any case, highly unlikely. Certainly, ethnic and religious quarrels, domestic strife, and intraregional rivalries among Persian Gulf states are more probable sources of conflict and instability. Some experts believe that the United States does not now possess sufficient mobile forces with adequate "forcible entry" capability to handle some of these contingencies. To be able to do so, they argue, the United States must procure more light-weight armored vehicles, logistics ships, helicopters, and vertical takeoff aircraft, recall old battleships or heavy cruisers into active service, and be able to convert merchant ships into mini–aircraft carriers —all multibillion dollar propositions.[27] But how useful would such military forces be in resolving complex political problems? Could U.S. forces protect the oil fields against hostile populations? Could these modernized marines stabilize unpopular Arab governments—or would their entry set off an anti-American reaction throughout the region?

Behind the argument for politically oriented intervention forces lies the implicit assumption that the fall of "friendly" Arab governments could well be fatal to U.S. economic and diplomatic interests in the Middle East. History suggests that such fears are exaggerated. In Algeria, Libya, and Iraq, "radicals" in power have kept the oil valve wide open. Arab nationalism, and even Islamic fundamentalism, contains healthy strands of economic developmentalism. Nationalist governments might elect growth strategies that would postpone a portion of oil production, but just as likely is the choice of a more ambitious strategy demanding rising export revenues. Nor does political change guarantee a Soviet diplomatic victory. Arab radical socialists have become increasingly disillusioned with the Soviet Union's sparse economic and faltering military contribution to their causes. For its part, Islamic fundamentalism is profoundly anti-Marxist. However, the dramatic appearance of U.S. troops in the midst of a revolutionary upheaval could present the Soviets with fresh opportunities.

Some proponents of an expanded version of traditional U.S. mobile intervention forces—the highly touted Rapid Deployment Force—recognize the RDF's questionable usefulness for protecting governments and oil fields in the Middle East. Rather, their vision is global. They see an RDF as potentially useful throughout the Third World.[28]

SEIZING THE OFFENSIVE

The current military buildup will increase the American capacity to fight in the Middle East and elsewhere in the Third World. The bulk of military spending, however, is targeted directly at the Soviet Union.

To the extent that these forces are needed to deter Soviet aggression, they are essential. To the extent that the aim is to establish superiority over the Soviet Union, or to give the United States offensive capabilities, they are expendable.

Why would the United States strive for a "margin of safety" in its war-fighting capabilities against the Soviet Union? Part of the answer lies in the logic that the best defense is a good offense. The navy, for example, thinks that the best way to keep sea lanes open is to be able to destroy the enemies' fleet. Fearing Soviet conventional superiority in central Europe, the Pentagon looks for offsetting pressurepoints. Another explanation lies in technological advances, such as enhanced guidance systems. Presented with the scientific capability to build more accurate missiles, the Defense Department naturally pushes to develop them. But an additional reason may lie behind the desire to possess a margin of superiority over the Soviet Union. The Soviets backed down in the Cuban missile crisis, the thinking goes, because the United States possessed unquestionable military superiority. In the 1970s, as the Soviets obtained nuclear parity and perhaps conventional superiority, they became more daring in the Third World. The United States, according to this view, needs to restore its earlier superiority if it is to halt Soviet adventurism in Africa, Asia, and the Caribbean. As Alexander Haig told an audience at the Georgetown University Center for Strategic and International Studies on 6 April, 1982, the military balance "casts a shadow over every significant geopolitical decision. It affects on a day-to-day basis the conduct of American diplomacy. It influences the management of international crises and the terms on which they are resolved."

Strategic superiority could provide the shield behind which the United States could respond more assertively in the Third World. The Soviets and their allies, according to this view, would be less likely to risk supporting revolutionary movements, or to match firm U.S. moves on behalf of our friends in the Third World. Moreover, the combination of enhanced rapid deployment forces and strategic superiority would make feasible a strategy of "horizontal escalation" against targets of our own choosing. As Defense Department officials have said, "If

Soviet forces were to invade the Persian Gulf region, the United States should have the capability to hit back there or in Cuba, Libya, Vietnam, or the Asian landmass of the Soviet Union itself."[29] If the Soviets or one of their allies commits aggression, U.S. forces could seize or destroy vulnerable Soviet "assets" in the Third World. Our nuclear superiority could inhibit the Soviets from launching a counterattack against the United States. The United States could call the Soviet's bluff and expect a rational Soviet leadership to back down. Why would they defend a Third World client if such action risked military escalation to levels where the Soviet Union would be at a disadvantage?

Such reasoning is risky and has several flaws. It assumes that the United States can obtain a sufficient margin of superiority and that the Soviet leadership will be "rational." It calculates Soviet behavior in the Third World to have been often determined by the global, strategic balance. Contrary to the evidence presented in chapter 3, it imagines that the Soviets have been highly successful in the Third World. It also presumes that various Third World regimes friendly to the Soviet Union are nothing but Soviet "assets," are strategically important, and cannot be shaken loose by less drastic measures. Yet, such misconceptions regarding Soviet policies and Third World politics appear to be a motivation, or at least a rationale, for the current military buildup.

THE BUDGETARY IMPACT

The Reagan military budget calls for authorizations of $1.6 trillion between 1983 and 1987. The percentage of GNP devoted to military spending is to rise from the 5.6 level of 1981 to 7.8 percent by 1987. The percentage of the budget devoted to military affairs will jump from 22 percent to over 35 percent.[30] Even these amounts may be insufficient to gain the military edge that the Reagan administration seeks. One study leaked from the Defense Department placed the price tag at $2.2 trillion.[31]

A defense strategy less concerned with beefing up intervention forces or with establishing superiority over the Soviet Union would be considerably less costly. A Brookings Institution analyst argued that the United States could adequately modernize its nuclear and conventional forces and shave $188.5 billion from the Reagan budget between fiscal years 1983 and 1987.[32] This alternative budget is hardly austere. It allows for a real growth in outlays in excess of the nearly 5 percent real increase programed by President Carter in his last budget, although less than the 8.1 percent increase in Reagan's five-year defense plan. The Brookings study presents a second alternative to the Reagan budget that would save $265.8 billion, but suggests, inconclusively, that it might not be sufficient.

How much could be saved if unnecessary expenditures on intervention forces were cut? Two students of military affairs, Barry Posen and Stephen Van Evera, calculated that, roughly, between 15 and 25 percent of the U.S. military budget was absorbed by forces optimized for intervention in the Third World. They made this estimate before the Reagan buildup of conventional forces. Forces "optimized for intervention" would look substantially different had they been tailored for action against the Soviets. According to Posen and Van Evera, such forces would have cost some 50 percent less if their sole mission were to respond to Soviet aggression. That leaves approximately 10 percent of the military budget directed toward preparing for Third World interventions.[33] Thus, over the five-year period of the Reagan budget (1983–87), roughly $164 billion will be authorized for intervention forces. The leaner budget would still provide for the Army's 101st and 82nd Airborne divisions, leaving the U.S. with considerable rapid deployment capabilities.

THE BROADER COSTS

The U.S. economy has been declining relative to its major economic competitors. In an expanding list of countries, per capita production is surpassing our own. In Western Europe, Japan, and some of the aggressively industrializing developing countries, productivity of labor —output per hour worked—has been growing much more rapidly than in the United States. As a result, many American goods have become less competitive, and wages paid to U.S. workers have increased less rapidly or even declined. In light of these disturbing trends, it is especially imperative that military budgets be scrutinized carefully for their potential impact on civilian productivity. U.S. firms must regain their international competitiveness if the American work force is to be more fully employed and if living standards are to rise.

How serious is the drain on the civilian economy caused by excessive military spending? The two main sources of economic growth are capital and technology; bloated military budgets eat at both.

Suppose the $188 billion in programed military spending that the Brookings study suggests is unnecessary were instead devoted to civilian industry. The $38 billion available each year could have a significant impact on the nation's economic development. In 1981, the U.S. spent $328.9 billion on nonresidential plant and equipment.[34] The $38 billion saved by a less frantic military buildup could increase the nation's productive investment by a handsome 11 percent. The share of GNP devoted to investment would rise by over 1 percent. The rate of investment, at 15 percent of GNP, has been remarkably constant over time in the United States. A jump by more than a full percentage point would be a major accomplishment.[35]

If U.S. military forces were targeted more directly at our chief military rival, the Soviet Union, and excessive Third World intervention forces were trimmed, further savings would be realized. The calculations based on the Posen and Van Evera approach, allowing for a 5-year savings of $164 billion, would release $33 billion a year. Investment in plant and equipment could jump by 10 percent. Since the cuts recommended by the Brookings and Posen/Van Evera approaches overlap, it would be incorrect simply to sum the two. The overlap, however, is far from total. If both recommendations were implemented, the gains would substantially exceed the capital saved by each alone.

The windfall savings could either be used to reduce the fiscal deficit or be funneled to private firms as loans and grants. Either way, the amount of capital available for private investment would be increased.

Other things being equal, the cost of capital would fall. All firms would benefit as their cost of funds declined. Firms that are small or just beginning might further benefit by an expansion of available capital. These firms often enjoy less ready access to private capital markets than do large, established companies. As banks become more flush with finance, loans are more likely to trickle down to smaller and newer businesses. Such firms are often the most dynamic innovators of new technology, as well as the least-cost creators of new jobs.

Inflated military budgets will sap the second source of economy growth—technological advancement. The Defense Department (DOD) will be siphoning off a growing share of the nation's scientists and engineers. Already DOD accounts for 60 percent of government research and development outlays, and over 30 percent of the U.S. total. In the past, the results of some DOD-contracted research were transferable to civilian uses. U.S. success in commercial aircraft was due, in large measure, to prior DOD financing of research and development and procurement of military aircraft.[36] But the advanced designs required by tomorrow's elaborate military hardware—designs incorporated into precision-guided munitions (PGMs), night-vision equipment, and missile-tracking devices—may be less easily adaptable to commercial uses.[37]

Even where adaptation of military designs to commercial uses is possible, it may not happen. DOD itself has little incentive to diffuse technology throughout the economy, or to spur the additional research and development needed for commercialization. Take the example of the video cassette recorder. It was first developed in the United States, but it was perfected—miniaturized—in Japan. DOD did devote considerable resources to designing miniature circuits, so crucial for warhead guidance systems in missiles. But no American firm applied miniaturization to video cassette recorders. The Japanese are unable to send missiles speeding toward distant targets with deadly accuracy, but they did produce a small, reliable, and relatively inexpensive video cassette recorder for the commercial market. All of the two million sold commercially in the United States between 1978 and 1980 were made in Japan.

The danger is great that this example will be replicated in other technologies and products. The Defense Department will be spending large sums on developing industrial robots, lasers, computers, and semiconductors. So will the Japanese government—but with the clear purpose of helping its high-technology firms to gain a competitive edge in the growth markets of the future. The Japanese objective is to develop commercial products for international consumption. DOD plans are largely disconnected from commercial strategies.

The defense buildup will divert American brains from commercial designs at an alarming rate. Between 1982 and 1987, defense spending for semiconductors will increase by 18.3 percent a year, while commercial purchases will rise by less than 12 percent.[38] A similar story will be told for computer sales, engineering and scientific equipment, and sales of communications technologies.

Capital and technology are not the only sources of growth. Productivity depends upon many other factors, including the distribution of investment among the various economic sectors, the rate of capacity utilization, and the ability of the work force to move rapidly down the learning curve. The pattern of investment in recent years, the chronic existence of excess capacity, and the failure to incorporate new techniques could account for a substantial portion of the productivity slowdown that the United States is already suffering.[39] Nevertheless, an increase in the rate of investment, and a more rapid development and commercialization of new technologies, would be important elements in a broad-gauged attack on slumping productivity.

In the 1980s, the United States will be the only noncommunist industrial country undergoing a major military buildup. Our European and Japanese competitors will be increasing their military budgets at a much less hectic pace. The United States already shoulders a defense burden that is disproportionately large. Our NATO and Japanese allies are spending a much lower percentage of their GNP on defense. The unfair division of military labor will widen, to the detriment of U.S. commerce.

In the past, an inverse relation has existed between the proportion of GNP that a country devotes to military spending and the growth in productivity of its manufacturing firms. From 1970 to 1979, the United States allocated nearly 6 percent of its GNP to defense, as compared to about 4 percent for France and Germany and under 1 percent for Japan. Productivity increases ranked in opposite order, with the United States gaining only 1.1 percent per year and Japan boasting an annual rate of increase of 4.5 percent.[40] Of course, correlation is not causation, and other factors explain a part of these trends. But in a world where capital and technological expertise are scarce, the allocation of resources for defense logically detracts from inputs available for other endeavors.

U.S. firms are increasingly being challenged by factories located in the Third World. Exports from South Korea, Brazil, and the Philippines are flooding international markets, and have become commonplace in the American home. Most of these developing countries are spending a much lower percentage of their GNP on defense than the United States.

THE TEMPTATION TO RETREAT

The United States has been losing world market shares for a lengthening list of products, including basic steel, shipbuilding, natural-fiber textiles, petrochemicals, and aluminum. The U.S. market has been deeply penetrated by foreign automobiles, steel, cameras, television sets, stereos, textiles, shoes, and food processors. Those businessmen and workers adversely affected by these trends look, not surprisingly, to their government for assistance. The quickest and ostensibly most economical official response is to erect barriers to the entry of competing imports. The proliferating forms that protectionism now takes seem to be limited only by the imagination of lobbyists, corporate lawyers, and government bureaucrats. No longer relying primarily on tariffs, declining firms now look to "non-tariff barriers," such as quotas, orderly marketing arrangements, "buy American" requirements for government procurement, and health and safety standards designed to keep foreign products out.

Protectionism can be in the public interest if it is temporary and is accompanied by measures that will help the afflicted firms and workers to adjust to the new international environment. Displaced companies and laborers must find ways to produce goods that are higher up on the ladder of international competitiveness. Firms may need help in restructuring their operations around select product lines. Workers may need training in new skills and allowances for relocation to cities where opportunities are greater.

Protectionism that is purely negative, however, is destructive to the U.S. economy and to U.S. diplomacy. Neither U.S. firms nor workers benefit over the longer run, since they lose incentives to modernize their plants and upgrade their skills. American consumers, forced to pay higher prices for goods that are often of less quality, also lose, at least until foreign products become so superior that they crack the walls of protectionism. In addition, U.S. diplomacy suffers. A declining and increasingly insular United States forfeits the ability to exert leadership over international economic matters. Worse still, other nations are likely to retaliate, and what begins as modest rockslides could quickly become a global avalanche of protectionism. While the Great Depression analogy might be exaggerated, a conflictive and stagnant international economy is an all-too plausible scenario. The linchpin of U.S. diplomacy could come unstuck.

The stated purpose of the U.S. military buildup is to increase our security and to augment our influence over world events. Yet, the economic consequences of sharply higher military budgets threaten to produce the opposite outcome. Bloated military programs suck capital and scientific resources away from the commercial sphere, leaving U.S. firms at an international disadvantage. As the relative performance of U.S. industry declines, the pressures for protectionism grow. A United States that decreases its participation in the international economy is a less relevant and less influential power.

The choice is not between guns and butter, but rather between two visions of national security. One relies heavily on military might to protect U.S. interests. Alternatively, while the United States needs to maintain a strong defense against the Soviet Union, U.S. strength can be understood to depend importantly on the performance of our civilian industries in global markets. First, our military machine will be better fed by a prosperous economy. Second, the American public may be more willing to sustain a steady level of military spending, and not imitate the lurches of the past. And third, U.S. firms must be able to compete in world markets if a smoothly functioning international economic system is to be the backbone of our diplomacy in the Third World. From this latter perspective, our overall position in the Third World will be better secured by balancing the allocation of resources between military and economic revitalization. This balanced strategy is more responsive to the real challenges and opportunities that face the United States today.

Husbanding Our Psychic Reserves

Just as a nation and its government do not possess unlimited economic resources, so are their psychic reserves bounded. The United States can concentrate obsessively on military strength, or it can gear a major share of its mental energies toward revitalizing the economy. This task will require, in addition to increased levels of savings, investment, and technological innovation, a major rethinking of how the workplace is organized, how firms and banks make investment decisions, and how the government and the private sector interact.[41] In each of these important and complex matters, the U.S. has failed to adjust rapidly enough to new realities. As chapter 2 suggested, other nations have been experimenting with more innovative and flexible industrial policies.

This exercise in national self-examination and reformation will consume tremendous amounts of psychic energy. In particular, it will demand the attention of public officials and the sacrifice of political capital. If Americans squander their resources on great military buildups and on dreams of reasserting control over Third World politics, the domestic economy will suffer. The nation will squander its energies in pursuing a chimera of foreign "greatness" while its base of operations deteriorates.

Over time, a decaying economic base will endanger the social cohesion required to conduct a coherent foreign policy. American democracy has prospered in the context of a growing economy. Interest groups have been able to take larger slices out of an expanding pie without reducing the living standards of competing parties. If the economy enters into a period of prolonged stagnation, American politics could enter a new, more conflictive stage. A social fabric busy tearing at itself is a poor backdrop against which to conduct international affairs. A nation torn by social strife will have great difficulty in implementing a consistent and affirmative foreign policy.

5 *A New Realism*

The United States is fortunate that, at a time when our ability to control events abroad is irreversibly declining, when the costs of intervention are rising, and when shifting international challenges demand that resources be spent on civilian industry, U.S. interests can safely be guarded in the Third World. Both our economic and security interests can be protected, if only the United States sets the right priorities, separates imagined from genuine dangers, and learns to turn recent trends to advantage.

Too much attention has been focused on negative developments in the Third World—its rhetoric, voting patterns in the United Nations, the decline of political liberalism. Other trends are more positive and profound. A growing number of Third World leaders see their self-interest as best served by participating actively in the one-world economy. The expansion of the international banking network, the greater flexibility of multinational enterprises, and the ideological tolerance of the financial and trading systems have made the global economy more enticing to a wide variety of Third World states. In addition, the dynamism of the international economy has produced another political dividend: developing countries are achieving the self-confidence and maturity they need to assert their national interests against any external exploitive force, including the Soviet Union. For their part, the Soviets are adjusting poorly to these trends, and are stumbling badly in their bids for greater influence.

Instead of welcoming these trends and subtly exploiting them, the Reagan administration has ignored or even sought to negate them. Never in the postwar period has an administration given lower priority to international economics. The administration has tended to view international finance and trade as convenient tools with which "to punish" the Soviet Union and its "proxies," thereby exerting unnecessary stress on the entire system. It is as though the productive potential of electricity were to be used only to build and power electric chairs. Rather than recognizing the advantages of independent Third World states, the administration has sought to build "strategic consensus" as a way of pulling developing countries into U.S.-centered alliances. And rather than responding to Soviet expansionism with a strategy based upon our own strengths, the administration has mirrored Soviet behavior by emphasizing military force.

A foreign policy can swim against powerful historic currents only at the sacrifice of energy, resources and effectiveness. Grounded in an understanding of the broad forces at work in the world, an efficient foreign policy would amplify the favorable trends, while dampening the disadvantageous ones. The neorealist policy advocated here would magnify U.S. strengths while working to shrink potential weaknesses. A neorealist strategy would elevate economics, welcome nationalism, deflate ideology, accommodate changes, and generally seek to defuse tensions in the international system.

Neorealism offers criteria for reformulating U.S. policies in the Third World, while eschewing rigid prescriptions. Policy principles should be useful guidelines, not straightjackets that constrict creativity; operational tenets must be flexible, adjusting to the particular case at hand. There will be exceptions to almost every rule. Indeed, neorealism is intended to free the United States from unyielding canons that have sometimes forced policymakers to act against their better instincts.

The Two Wedges

Neorealism recognizes that a wedge exists between the domestic political economy of states and their mode of participation in the international economy. That is, whether a nation's political institutions be authoritarian or liberal, its economy more statist or decentralized, a break occurs at the shoreline of the international economy. That vast sea blurs differences in local political economics, allowing nations to pursue mutual gains. Neorealism would reinforce this ameliorating tendency by adding yet another wedge: this time between a nation's political economy and its international diplomacy. Regardless of internal class structure and professed ideology, nations should not feel the need to seek the protection of the Soviet Union for security.

A neorealist strategy places the two wedges at the center of policy. The effect of the first wedge, which keeps separate many internal political choices from decisions that influence a nation's participation in the international economy, is (as chapter 2 has emphasized) already a fact of life in the Third World. Its full implications remain unrealized because U.S. policymakers are only dimly aware of its existence and underestimate its advantages. The United States has wisely exploited the second wedge, which divides domestic politics from diplomacy, in particular instances, notably Yugoslavia and China. As chapters 3 and 4 suggested, the United States has not perceived the potential of turning this effect into an organizing principle of U.S. diplomacy. We have generally assumed that a government's professed ideology and institutions preordain its international alignment. As a result, we have lost opportunities to drive the second wedge deeper.

The American Right and Left either deny the existence or downplay the utility of the two wedges. Many on the Right would force countries to alter their domestic structures as a condition for participating fully in the international economy. The Left and some liberals persist in seeing fundamental contradictions between national interests and transnational corporations and banks. The Right often brushes aside the importance of the second wedge by assuming that Third World leftists are inherently pro-Soviet or at least hopelessly anti-American. Many American Leftists tend to ignore the East-West dimension altogether. The visions of both the Left and the Right are obscured by ideological blinders.

American businessmen understand the openings created by the first wedge. David Rockefeller, the retired chairman of Chase Manhattan Bank, told reporters after a ten-nation tour of Africa that dealing with socialist or self-professed Marxist countries "really does not cause us any problem at all. . . . We do business with at least 125 countries in the world, governments ranging over the whole political spectrum."[1] Rockefeller added that ideological categories are no longer definitive: so-called capitalistic and socialistic economic systems vary widely among themselves, and also share many similarities with each other.

Unaware that the first wedge has opened a cleavage that makes it easier to hammer in the second, some security-oriented observers, paraphrasing Lenin, have attacked business for "selling the rope with which we will all be hung." Business is accused of being short-sighted, of putting private interests before national security. In fact, by helping to implant the first wedge, pragmatic businessmen have been trailblazers for U.S. diplomacy. This is not the first time that the private sector has been more responsive to changing circumstances, and less wedded to fixed ideas than the government. Government bureaucrats are more removed from the changing realities of the world market, and generally receive little reward for advocating innovative adjustments. Politicians are often prisoners of popular sentiments that lag behind events, especially those occurring overseas. Of course, not all businessmen preach what they practice. The Reagan administration is especially replete with businessmen whose firms work closely with governments around the world, but who still decry "government intervention in the free market."

In their actions, businessmen have opened new paths for U.S. diplomats to follow. Far from jeopardizing U.S. security, the first wedge creates new possibilities for U.S. diplomacy. Indeed, the two wedges make possible a secure America, safe in a world drawn together by a cohesive and hospitable economy, where Soviet influence can be managed without undue strain.

To begin, the United States must rid itself of outmoded perceptions of what we must do to protect ourselves in today's world. The appeal of Ronald Reagan's call for a return to U.S. global preeminence suggests that many Americans prefer to avoid confronting the decline of U.S. power. When the hostages returning from Iran paraded in the streets of Washington, the crowd chanted, "We're number one, we're number one."

Nationalism can be healthy. It can instill pride in one's culture, foster greater social cohesion, and reinforce democratic values. Nationalism, however, has a darker, more dangerous side. In a great power, nationalism can stimulate flashfloods of arrogance and aggressiveness that overflow into chauvinistic and rigid foreign policies. Policy makers will be swept up by an emotional public clamoring to project their sense of self onto the rest of the world.

The American public, to whose shifting moods Washington is so sensitive, must fashion a new self-identity. We must learn to enjoy our own institutions and values without feeling the need for others to duplicate them. We should not expect that the demanding morality of interpersonal relations will be acted out on a world stage. Satisfaction must come less from the exercise of raw power, and more from working with others to manage the global economy and to reduce international tensions. Americans should feel secure enough that the revelation of a Soviet gain in some distant Third World land does not discredit a presidency.

If we revamp our self-definition to mesh with new realities, we may have accomplished our most difficult task. We would be free to devise strategies that benefit fully from the double-wedged reality of the 1980s. Such policies imply new priorities. First, the United States must work harder to assure that the international economy functions smoothly. This will require reforms in the management of the U.S. economy. Second, the United States must be willing to abandon ties with certain groups and individuals within Third World states. At the same time, opportunities for us to build relations with the state bureaucracies who will mediate between their nations and the international system must be taken advantage of as they arise. Third, the United States can work to dampen those tendencies in the system that create opportunities for the Soviet Union. In consort with other powers, U.S. diplomacy can seek to reduce regional tensions, support peacekeeping efforts, and oppose aggressive actions by expansionist Third World states. By leaving room for independent nationalism, the United States can bolster favorable systemic tendencies; sometimes the best way to reduce Soviet influence will be for the United States to do less. Finally, we must recognize that a *Realpolitik* of human rights and an accommodationist posture toward young revolutions are the best approaches to the managing of inevitable change.

Economic Responsibilities

U.S. safety, the neorealist worldview, and the two-wedge strategy require a stable and expanding international economy. It is the web of capital and trade flows that binds the one-world system together to create a mutuality of interests between sellers and buyers, exporters and importers, lenders and borrowers. Maintaining the delicate strands that hold this system together is as important to U.S. security as the global military balance.

Economics must be elevated to the status of so-called "high politics" security issues, and adequately trained personnel must be appointed to positions of power. In the United States, international economics has typically been considered "low politics." Until the appointment of George Schultz, none of the recent secretaries of state—Kissinger, Vance, Muskie, Haig—or NSC advisers—Scowcroft, Brzezinski, Allen, Clark—have known or seemingly cared much about economics. In contrast, many European and Third World leaders are well informed about economics, often having held portfolios in finance or industrial policy.

When we open our eyes, what will we see? The gravest threat to the international economic system comes from the accumulating, massive financial imbalances discussed in chapter 2. The system can adjust automatically to these disruptions. Countries can lower their deficits and learn to live within their means by cutting imports and living standards. But this is an extreme solution. It is as though a man whose suit had shrunk from a sudden downpour was referred to a surgeon to make the body fit the suit.

Moreover, the deflationary solution diminishes the political "pull" of the international system. Ideology is no longer muted by economic expansion; indeed it may roar as politicians try to survive the chronic austerity. As political instability and polarization increase, so does the potential influence of the Soviet Union. It is in our interest to dry out the suit, stretch it, or let out its seams.

As chapter 2 suggests, the United States needs to help assure adequate global liquidity, facilitate capital availability, strengthen the multilateral financial agencies, and institutionalize mechanisms for debt rescheduling. These problems are complex but are within our reach. If the United States allocated a portion of the resources and energies being devoted to weapons systems and defense toward enhancing international economic security, the system could at least be managed. The United States, acting with other industrial and oil-surplus states, has the financial resources to lift the cloud of chronic austerity—and the no-win choice of default or destitution—that darkens the futures of a growing number of developing countries. The resources of the multilateral development banks and the International Monetary Fund, for example, can be increased vastly at little real cost to the U.S. budget.[2] The necessary funds can largely be borrowed from private capital markets, from governments with excess reserves, like Saudi Arabia, or simply be created by fiat. Risking additional resources in emergency safety nets, or in actual bailouts of debtor countries or commercial banks, would still be far cheaper than the costs of a prolonged global slump. Moreover, making such funds available increases the attractiveness of the international economic system, whereas a collapse can only benefit Soviet diplomacy.

Of course, economic growth by itself does not guarantee political stability. One certain advantage of economic progress, however, is that as states become wealthier, the Soviet Union becomes an even less attractive economic alternative. Moreover, the Soviet Union is unlikely to have or want to devote the surplus resources needed to sustain an upper-income developing country. Only very underdeveloped nations can even consider replacing their ties to the international economy with a mixture of ties to COMECON and a new self-reliance. W. W.

Rostow, in his 1950s theory of economic growth, warned that the earlier stages of development carried the greatest dangers, because the strain of modernization provided fertile ground for radical leaders. A contemporary disciple of Rostow would offer an amendment: that the risk of Soviet encroachment is also greater when nations are still poor and unformed. Once a nation reaches a certain level of maturity and economic wealth, the Kremlin's instruments of influence are of limited value.

NATIONAL INDUSTRIAL POLICY

If the United States wants to preserve the one-world economy, it needs domestic economic policies that are consistent with its international objectives. This reverses the traditional dictum that has a Great Power etching onto the world scene an international economy consistent with its domestic economic interests. U.S. participation and leadership in the international economy require a domestic economic structure that adjusts quickly and smoothly to the rapidly shifting demands placed upon it. The U.S. economy must be dynamic enough to survive in a highly competitive world. Otherwise, uncompetitive firms and their workers and representatives in Washington will lobby for a product-by-product withdrawal from the international economy.

Contrary to the neoclassical orthodoxy, U.S. commitment to open markets abroad now requires an activist government at home. As suggested in the previous chapter, the United States needs a national industrial policy to speed and cushion the adjustment of markets, firms, and workers to international competition.[3] A constructive industrial policy promotes rather than resists market forces by accelerating an efficient and socially less costly adjustment of the American economy to structural changes in the world economy.

A positive industrial policy would assist a declining industry in devising a systematic plan to salvage potentially competitive parts of an industry. To minimize hardships to displaced workers, the government could expand existing programs to help workers find new jobs and acquire the requisite skills. To attract new industry to depressed regions, the government could target tax benefits, loans for capital investments, and training grants. These measures to assist firms, workers, and communities would diffuse pressures for the protection of dying industries.

A dynamic industrial policy would also provide loans and tax credits for projects that show promise of international competitive success, but whose risks, high capital requirements, and slow payback have inhibited companies from moving forward on their own. Government can also subsidize research and development on new technologies with commercial application. A national development bank could provide funds for such "supply side" projects.

The United States already has an industrial policy, but it is ad hoc, and sometimes protects and subsidizes inefficiency. The Office of Management and Budget, or a new government agency, should be charged with scrutinizing the mass of detailed government tax and credit subsidies, patent laws, trade regulations, loan guarantees, and fiscal expenditures, including defense programs, to assess their impact on the availability and distribution of investment capital. Confronted with an increasingly competitive international environment, the United States can no longer afford uncoordinated and unfocused economic policies. Just as good diplomats coordinate tactics and strategies around a definition of the national interest, so should our economic policymakers be guided by a strategic vision. Furthermore, the diplomatic and economic strategies of the United States should be mutually reinforcing. An outward-looking, growth-oriented industrial policy would buttress a neorealist foreign policy.

U.S. industrial policy should be consistent with maintaining an open world trading system. An industrial policy that emphasizes accelerating market forces, increasing productivity, and easing adjustment to a changing international environment, while strenuously avoiding prolonged protection of hopelessly troubled businesses, would contribute to a healthy global economy. Such an industrial policy does not conform to a laissez-faire liberalism, but, as we saw in chapter 2, neither does the existing international trading system. Moreover, firms and workers, in the United States and elsewhere, are only likely to accept dynamic international trading if governments actively buffer the inevitable dislocations.

Although interdependence generally furthers our interests, in one area the United States should try to insulate itself from potential disturbances in the world economy. The stockpiling of critical raw materials reduces U.S. vulnerability to political shocks in supplier states. Stocks are already adequate for many commodities but should be deepened for some others.

The United States must view the stability of the international economy as a primary interest. An expanding international economy creates opportunities for our own prosperity. Recognizing that predictability is important to traders and investors, the United States should avoid interrupting the system for immediate political gain. International economic integration is no mere device for coercive U.S. behavior. Rather, it is a system that, by its very nature, deprives the Soviet Union of the ability to impose its control. It is a system that allows the United States to outperform the Soviet Union economically, while it limits Soviet power in the Third World.

Political Strategies

Political activism, sometimes rooted in ideology, has caused many of America's problems in the Third World. By concentrating on internal politics and personalities we are blind to the wedge separating local politics from international economics. Our active hostility toward authoritarian regimes then dissolves that wedge and creates a link between nationalism and Sovietism.

Whenever I have discussed the preceding chapters with members of the policy-making community, they may nod in agreement with the analysis, but they almost invariably query: "Fine, but what are your positive recommendations? What should we be doing?" They recoil from the logic that "less may be more": or, more horrifying, that "nothing may be best." It is hard for Americans in general, and for bureaucrats writing "Action Memoranda" in particular, to sit back and let events run their course. Yet, if—as chapter 4 explained—the United States had not lavished attention on its friends, been so intent on demonstrating credibility, taken sides in regional disputes, and been as hostile toward alleged enemies, we might often have been better off.

The best response to a Soviet inroad may be to give the Soviets time to make their own mistakes. While exercising restraint, government officials could temper their frustration by reminding themselves that future developments may afford more favorable opportunities for U.S. diplomacy. Many Soviet gains have been reversed by events not triggered by the United States. The higher their profile, the uglier the Russians become. When local discontent with their Soviet guests mounts, the time may be ripe for a U.S. counteroffer.

As discussed in chapter 2, U.S. diplomats will often devote their energies to sponsoring local businessmen. The reflex is rarely questioned within the U.S. bureaucracy. When viewed in the context of our two wedges, the question is whether the reflex should still be automatic. Businessmen do offer advantages; but they also carry liabilities.

By definition, businessmen seem more predisposed than other groups to participate in the international economy. The difference between businessmen and their opponents on this crucial issue is often more rhetorical than real, however. In fact, what separates many businessmen from politicians, intellectuals or the military is less the intensity of their nationalism than their practical experience in the limits of their nation's power. In many developing countries, businessmen may be even more anxious than their opponents to use the state to protect local markets from the international economy.

Businessmen appear to offer a second advantage. While they may be willing to make profits by trading with the Soviet Union, their culture and broader economic interests inoculate them against pro-Sovietism. The dilemma for policymakers is that, by placing its bets on local businessmen, the United States runs the risk of generating the very dynamic it wishes to avoid. When the U.S. bankrolls local allies, their competitors must find ways to match the ante. In a self-fulfilling prophecy, the Soviets may be invited to pull up a chair and join the match.

Betting on private businessmen can be an unwise wager. Historically, businessmen often fail to gain and consolidate political power. Even when they do, they are also motivated by national and self-interest. They may betray the trust the United States naively placed in them and turn against us. Total U.S. identification with particular local interests can generate resentments among future rulers that will complicate U.S. diplomacy. Why create unnecessary tensions? Why generate self-defined failures?

The arguments for allying automatically and closely with local officer corps are even weaker. Their understanding of the international economy is often rudimentary. Even worse, their hunger for weapons can drive them toward Moscow, which is better equipped and more willing to provide military than economic assistance. Not only are they not a guarantee of stability, but their political awkwardness can actually generate instability. Again, the Soviets may find an open door.

If the United States were more aware of the openings created by the two wedges, it would feel less compelled to rally by the side of particular local interests. Once the U.S. realizes that its essential interests do not generally depend upon which social group controls resources or power within Third World states, it could view local power struggles with more equanimity. Having learned from past mistakes, and more aware of new realities, this approach would be less risky, less costly, and more effective in containing Soviet imperialism than apparently "tougher" policies.

THE PERMANENT BUREAUCRACIES

Americans like to think of themselves as pragmatists, and U.S. foreign policymakers are no exception. Yet, too often we have viewed the world through thick, ideological lenses. The ideological and cultural biases of U.S. diplomats and policymakers have contributed to the reflexive identification of U.S. interests with local business elites and —to a less degree—with military officers. Once these biases may have been reliable; they were like sea maps in an old logbook. Now these old values no longer accurately chart the world's oceans.

A new force has emerged in Third World countries that requires nurturing, but that ideology still obscures. This force is the governmental bureaucracy. Both American foreign policymakers and Marxists tend to view governments as instruments of vested social classes or powerful leaders. But today in the Third World, governmental bureaucracies have become a force in their own right. One of their functions is to negotiate the terms on which their nation will participate in the international economy.

Especially in the more institutionalized developing countries like Argentina, Brazil, India, Mexico, and South Korea, the governmental bureaucracies have demonstrated impressive staying power. Composed of sophisticated technocrats, these bureaucracies provide the ideas that frame how countries view their basic national interests. In turn, these frameworks tend to limit the behavior of particular administrations. While not immutable, they do reflect rational calculations of the country's geopolitical setting and economy and thus tend to persevere over time. In Mexico, where one party has dominated official life since the Revolution, the bureaucracy is especially powerful. The Mexican president and his coterie are products of the bureaucracy and of the official party. The party itself is dependent upon and integrated into the governing structures. In countries such as Argentina, where ruling parties change, the bureaucracy remains. Even under the post–1976 junta, which represented the "liberal" tradition in Argentine economic and foreign policies, the state bureaucracy continued to play a major role.[4] This was most apparent in the continuing development of hydrocarbons and nuclear power, in the arrangement of bilateral trade deals, in the production and purchase of armaments, and in the maintenance of an ambiguous foreign policy aligned neither with the industrial states nor with the more strident LDCs.

In some African and Asian states, where local business elites are weak, the United States has recognized the importance of the state bureaucracy but has usually relied on personal ties to safeguard U.S. interests. The underlying assumption has been that such nations naturally need personalized autocracies. But these autocratic leaders actually are much more fragile than the bureaucracies they rule. They can, however, gradually corrode the bureaucracy's efficiency and morale, while years of corruption and repression can alienate the population enough that, in exorcising the autocrat, revolutionaries simultaneously wreck the bureaucracy. Thus, the persistence of an unpopular tyrant may actually endanger the continuity a bureaucracy implies. To some degree this happened in Iran and is happening in Zaire under Mobutu. By propping up rulers long after they have lost their legitimacy, the United States risks much more radical destruction of existing institutions.

Bureaucracies promise to be more lasting and truly representative of the nation's interests. They are a firmer, less controversial foundation for U.S. diplomacy. Moreover, bureaucrats in the Third World are likely to resist close ties to the Soviet Union. Whether they came to their posts through competitive examinations, patronage, or revolutions, bureaucrats in the Third World tend to be interests in hierarchy, consumerism, and modern technology. Given these concerns, it is not surprising that bureaucrats have proven to be elusive targets for the Soviets.

Of course, no foreign power can hope to manipulate state bureaucracies as they might a political party or a small group of business or military leaders. Rather than continuing to pursue the chimera of control through alliances with the traditional political instrumentalities, the United States needs to devote greater attention to developing personal and policy influence with the more permanent bureaucracy. Some embassies already strive to penetrate local bureaucracies, but most could do more. In cases where military and business groups remain powerful within a society and its governmental bureaucracy, the United States may still wish to cultivate their friendship. Indeed, immediate diplomatic objectives will sometimes require that we do so. But our eyes should be kept on the less visible, and more mundane, state apparatus. American businessmen have long pursued a policy of lobbying the working levels of Washington's many agencies, while simultaneously seeking to exploit White House and Cabinet-level contacts. The more adept firms also follow a similar two-tier strategy overseas. U.S. diplomats must learn to present themselves persuasively not only in the palaces of presidents and monarchs, but also in the drab offices of ordinary functionaries.

LIMITED ENGAGEMENT

Our relations within countries should be broadly based, to include ties with bureaucrats, opposition figures, and clerics, as well as businessmen and military officers. But the United States must still find a way of dealing with Third World governments without falling into the traps of the commitment/credibility syndromes. Rather than thinking in terms of friendly governments to whom we are emotionally and absolutely committed—and hostile governments that should only be ignored or harassed—we should develop more circumscribed, nuanced relationships. We should feel free to enter into mutually beneficial agreements on particular issues, without having to enter into a general obligation. Governments should neither assume our blind allegiance, nor should they anticipate automatic belligerence. We do not want governments to take our support for granted: for us to feel that we must support their interests; or for them to presume that they can act against our interests with impunity. Conversely, governments that find the doors to the State Department firmly shut have little incentive to please us.

One issue where the United States will want to work actively with other governments is dispute settlement. As Great Powers lose their grip on the Third World, local wars may become more common. Conflicts between developing countries pose a threat to several U.S. interests. Armed conflicts cause countries to place security first, thereby opening opportunities for the Soviet Union. Local wars can escalate into a threat to world peace, should the superpowers be drawn in behind opposing sides. In addition, increasingly destructive arsenals give Third World countries growing capabilities to damage each other's productive apparatus. The ability of the battling countries to fulfill their international economic obligations could be jeopardized. The use of more effective lethal weapons also enlarges the scale of human suffering.

When we are engaged in trying to settle regional disputes, we may find it necessary to court governments. We will surely need to work closely with the other, interested parties. The Camp David accords, which reduced the chances of a full-scale war in the Middle East, required the agreement of Sadat. The Carter administration's wooing of Nigeria paid dividends during the negotiations on Zimbabwe. Nevertheless, such tactical engagements should not become open-ended commitments. We should think of them as collegial relationships, or as temporary liasons, rather than as binding marriages.

FLEXIBLE DISENGAGEMENT

This more flexible attitude toward foreign relations will make it easier to accept inevitable setbacks in our relations with particular countries. Presidents will no longer fear that the collapse of a friendly government could endanger their own administration. Our honor and our credibility will not be hostage to events that we cannot control.

A president should explain that the downfall of a government with which we worked in the past was due primarily to an internal dynamic beyond the influence of the United States. Warren Christopher, who negotiated the release of the American diplomats held hostage in Teheran, later drew this lesson from the Iranian crisis:

> The Irani experience should encourage a sense of realism in our dealings with developing countries. For their internal politics are shaped almost wholly by internal forces, and very little by external pressures. A wise nation, however powerful, understands the peril it invites in confronting the will of another people. Outside powers have an affect, if any, only at the margins."[5]

Similar words ought to be repeated the next time an administration suffers a "loss" in a Third World nation.

To critics who blame the administration for not having acted with sufficient vigor to save the fallen regime, officials may respond that feasible adjustments in U.S. policy, even sudden increases in arms or economic aid, would not have saved the tottering government; furthermore, the remaining recourse—military intervention—would have violated the principle of national sovereignty. Public opinion polls suggest that, while Americans want a "strong" foreign policy, many also favor nonintervention in the affairs of other states.[6] Nor do they want to spill American blood if U.S. national security itself is not at stake.

To further defuse the issues of strength and prestige, an administration should be careful not to exaggerate the setback, nor to inflate any increase in Soviet influence. Typically, it will be possible to argue that no vital U.S. interest has been threatened. Moreover, when events have settled and a new government consolidates itself, history suggests that it, too, will eventually want to normalize relations with the United States. The new rulers will need the United States, it should be argued, more than we will need them.

To articulate convincingly such a new interpretation of U.S. interests and how best to defend them, an administration must be clearheaded and united. If its language is ambiguous, its pronouncements divergent, or its actions contradictory, it will be overwhelmed by a confused and angry public opinion. But if it succeeds, it will have freed itself and the country from having to pass through yet another trauma of nasty accusations and self-flagellation. It will also have placed American diplomacy on a firmer, more realistic footing.

OVERT AGGRESSION

The United States needs to distinguish between essentially internal conflicts and external aggression. U.S. interests require an active diplomacy to settle or at least manage regional disputes. But peacekeeping efforts may fail, and one state may attack another. The appropriate U.S. response to a case of overt aggression can, however, only be decided on a case-by-case basis. In determining the nature and intensity of its reaction, the United States should take into account the historical background to the conflict, the character and stability of the contesting governments, the attitudes of other governments in the region and of our NATO allies, the tangible U.S. interests at stake, U.S. military capabilities in the area, and the degree of Soviet involvement. A diplomatic solution may still be possible, and the U.S. should be predisposed to participate in multilateral peacekeeping forces. In the absence of such an international accord, arms transfers are more likely to be commensurate with the U.S. stake than sending U.S. troops. When a military response is required, it must be undertaken in the context of a broader diplomatic strategy.

A conflict can still be essentially internal even if some foreign meddling is detected. We should avoid assuming that the external backers of either of the contending parties are in control of their side, or would be able to maintain whatever influence they currently exert if their friends prevail. Washington should keep in mind the ability of the United States, Western Europe, or independent regional powers, to regain influence once stability is restored.

NONALIGNMENT

The U.S. interest in raising barriers to Soviet control is served when Third World states choose strategic nonalignment. Our goal is not to populate the Third World with automatons but to prevent the Soviets from doing so. Moreover, accepting nonalignment will facilitate our engagement with a broad array of Third World governments. As long as the one-world economy functions, political nonalignment occurs within a larger framework of shared interests.

The acceptance of nonalignment is the international equivalent of tolerance toward internal political choices. The search for close allies creates strong pressures to favor those political factions most favorable to the United States, and to oppose those who prefer a more independent posture. While circumstances may arise when an overriding U.S. interest requires such choices, they should be the exception rather than the rule.

The first principle of nonalignment is that countries follow their own national interest. Nonalignment does not, however, deny all of a Great Power's influence. Mere participation in the one-world economy guarantees some influence, however diffuse, to the industrial powers that provide commodities and credits. Soviet power will also be felt in some regions. A nonaligned nation may even use a limited Soviet presence to help offset a stronger Western one. Genuine nonalignment is inconsistent with Soviet control, but does not require the elimination of all Soviet interchange. While Cuba is not genuinely nonaligned, Brazil, India, and Iraq do qualify.

Nonalignment does not imply that countries always vote against the Soviet Union in the United Nations. On the contrary, the Soviets are able to support key nonaligned positions. On such "anti-imperialist" issues as South Africa, Israel, Puerto Riço, and Chile, Soviet interests (but not necessarily motives) coincide with the Third World majority. In these cases, at least, the Soviets have little interest in preserving the status quo. The Soviets also find it rhetorically easy to support demands for a new international economic order—so long as they don't have to contribute hard currency. On many of these issues, however, the Soviets are following the lead of the Third World. The Kremlin neither creates the issue nor controls its content and direction. Moscow may gain some diplomatic points, but the Third World could reasonably consider that it is the Soviet Union that is being used.

By accepting nonalignment, the United States can overcome the legacy of containment that led many in the Third World to conclude that both superpowers were equally interested in preserving and extending their own power at the expense of smaller nations. If the United States could build a record over time of genuinely supporting the independence of Third World states, those U.S. involvements that are undertaken would receive wider acceptance. On behalf of sovereignty, the United States could provide measured amounts of security assistance to countries threatened by their neighbors. Furthermore, should the Soviet Union undertake an illegitimate military intervention, a U.S. decision to assist rebels fighting for national independence might be widely approved. (Such aid, however, would best be extended only when the rebels showed a reasonable chance of success. When clients lose, so do their sponsors. Moreover, if aid is provided merely "to bleed the Soviets," the United States will be perceived as just another Great Power cynically seeking to weaken its adversary by using others as cannon fodder.)

The best strategy for fostering genuine nonalignment is to hammer hard at the two wedges. Keeping the international economy healthy ensures the West's continuing appeal. When the United States helps a country protect its borders, regardless of its internal politics, the potential usefulness of the Soviet Union is reduced. Again, a policy based on the two wedges will be more effective in closing doors to Soviet diplomacy than the more traditional, "tougher" tack of close alignment with friends and hostility toward alleged enemies.

U.S. officials often claim to accept and even advocate nonalignment, just as they profess to adhere to the principle of nonintervention in Third World internal politics. The record of U.S. behavior argues otherwise, as indeed it must so long as our interests and the threats they face are defined too broadly. But once U.S. interests are properly narrowed, the fostering of nonalignment, defending of national sovereignty, and tolerating of ideological diversity become the most efficient means of protecting those interests.

REGIONAL POWERS

Regional powers tend to be leery of Great Power intervention in and around their own spheres of influence. These countries may try to gain some limited advantages from the Great Powers, but will perceive a large, direct presence as a challenge to their own influence. They will also worry that such a presence will engage the other superpower and that it will become increasingly difficult to avoid becoming a pawn in an East-West confrontation. Thus, while Iraq and India have sought arms and some diplomatic backing from the Soviet Union, they have also worked to limit Soviet influence in their regions. Each seeks to expand its own power at the expense of both Moscow and Washington.

The United States should assist regional powers to enhance their own independence. The United States and Western Europe can provide them with limited amounts of weapons appropriate for their self-defense. We can assist in the settling of regional boundary disputes. We can offer protection against the blatant aggression of others. We can support regional schemes to increase economic integration or strengthen diplomatic cooperation. Locally inspired organizations, like CARICOM (Caribbean Community) and ASEAN (Association of East Asian Nations) fit this formula.

The United States should associate with regional powers on particular issues, but should generally avoid pacts and alliances, except those of a clearly defensive nature. They compromise the image, if not the reality, of the weaker member's independence. They invite neighboring states to seek alternative external protectors. Alliances also risk U.S. credibility and can create pressures for U.S. responses where our interests are not at stake. Certainly, the United States should not seek offensive surrogates in the Third World. Establishing surrogates runs contrary to the central objective of fostering independence and nonalignment. The ground they churn up becomes fertile soil for Soviet expansionism.

The Nixon doctrine recognized the potential of regional powers, but sought to tie them to an American definition of the threats to their region. The United States is more likely to be successful if it encourages local powers to play an active and independent role in their own regions. The Carter administration generally understood this but was not always willing to accept some of the logic consequences. Mexico, for example, sees Central America as its natural sphere of influence, and has become increasingly involved in trying to reduce tensions within and between the five small Central American republics. Although Mexico may wish to increase its own influence at the expense of the United States, it also wants Central America to remain integrated into the international economy without becoming more enmeshed in the East-West conflict. Unfortunately, both the Carter and the Reagan administrations have been so concerned with Mexican acquiescence to more authoritarian or to leftist regimes that they have sought to frustrate or work around Mexico. By placing ideology first, the U.S. has neglected an opportunity to safeguard its fundamental interests.

A policy of devolution, whereby the U.S. relinquishes influence to a regional power—or in some cases, to another industrial power—resolves many of the problems facing U.S. policy. The costs incurred by an active U.S. involvement are avoided. At the same time, the United States benefits indirectly, since the regional power will generally seek to contain local tensions and will jealously guard against Soviet encroachment. We must accept that, even when the regional power shares the fundamental interests of the United States as defined here, direct U.S. influence will still decline. Moreover, the regional power may tolerate or even facilitate domestic political outcomes that we do not like. Such are the costs of the loss of control.

Human Rights and Revolution

Throughout this argument, a central theme has been the challenge presented to U.S. foreign policy by social change in the Third World. A foreign policy that tries to forestall all change is bound to end in costly failure. Indeed, in the 1980s, a less predictable economic environment will make life precarious for many governments.

A carefully designed human rights policy offers the best preemptive response to the pressures for change in the Third World. Governments that are highly repressive and are systematically violating human rights often do so because they fear change. While repression can sometimes control dissent, it seldom eliminates it. Over time, if the regime fails to accommodate at least some of the dissident elements, renewed and more vigorous unrest may well appear.

The United States can disassociate itself from grossly repressive regimes by reducing or eliminating official military transfers and by not sending any signals of approval or acquiescence. When a country is already moving toward more open political institutions, the United States can publicly encourage the process, while not identifying with any particular personalities or parties. In either case, the United States may help to prevent or reverse real or de facto civil wars and to open avenues for stabilizing reform.

President Carter's human rights policy was essentially based on such tactics. The policy was relatively successful in Latin America, where it was implemented most seriously and where U.S. influence is greatest. The most notable triumphs occurred where U.S. policies reinforced already strong domestic currents. In Ecuador, Peru, Honduras, and the Dominican Republic, incumbent military regimes were widely viewed as corrupt and exhausted, and strong civilian parties were poised to assume power. In Brazil, U.S. policies fortified the powerful internal currents demanding political liberalization.

Carter's human rights policy encountered tougher obstacles where authoritarian regimes were firmly entrenched and opposed to accommodation even with centrist opponents. In the Southern Cone—Chile, Argentina, Uruguay—authoritarian regimes had recently come to power in the wake of severe institutional crises and profound social conflicts. They were intent upon remaining in power until their nation's psyches and institutions were reshaped. The Carter administration may have had some success in saving individuals persons from prison and execution, but general political and civil liberties remained tightly controlled. The administration's human rights policies were even less successful in Central America, where entrenched military regimes in Nicaragua, El Salvador, and Guatemala preferred to respond to discontent with heightened repression until pressures were too great to be relieved by moderate reforms.[7]

Carter's human rights policy did yield diplomatic returns.[8] In a remarkably short period of time, President Carter removed the venom in U.S.-Latin relations that was the legacy of the Nixon/Kissinger policies of a general neglect interspersed with specific interventions. The Carter administration was able to forge a series of useful relationships with more democratic governments. These new associations enhanced U.S. stature and influence in the hemisphere. For example, the combination of an improved image and these new diplomatic ties enabled the United States to win the backing of the OAS for the 1978, U.S.-led mediation that hoped to resolve the emerging Nicaraguan crisis. The more democratic states would almost certainly not have entrusted the Nixon administration with such a task force. Carter's human rights policy also made it more difficult for nationalist forces to cast the United States government as the foreign devil behind local problems. Whereas the center-left party of Michael Manley had successfully directed nationalist wrath against the United States in the 1976 Jamaican elections, the tactic was both less pronounced and less effective in the 1980 elections.

Throughout the hemisphere, centrist and center-left political forces, and even some leftist elements, came to view the United States as a benevolent or at least neutral power. The human rights policy permitted U.S. embassy officials to associate with opposition elements, for it was their rights that were being monitored. The United States could thereby collect information on a wide range of political factions, while establishing better relations with them. Had these forces come to power —or should they succeed under a future, human rights-minded U.S. administration—the United States should be able to avoid the diplomatic disruptions that can accompany governmental changes.

In sum, the Carter experience suggests that a human rights policy can sometimes help to reduce political tensions, facilitate peaceful change and benefit U.S. diplomacy. The United States may find itself powerless, however, once the process of polarization is too far advanced.

Carter's policy relied heavily on rhetoric, diplomatic signals, and small amounts of bilateral military and economic aid. Carter did not try to withhold private-sector trade and credits. While his motivations may have been primarily political—not wanting to offend U.S. firms and banks—the policy was basically correct. The health and integrity of the international economic system would have been damaged if it had been routinely manipulated to punish or reward the large number of Latin states that were targets of the Carter human rights policies.

In the 1980s, U.S. diplomacy in the Persian Gulf could benefit from a human rights policy properly adapted to the region's sensitivities and problems. The likelihood of sharp political discontinuity in Saudi Arabia, Kuwait, Bahrein, the United Arab Emirates, and Oman could be reduced if governments develop or expand existing institutional channels open to the participation of widening sectors of the population. Rapid economic growth is generating newly aware social forces that will have to be accomodated if upheaval is to be avoided. Similarly, a widespread distribution of the fruits of development could deflate tensions generated by new wealth.[9] Nevertheless, even if the United States uses its limited ability to influence the political decisions of the Persian Gulf states in a properly low-key, astute fashion, the pressures from extremely swift modernization may overwhelm some of the Arab potentates.

ACCOMMODATING REVOLUTION

With or without a U.S. human rights policy, some countries will still undergo upheavals and revolutions. The United States lacks the wisdom, subtlety, and power to steer many of the social forces unleashed in the Third World. We may prefer peaceful change, but a foreign policy that rules violent change "unacceptable" will oppose the basic historical experiences of an ever-growing list of countries. How should the United States respond to revolution?

First, we should cut losses. We should be willing to sever ties with old but tottering friends and open communication with emerging winners. If we do not bind U.S. credibility to the defense of particular rulers, we can avoid the traumas of self-inflicted defeat and guilt.

Second, we should be circumspect and cautious in placing our bets on alternative ruling groups. The reliability and durability of local business groups and militaries should not be overestimated. The United States should, however, seek to maintain good relations with the permanent bureaucracy, and with as wide a range of political factions as possible.

Third, we should not automatically panic if more radical groups ascend to power. In the euphoria of revolution, their rhetoric is bound to be heady and may be highly nationalistic. They will be hypersensitive to any foreign criticism or signs of external interference. Their knowledge of more technical subjects, including economics and even diplomacy, may be no more than rudimentary. The new leaders will need a grace period to purge past frustrations and learn the new realities of governing.

Fourth, we should generally participate in economic assistance programs. Countries undergoing social change are among those most in need of official aid. Private capital—both foreign and domestic—is unlikely to invest in a politically uncertain environment. Without external finance, the economy may deteriorate and thereby exacerbate political conflict. Official aid can help to alleviate internal tensions and to maintain more normal links to the international economy. The International Monetary Fund and the World Bank can provide the credits needed to maintain economic activity and meet debt service and other external obligations. These loans may be conditioned upon responsible fiscal and monetary management, but should not dogmatically require a particular mix between the public and the private sectors. These loans should be seen less as levers to obtain immediate political concessions than as bridges connecting the country with the international economy.

Diplomatic normality may be impossible, however, if the regime undertakes massive killings of its opposition. In the case of Pol Pots and Pinochets, only humanitarian assistance will be consistent with a human rights policy. Over time, such governments generally will either moderate themselves or be overthrown. The United States can then reappraise its posture.

Fifth, the United States should encourage the peaceful settlement of regional disputes or other external threats facing the country in question. If these disputes cannot be resolved, they can perhaps at least be dampened. The United States should do whatever it can to prevent security concerns from overwhelming economic concerns in determining a regime's behavior. Providing defensive weapons may alleviate such fears. In some cases, the Western Europeans or regional powers may be better placed to provide security and economic aid and peacekeeping services. In such instances, the United States should be willing to follow their lead.

Sixth, the United States should make clear its opposition to interference in the internal affairs of neighboring states. While some spillover may be inevitable, the revolutionary government should seek to contain its more effervescent elements. Otherwise, the United States might extend measured security assistance to the threatened regimes.

In essence, the United States should grasp the opportunities offered by the two wedges. By eschewing alliance with particular factions, we can drive a wedge between how the new regime organizes domestic institutions and how it interacts with the international economy. By reducing its fears, we can increase the likelihood that economics will be emphasized over security. By accepting nonalignment, we can lessen the danger that the new-born government will look to the Soviet Union for protection: and the probability that such an action could credibly be justified under the banner of nationalism.

The revolutionaries may still turn to Moscow for arms. The legacy of past involvements may make it impossible for the West to overcome the regime's distrust. Regional conflicts may spin out of control. The regime may fear renewed civil strife and see aid from the Soviet Union or another socialist state as more politically compatible. Even then, the West should seek to keep the country integrated into the international economy and gradually to drive home the two wedges. Time is on our side.

The Agenda

The foregoing recommendations call for a reduction in certain traditional modes of American activism. They do not call for passivity or isolationism, nor do they ignore our interest in containing Soviet power. Neorealist foreign policy requires major initiatives in domestic and international economic policy, an alertness to opportunities to dampen regional disputes, and consistent efforts to lessen polarization within states and between the United States and revolutionary movements. These tasks will more than fill the days of the watch officers in the State Department's information center and of the top policy officials on the seventh floor.

A policy grounded in a neorealist appreciation of U.S. interests would reduce tensions between the industrial and the developing world, without indulging irresponsible rhetoric for a "New International Economic Order." A genuine program to regenerate the international economy and foster nonalignment would also be in the interests of the Third World. This convergence of fundamental interests may not erase all differences; it will make the world more hospitable for everyone.

Neorealism will require some adaptation of the American consciousness. However, a neorealist vision adheres to values central to the American culture: pragmatism, materialism, democratic nationalism, benign internationalism. Under its sway, America's ideological projection abroad would be based appreciably less on efforts to shape other people's institutions. Instead of exporting our values wholesale, we could take the opportunity to set a compelling example.

The United States can adopt to new realities graciously, or we can thrash about noisily. It is time to stop churning and end the melodrama; our task is not to change the course of history, but to smooth the transition from one era to another, for ourselves and, within our capabilities, for and with others. The neorealist prescription offers new outlets for American energies in making the world safer and more prosperous during the remainder of the twentieth century.

Notes

INTRODUCTION

1. Henry Kissinger, address before the annual convention of The American Society of Newspaper Editors, Washington, D.C., 10 April 1980.

2. Alexander Haig, "A New Direction in U.S. Foreign Policy," address before The American Society of Newspaper Editors, Washington, D.C., 24 April 1981; printed as Current Policy No. 275, Bureau of Public Affairs, Department of State, Washington, D.C.

3. "Transcript of Prime Minister Begin's Statement to the U.S. Envoy to Israel," *New York Times,* 21, December 1981.

4. Kissinger, 10 April 1980 address.

5. Numerous writers have tried their hand at analyzing and defining the concept of "national interest." Realist interpretations can be found in Klaus Knorr, *The Power of Nations: The Political Economy of International Relations* (New York: Basic Books, 1975), especially chap. 2, and in Hans J. Morgenthau, *In Defense of the National Interest* (New York: Methren 1951). The classic "materialist" interpretation, which stresses the role of economic interests in shaping foreign policy, is Charles A. Beard, *The Idea of National Interest* (New York: MacMillan, 1934). See also William Appleman Williams, *The Tragedy of American Diplomacy* (New York: Dell, 1959), for a discussion of commercial motivations behind the "open door" policy. For an effort by the "complex interdependence" school to grapple with the idea, see Alexander L. George and Robert O. Keohane, "The Concept of National Interests: Uses and Limits," in *Presidential Decisionmaking in Foreign Policy: The Effective Use of Information and*

Advice, ed. Alexander L. George (Boulder, Colorado: Westview Press, 1980). Other useful studies are Joseph Frankl, *National Interest* (New York: Praeger, 1970), and Donald Neuchterlein, *National Interests and Presidential Leadership: The Setting of Priorities* (Boulder, Colorado: Westview Press, 1980).

6. U.S., Department of State, National Security Council (NSC)–68, *Foreign Relations of the United States, 1950* (Washington, D.C.: Government Printing Office, 1950)

7. Cited in John Lewis Gaddis, *Strategies of Containment: A Critical Apprisal of Postwar American National Security Policy* (New York: Oxford University Press, 1982), p. 241.

8. Aside from Morgenthau, these individuals were mostly "practical realists," in the sense of being men of affairs rather than pure theoreticians. Their realism offered both a description of the world, and a prescription for U.S. foreign policy. The classic work on realism is Hans J. Morgenthau, *Politics Among Nations* (New York: A. A. Knopf, 1948). See also Walter Lippmann, *The Cold War: A Study in U.S. Foreign Policy* (New York: Harper & Row, 1947); George F. Kennan, *Memoirs, 1925–1950* (Boston: Little, Brown, 1967); and George Ball, *The Discipline of Power* (Boston: Little, Brown, 1968).

9. Morgenthau, *Politics Among Nations,* 5th rev. ed., p. 11.

10. A good textbook review of the realist-idealist debate can be found in J. Dougherty and R. Pfaltzgraff, *Contending Theories of International Relations* (New York: Lippincott, 1979), especially chapters 1 and 3. Also, see Robert E. Osgood, *Ideals and Self-Interest in America's Foreign Relations* (Chicago: University of Chicago Press, 1953). A recent exposition of "world order" idealism is Robert C. Johansen, *The National Interest and the Human Interest* (Princeton: Princeton University Press, 1980).

11. The author first used this term in a paper entitled "United States' Interests and Options in Central America," delivered at a conference sponsored by the Friedrich Ebert Foundation, Bonn, West Germany, October 1980. A revised version of the paper was published in *Change in Central America: Internal and External Dimensions, eds. Wolf Grabendorff, J. Todt, and H.W. Krumwiede (Boulder, Colorado: Westview Press, 1983).* At the same time and working independently, Tom J. Farer used the term neorealism in his important essay, "Searching for Defeat," *Foreign Policy,* no. 40 (Fall 1980), pp. 155–74.

12. The "complex interdependence" school also emphasizes the importance of "non-state actors," for example, multinational corporations and banks; see Robert O. Keohane and Joseph S. Nye, *Power and Interdependence: World Politics in Transition* (Boston: Little, Brown, 1977).

13. Lloyd C. Gardner, *Economic Aspects of New Deal Diplomacy* (Madison, Wisconsin: University of Wisconsin Press, 1964), p. 51.

14. Ibid, p. 47.

CHAPTER 1

1. See, for example, Norman Podhoretz, *The Present Danger* (New York: Simon and Schuster, 1980); W. Scott Thompson, ed., *The Third World: Premises of U.S. Policy* (San Francisco: Institute for Contemporary Studies, 1978); Robert W. Tucker, "America in Decline: The Foreign Policy of Maturity," *Foreign Affairs* 58, no. 3 (1980), pp. 449–84.

2. World Bank, *World Development Report 1981* (Washington, D.C.: World Bank, 1981), p. 164, table 16.

3. *Organization for Economic Cooperation and Development, Development Co-operation 1980* (Paris: OECD, 1980), p. 186, table A–9; and ibid. (1972), p. 218, table 5.

4. ibid. (1980), p. 199, table A–15. Figures are based on net disbursements.

5. See Simon Serfaty, *The United States, Western Europe and The Third World: Allies and Adversaries* (Washington, D.C.: Georgetown University Center for Strategic and International Studies, 1980).

6. For detailed analysis of numerous case studies, including India, Pakistan, Brazil, and Argentina, see Joseph A. Yager, ed., *Nonproliferation and U.S. Foreign Policy* (Washington, D.C.: Brookings Institution, 1980).

7. For a recent version of this argument, see James Chace, *Solvency: The Price of Survival* (New York: Random House, 1981).

8. Thomas Bailey, *A Diplomatic History of the American People,* 9th ed. (Englewood Cliffs, New Jersey: Prentice-Hall, 1974), p. 923.

9. This account draws heavily upon Scott Armstrong's detailed description of U.S. policymaking during the period immediately preceeding the Shah's downfall. *The Washington Post,* 25–30 October 1980.

10. An official interagency study undertaken after the Shah's downfall identified several shortcomings of existing intelligence practices, including an overconcentration on contacts with ruling elites. Richard Burt, "U.S. Seeks Ways to Gauge Foreign Nations' Stability," *New York Times,* 29 January 1979, p. 192.

11. Armstrong, *The Washington Post,* 27 October 1980, p. 1.

12. For theoretical discussions of this problem, see Robert Jervis, *Perception and Misperception in International Politics* (Princeton, New Jersey: Princeton University Press, 1976); and George, *Presidential Decisionmaking.*

13. For a diplomatic history of the Vietnam war by a State Department participant, which emphasizes ignorance at the top, see Paul M. Kattenburg, *The Vietnam Trauma in American Foreign Policy, 1945–1975* (New Brunswick: Transaction Books, 1980).

14. In the first volume of his autobiography, *White House Years* (Boston: Little, Brown, 1979), Henry Kissinger notes this problem area for U.S. policy,

but fails to draw any policy lesson (see pp. 845–47). The Reagan administration's decision to enter into a massive economic and security aid relationship with Pakistan further complicated U.S.—Indian relations.

15. For a warning that the suppression of the Shaba rebellion has not resolved U.S. problems in the bankrupt and unstable Zaire of Mobutu, see Robert M. Price, *U.S. Foreign Policy in Sub-Saharan Africa: National Interest and Global Strategy* (Berkeley, California: University of California Institute of International Studies, 1978), pp. 51–58.

16. Those who argue that we ought to have supported Somoza ignore these essential facts. Also, it is naive to imagine that we could have maintained Somoza in power until the scheduled 1981 elections; even in the unlikely event that massive weapons shipments and U.S. advisers had enabled Somoza to retain control of Managua, genuine elections could never have been held in those circumstances. For an example of such an uninformed critique of U.S. policy see Jeane Kirkpatrick, "Dictatorship and Double Standards," *Commentary,* November 1979, pp.34–35.

17. U.S., Congress, House of Representatives, Committee on Foreign Affairs, *Statement before the Subcommittee on Inter-American Affairs,* 96th Cong., 1st sess., 26 June 1979.

18. On Mexican motivation in Central America, see Mario Ojeda and Rene Herrera, "Petroleum and Mexican Policy in Central America," in *Central America: International Dimensions of the Crisis,* ed. Richard E. Feinberg (New York: Holmes and Meier, 1982); and Richard E. Feinberg, "Central America: No Easy Answers," *Foreign Affairs,* Summer 1981, pp. 1121–46.

19. Brazil's U.N. voting reflected its tilt away from the United States and toward third-world positions: In U.N. plenary voting for 1974–75, on all substantive issues Brazil agreed with the United States less than one-third of the time—an unusually low correlation. Wayne A. Selcher, "Brazil's Candidacy for Major Power Status," *Intellect,* June 1977, p. 404.

20. For a bibliographic essay on earlier dependency literature, see Ronald H. Chilcote, "A Critical Synthesis of the Dependency Literature," *Latin American Perspectives* 1, Spring 1974. For an earlier conservative view, see Nelson Rockefeller, *The Rockefeller Report on the Americas* (Chicago: Quadrangle Books, 1969); and, for a forceful presentation of the current administration's implicit return, in important respects, to this earlier perspective, see Ronald Reagan, Remarks before the World Affairs Council of Philadelphia, Philadelphia, 15 October 1981.

21. For a series of interesting case studies, see Stephen Krasner, *Defending the National Interest: Raw Materials Investment and U.S. Foreign Policy* (Princeton, New Jersey: Princeton University Press, 1978).

22. A critical evaluation of traditional U.S. assumptions can be found in

C. Fred Bergsten, T. Horst, and T. Moran, *American Multinationals and American Interests* (Washington, D.C.: Brookings Institution, 1978). Bergsten became the Assistant Secretary for International Affairs in the Treasury Department under Carter.

23. For a case study of local business aligning in a "national bourgeois" statist coalition in favor of nationalization of raw materials resources, see Theodore Moran, *Multinational Corporations and the Politics of Dependence: Copper in Chile* (Princeton, New Jersey: Princeton University Press, 1974), pp. 172–215.

24. Jorge Dominguez, "Is There a National Bourgeoisie?: Elite and Mass Opinion Toward Private Direct Foreign Investment in Latin America," mimeographed, Harvard University.

25. The following accounts of Nicaragua and El Salvador rely heavily upon personal observations. Accounts of the periods discussed can be found in: William Leogrande, "The Revolution in Nicaragua: Another Cuba?" *Foreign Affairs,* Fall 1979, pp.28–50; U.S., Department of State, "The Violent Overthrow of Authoritarian Governments: The Central American Case," prepared under an External Research Grant by Frederico Gil et. al., 1981; and George Lawton, "U.S. Policy Toward Nicaragua," Ph.D. dissertation, Johns Hopkins-SAIS, Washington, D.C., forthcoming. See also Richard E. Feinberg, "The Recent Rapid Redefinitions of U.S. Interests and Diplomacy in Central America," in Feinberg, *Central America.*

26. These clashes cannot simply be attributed to the peculiarities of the Carter administration. More conservative administrations would have been even more appalled at the willingness of Nicaraguan businessmen to align with the FSLN. While some Republicans in 1979–80 had been more sympathetic to Salvadoran business sentiment, once in power the Reagan administration chose to support the Christian Democrats in the junta and the agrarian reform.

27. For an early, if ambiguous, critique of U.S. reliance on Latin militaries, see Edwin Lieuwen, *Arms and Politics in Latin America* (New York: Praeger, 1960).

28. For a passionate discussion of these perceived threats, see Kissinger, *White House Years* pp. 653–83.

29. By the end of the 1970s, Brazil's annual arms production was approaching $5 billion, and arms exports were expected to surpass $1 billion by the early 1980s. Stockholm International Peace Research Institute, *World Armaments and Disarmaments SPIRI Yearbook 1980* (London: Taylor and Francis, 1980), p. 88.

30. See Robert L. Paarlberg, "Lessons of the Grain Embargo," *Foreign Affairs,* Fall 1980, pp.144–62.

31. The two classic studies of that period on the political role of the Latin

military are: Lieuwen, *Arms and Politics,* cited above; and John J. Johnson, *The Military and Society in Latin America* (Stanford: Stanford University Press, 1964). See also John J. Johnson, *The Role of the Military in Underdeveloped Countries* (Princeton: Princeton University Press, 1963). A critique of these "liberal academic hopes" based on the experience of the last 20 years in Latin America and the rest of the Third World can be found in S.E. Finer, "The Military and Politics in the Third World," in *The Third World: Premises of U.S. Policy,* ed. W. Scott Thompson (San Francisco: Institute for Contemporary Studies, 1978).

32. For one survey, see Eric Nordlinger, "Soldiers in Mufti: The Impact of Military Rule upon Economic and Social Change in the Non-Western States," *American Political Science Review* 64 no.4 (December 1970), pp.1131–48.

33. For a series of insightful theoretical papers and country case studies, see Guillermo O'Donnell, Philippe Schmitter and Lawrence Whithead, eds., *Transitions from Authoritarian Rule,* forthcoming; and Abraham Lowenthal, ed., *Armies and Politics in Latin America* (New York: Holmes and Meier, 1976).

34. See Alfred Stepan, *The State and Society: Peru in Comparative Perspective* (Princeton, New Jersey: Princeton University Press, 1978).

35. For an earlier indication of such problems inherent in military rule, see Alfred Stepan, *The Military in Politics: Changing Patterns in Brazil* (Princeton, New Jersey: Princeton University Press, 1971). A more recent discussion can be found in Margaret E. Crahan, "National Security Ideology and Human Rights," in *Human Rights and Basic Needs in the Americas,* ed. Margaret E. Crahan (Washington, D.C.: Georgetown University Press, 1982).

CHAPTER 2

1. For example, see Peter T. Bauer, *Dissent on Development* (Cambridge: Harvard University Press, 1976); P.T. Bauer and Basil Yamey, "Against the New Economic Order," *Commentary,* April 1977, pp.25–33 Martin Brofenbrenner, "Predatory Poverty on the Offensive: The UNCTAD Record," *Economic Development and Cultural Change,* July 1976, pp.825–31 and Edwin Feulner, *Congress and the New International Economic Order* (Washington, D.C.: The Heritage Foundation, 1976).

2. U.S., Department of State, Bureau of Public Affairs, "A Strategic Approach to American Foreign Policy" (Speech delivered in New Orleans, 11 August 1981.) For an alarming assessment by the chairman of President Reagan's Strategic Minerals Task Force, see R. Daniel McMichael, "Strategic Minerals: Life Subsystem of Resource Dependency," in *Seapower: The Nation's Lifeline* (Pittsburgh: World Affairs Council of Pittsburgh, 1981).

3. Address before the Foreign Relations and National Security Committee of the American Legion, Honolulu, 29 August 1981.

4. For advocacy that U.S. military forces ought to be configured for intervention against governments closing their markets to the U.S., see Maxwell Taylor (former chairman of the Joint Chiefs of Staff), "Reagan's Military Policy is in Trouble," *Washington Post,* 3 November 1981, Op-Ed page.

5. Bank for International Settlements, *Annual Report* 51 (1981), p. 105. This figure excludes loans to offshore banking centers such as the Bahamas and Hong Kong.

6. World Bank, *World Development Report 1981* (Washington, DC: World Bank, 1981), p. 13.

7. Data on direct investment income is from the U.S. Department of Commerce, *Survey of Current Business* 61, no. 8, table 18, August 1981, p.38. Interest income is calculated from the same publication by subtracting line 30 from line 14 in table 10 (vol. 61, no. 6, June 1981, p. 64) and adding to the remainder banking income as presented in table 18 (vol. 61, no. 8, p. 38).

8. The ratio of debt service to exports for the twenty-five largest non-oil LDCs rose from 17 percent in 1975 to 24 percent in 1979; debt service as a ratio of GDP rose from 2.5 percent to 4.5 percent.

9. International Monetary Fund, *International Financial Statistics* (Washington, D.C.: IMF), monthly, various issues.

10. Of U.S. bank loans to developing countries outstanding at the end of 1980, 32 percent were to public borrowers and 33 percent were to other banks. Board of Governors of the Federal Reserve System, "Country Exposure Lending Survey," press release, 28 May 1981.

11. Bank for International Settlements, *Annual Report* 51 (1981), p. 105.

12. Karin Lissakers, "Money and Manipulation," *Foreign Policy,* no. 44 (Fall 1981), p. 112.

13. A survey of affiliates of 180 U.S.-based manufacturing firms found that the percentage of wholly owned affiliates fell from 58 percent before 1951 to 44 percent in the 1970s. For European and other non-U.S.-based MNCs, the drop was even more dramatic. See Isaiah Frank, *Foreign Enterprise in Developing Countries* (Baltimore: Johns Hopkins University Press, 1980), p. 21.

14. This idea is skillfully developed in Richard S. Newfarmer, ed., *International Oligopoly and Uneven Development,* forthcoming.

15. Frank, *Foreign Enterprise,* pp. 4, 157.

16. Ibid., p. 112.

17. *Washington Post,* 23 September 1981, p. A20.

18. For a summary of recent studies on MNC profitability, see Richard Newfarmer, "Multinationals and Marketplace Magic in the 1980s," in *The*

Multinational Corporation in the 1980s, ed. Charles P. Kindleberger and David B. Audretsch, forthcoming.

19. For several industry studies that argue that a strategy relying on overseas investment to maintain profit levels has, in the long run, harmed U.S. competitiveness, see the forthcoming book edited by John Zysman on issues in industrial policy.

20. *New York Times,* 26 July 1981, p. F5; and "New Restrictions on World Trade," *Business Week,* 19 July 1982, pp. 118–22.

21. For a description of how several administrations have used the slogan of "free trade" to restrain domestic protectionist pressures, see Robert A. Pastor, *Congress and the Politics of U.S. Foreign Economic Policy* (Berkeley: University of California Press, 1980), especially chapters 3–6.

22. Statement at the joint annual meetings of the IMF and the World Bank, Washington, D.C., 30 September 1981.

23. A World Bank study found that the following developing countries, among others, had price controls: Algeria, Bangladesh, Brazil, Chile, Colombia, Egypt, Guatemala, India, Indonesia, Iran, Ivory Coast, Mexico, Morocco, Nigeria, Pakistan, Papua-New Guinea, Senegal, Spain, Sudan, Tanzania, Turkey, and Yugoslavia. Armeane Choksi, *State Intervention in the Industrialization of Developing Countries: Selected Issues,* Working Paper no. 341 (Washington, D.C.: World Bank, 1979), p. 76, table 3.1.

24. For a clearheaded discussion of the interdependence of the public and private sectors by a World Bank economist, see Barend A. deVries, "Public Policy and the Private Sector," *Finance and Development* 18, no. 3 (September 1981), pp.11–15.

25. See World Bank, *The Capital Goods Sector in LDCs: A Case for State Intervention?,* Staff Working Paper no. 343 (Washington, D.C.: World Bank, 1979).

26. Council on Foreign Relations and the International Management and Development Institute, pamphlet, "New Directions in U.S. Foreign Policy," appendix, p. 3, 1980.

27. Ibid., appendix, p. 4.

28. A government-subsidized firm can accept minimal profits for ten years while cutting prices, increasing its market share, and adding capacity, thereby achieving a long-term competitive cost advantage. See Telesis, *A Framework for Swedish Industrial Policy* (Somerville, Massachusetts; Telesis, 1978), vol. 1, p. 69.

29. Newfarmer, *International Oligopoly,* chapter 11.

30. On German industrial policy, see Telesis, *Framework,* vol. 2, appendix 12.

31. For a thorough discussion of the Chinese modernization campaign

and its opening to the West, see Doak Barnett, *China in the Global Economy* (Washington, D.C.: Brookings Institution, 1981).

32. *Fortune,* 7 September 1981, p. 93.

33. Ibid., p. 91.

34. Lynn Feintech, *China's Modernization Strategy and the United States* (Washington, D.C.: Overseas Development Council, 1981), Development Paper 31, pp. 41–61.

35. Quoted in James H. Mittleman, *Underdevelopment and the Transition to Socialism: Mozambique and Tanzania* (New York: Academic Press, 1981), p. 121.

36. An early example of this thinking is Celso Furtado, *Obstacles to Development in Latin America* (Garden City, New York: Anchor Books, 1970). For a more recent appraisal, see Newfarmer, *International Oligopoly,* especially chap. 11.

37. Interestingly, bauxite was one of the commodities judged to be a good candidate for successful cartelization by C. Fred Bergsten in his foreboding article, "The Threat from the Third World," *Foreign Policy,* no. 11 (Summer 1973), pp.102–24.

38. See Douglas Woods and James Burrows, *The World Aluminum-Bauxite Market* (New York: Charles River Associates and Praeger, 1980).

39. See Adam Boulton, "Jamaica's Bauxite Strategy: The Caribbean Flirts with the International System," *SAIS Review,* no. 2 (Summer 1981), pp. 81–92.

40. The Joint Chiefs of Staff, *United States Military Posture for FY1982* (Washington, D.C.: Government Printing Office, 1981), supplement, p. 3.

41. Bureau of Mines, *Mineral Commodity Summaries 1981* (Washington, D.C.: Government Printing Office, 1981); Bureau of Mines, *Minerals and Materials* (monthly survey) (Washington, D.C.: Government Printing Office, 1981); Bureau of Mines, *Minerals Yearbook 1980* (Washington, D.C.: Government Printing Office, 1981), vol. 1.

42. See Stephen D. Krasner, "Oil is the Exception," *Foreign Policy,* no. 14 (Spring 1974), 68–83.

43. International Monetary Fund, *World Economic Outlook* (Washington, D.C.: IMF, 1981), p. 7.

44. Ibid., p. 17.

45. Ibid., p. 12.

46. On the need for increasing the resources of the World Bank and the IMF, see John Williamson, *The Lending Policies of the International Monetary Fund* (Washington, D.C.: Institute for International Economics, 1982); Economic Policy Council of the United Nations Association-USA, *U.S. Policies Toward the World Bank and the International Monetary Fund* (New York:

UNA-USA, 1982); and U.S., Congress, House of Representatives, Subcommittee on International Development Institutions and Finance, Committee on Banking, Finance and Urban Affairs, Report, *The Future of the Multilateral Development Banks,* 97th Cong., 2nd sess. (Washington, D.C.: Government Printing Office, 1982).

47. For a concise summary of the problems facing bank regulators, see Richard Dale, *Bank Supervision Around the World* (New York: Group of 30, 1982).

48. Among the better recent writings on debt rescheduling are Chandra S. Hardy, *Rescheduling Developing-Country Debts, 1956–81: Lessons and Recommendations* (Washington, D.C.: Overseas Development Council, 1982); Group of 30, *Risks in International Bank Lending* (New York: Group of 30, 1982) and Jeffrey E. Garten, "Rescheduling Sovereign Debt: Is There a Better Approach?", *World Economy,* forthcoming.

49. An Hungarian economist noted this relationship with candor and succinctness: "The Hungarian People's Republic is one of those small countries which do not have a decisive influence on the evolution of international economic relations and which are obliged to adapt to them." Mihaly Simai, *Interdependence and Conflicts in the World Economy* (Budapest: Academiai Kiado, 1981), p. 7.

CHAPTER 3

1. "Soviet Geopolitical Momentum: Myth or Menace?" *The Defense Monitor* 9, no. 1 (January 1980). The study listed the following countries as being under significant Soviet influence: Afghanistan, Angola, Bulgaria, Cambodia, Congo, Cuba, Czechoslovakia, Ethiopia, East Germany, Hungary, Laos, Libya, Mongolia, Mozambique, Poland, Romania, Syria, South Yemen, and Vietnam. Even some of these examples are arguable.

2. Robert H. Donaldson, ed., *The Soviet Union in the Third World: Success and Failures* (Boulder, Colorado: Westview Press, 1980).

3. International Monetary Fund, *Direction of Trade Statistics* (Washington, D.C.: IMF, published monthly).

4. Central Intelligence Agency, *Communist Aid Activities in Non-Communist Less Developed Countries, 1978* (Washington, D.C.: CIA, 1979) and Overseas Development Council, *U.S. Foreign Policy and the Third World: Agenda 1982* (New York: Praeger, 1982), annex F.

5. Basil Caplan, "Soviet Economy: Trade and Aid for the Third World," *The Banker,* July 1981, p. 42; and CIA, *Communist Aid Activities,* p. 11.

6. Orah Cooper and Carol Fogarty, "Soviet Economic and Military Aid to the Less Developed Countries, 1954–78," *Soviet Economy in a Time of*

Change (Washington, D.C.: Government Printing Office for the Joint Economic Committee, 1979), vol. 2, p. 649.

7. For an excellent discussion of this evolution in Soviet thought, see Elizabeth Kridl Valkenier, "The USSR, the Third World, and the Global Economy," *Problems of Communism,* July–August 1979, 17–33.

8. E. Korotkova, cited in Valkenier, "The USSR," p. 265, ftn. 8.

9. "Socialist Orientation in Africa," *International Affairs,* no. 9 (1979), p. 103.

10. See Joseph L. Nogee and John W. Sloan, "Allende's Chile and the Soviet Union: A Policy Lesson for Latin American Nations Seeking Autonomy," *Journal of Inter-American Studies and World Affairs* 21, no. 3 (August 1979): 339–68.

11. Edward Hewett and Herbert Levin, "The Soviet Union's Economic Relations in Asia," in Donald Zagoria, ed., *The Soviet Union in Asia,* forthcoming.

12. See Sheldon Simon and Donald Zagoria, "Soviet Policy in Southeast Asia," in Zagoria, *Soviet Union in Asia.*

13. See Ralph Clough, "The Soviet Union and the Two Koreas," in Zagoria, *Soviet Union in Asia.*

14. This section on Ethiopia is based on interviews with Americans involved with Ethiopia at the time and with a former Ethiopian government official; on David and Marina Ottaway, *Afrocommunism* (New York: Holmes and Meier, 1981), especially chap. 6; and Paul B. Henze, "Communism and Ethiopia," *Problems of Communism,* May–June 1981, pp. 55–74.

15. Ottoway, *Afrocommunism,* p. 137.

16. Jay Ross, "Ethiopia Leans Uneasily on Soviets as Reliable Source of Arms," *Washington Post,* 31 December 1981, p. A12.

17. Pranay B. Gupte, "Ethiopians' Links to Soviet Strained," *New York Times,* 12 December 1981, p. A7.

18. Ross, "Ethiopia Leans Uneasily."

19. For an excellent discussion of Soviet disillusionment with "revolutionary democrats," see Morton Schwartz, "The USSR and Leftist Regimes in Less-Developed countries," *Survey* 19 (Spring 1973), pp.209–44.

20. The following discussion is based largely on interviews conducted in Moscow in June 1981. See also the essays by Anatoli Gromyko and N. Kosukhin in *Present-Day Development of Africa* (Moscow: USSR Academy of Sciences, 1980).

21. For Western critiques of African socialism, see Carl Rosberg and Thomas M. Callagy, *Socialism in Sub-Saharan Africa* (Berkeley, California: University of California Institute of International Studies, 1979); and Ottaway, *Afrocommunism.*

22. Kosukhin, *Present-day Development,* p. 119.

23. The Soviet debate on the causes of the Pinochet coup is summarized in Jerry Hough, "The Evolving Soviet Debate on Latin America," *Latin America Research Review* 16 no. 1 (1980): 124–43.

24. Mohamed Heikal, *The Road to Ramadan* (New York: Ballantine Books, 1975), pp. 81–82.

25. Ibid., p. 167.

26. Anwar el-Sadat, *In Search of Identity* (New York: Harper and Row, 1977), p. 231.

27. Heikal, *Road to Ramadan,* pp. 166–87. See also Sadat, *In Search of Identity,* appendix A, pp. 317–24 for Sadat's message to Brezhnev listing some of the military equipment that he accused Moscow of having "embargoed."

28. Heikal, *Road to Ramadan,* p. 177.

29. Ibid., p. 170.

30. Sadat, *In Search of Identity,* p. 321.

31. Stephen S. Kaplan, *Diplomacy of Power: Soviet Armed Forces as a Political Instrument* (Washington, D.C.: Brookings Institution, 1981), pp. 661–62.

32. Francis Fukuyama, *The Soviet Union and Iraq Since 1968* (Santa Monica: Rand, 1980), especially pp. 35–37. On Soviet-Iraqi relations, see also Adeed Dawish, "Iraq: The West's Opportunity," *Foreign Policy,* no. 41 (Winter 1980/81), 134–53; and Claudia Wright, "Iraq," *Atlantic Monthly,* April 1979, pp. 12–28.

33. *Wall Street Journal,* 29 April 1981, p. 1.

34. *The Economist* (19 December 1981, p. 11) made this characterization and criticized it.

35. Robert H. Donaldson, *The Soviet-Indian Alignment: Quest for Influence,* Monograph Series in World Affairs, vol. 16 (Denver: University of Denver, 1979), pp. 32–33.

36. Survey by Canadian political scientist Stephen Clarkson, in *Economic and Political Weekly,* 14 April 1973, p. 723.

37. Donaldson, *Soviet-Indian Alignment,* p. 6.

38. Ibid.

39. Nick Eberstadt and Tom Ricks, "The Cost of Pax Sovietica," *The New Republic,* 30 December 1981, p. 16; also, Paul Marer, "Has Eastern Europe Become a Liability to the Soviet Union—The Economic Aspect," in *The International Politics of Eastern Europe,* ed. Charles Gati (New York: Praeger, 1976).

40. "Congo: Recent History," *Africa South of the Sahara, 1981–82* (Europa Publishers, 1981), p. 325.

41. G.I. Mirsky, as quoted in Charles C. Peterson, *Third World Military*

Elites in Soviet Perspective (Alexandria, Virginia: Center for Naval Analyses, 1979), Professional Paper 262, p. 31.

42. Andrew J. Pierre, *The Global Politics of Arms Sales* (Princeton, New Jersey: Princeton University Press and the Council on Foreign Relations, 1982), p. 82.

43. *Peking Review,* 19 January 1979, p. 16.

44. For a more detailed argument that Soviet military gains in Africa have been exaggerated, see Richard Remnek, *Soviet Strategic Military Concerns in Africa* (Alexandria, Virginia: Center for Naval Analyses, 1981). Remnek suggests that any Soviet bases in Africa would be highly vulnerable to Western attack in the event of war. The Soviets do not need bases in Africa to intercept the flow of Persian Gulf oil, as airfields located within the Soviet bloc are already within striking range of the oil fields and terminals.

45. Eberstadt and Ricks, "Cost of Pay Sovietica," place the subsidies to Eastern Europe at $20 billion, to Third World "proxies" at $10 bilion. The latter figure seems to include military aid.

46. In general, the overthrow of governments friendly to the Soviet Union has been primarily the result of internal forces. The United States has, however, played some role in the overthrow of several Third World governments perceived at the time as being too close to the Soviet Union, including Iran (1953), Guatemala (1954), and Chile (1973). In retrospect, these governments were more reformist and nationalist than Communist, although a Communist Party may have played a role in governing coalitions. Moreover, the subsequent regimes have proven to be less than stable. The U.S. gain has already been erased in Iran and is in clear danger in Guatemala.

CHAPTER 4

1. U.S., Department of Defense, *The Pentagon Papers (Senator Gravel Edition): The Department of Defense History of United States Decisionmaking on Vietnam* (Boston, 1971), vol. 2, pp. 58–59.

2. George Ball, "We Should De-escalate the Importance of Vietnam," *New York Times Magazine,* 21 December 1969, p. 36.

3. "The Present Danger," *Commentary,* March 1980, p. 31. Podhoretz cries out for a renewed American nationalism, willing once again to understand that Communism anywhere represents an expansion of Soviet power, that ideology and politics must take precedence over economics, and that a rearmed America must be prepared to intervene.

4. Stated by the Nigerian head of state, as quoted in Price, *U.S. Foreign Policy in Sub-Saharan Africa,* p. 40.

5. For a discussion of public disillusion with wars of attrition in Third

World states, see Andrew Mack, "Why Big Nations Lose Small Wars: The Politics of Asymmetric Conflict," *World Politics* 27 (1974–75).

6. "Dictatorships and Double Standards," *Commentary,* November 1979.

7. Speech to the American Society of Newspaper Editors, 25 April 1981. Reprinted in *New York Times,* 25 April 1981.

8. Kissinger, *White House Years,* p. 668.

9. As told to the author by an informed Soviet Latin Americanist, July 1981.

10. Address to the American Society of Newspaper Editors, 10 April 1980, Washington, D.C.

11. Fred Halliday, *Soviet Policy in the Arc of Crisis* (Washington, D.C.: The Institute for Policy Studies, 1981), pp. 84–90.

12. John B. Oakes, "Some History for Haig," *New York Times,* 6 April 1982, p. A19.

13. The story of the CIA-backed coup is told in Stephen Schlesinger and Stephen Kinzer, *Bitter Fruit: the Untold Story of the American Coup in Guatemala* (New York: Doubleday, 1982).

14. U.S., Congress, Senate, Select Committee to Study Governmental Operations With Respect to Intelligence Activities, *Covert Action in Chile, 1963–1973,* Staff Report, 94th Cong., 1st sess. (Washington, D.C.: Government Printing Office, 1975).

15. *New York Times,* 14 March 1982, p. 1.

16. Robert Carswell, "Economic Sanctions and the Iran Experience," *Foreign Affairs* 60, no. 2 (Winter 1981–82), p. 261.

17. Knorr, *Power of Nations,* p. 152.

18. Quoted in Barry Rubin, *Paved with Good Intentions: The American Experience in Iran* (New York: Penguin Books, 1981), p. 260.

19. Jennifer Seymour Whitaker, "Cairo: They Don't Miss Sadat," *The Atlantic Monthly,* January 1982, pp. 18–19.

20. *New York Times,* 9 February 1982, p. A5; and *Washington Post,* 21 December 1981, p. A23.

21. *New York Times,* 2 October 1981, p. A26.

22. Quoted in Rubin, *Paved with Good Intentions,* p. 276.

23. Quoted in Foreign Broadcast Information Service (FBIS), *Latin America,* 11 January 1982, p. 11.

24. Lippmann, *The Cold War,* p. 22. On the debate over postwar policies for dealing with the Soviet Union and the Third World, see Gaddis, *Strategies of Containment.*

25. This argument follows Barry R. Posen and Stephen Van Evera, "Defense Policy: Departure from Containment," in *Eagle Defiant,* ed. Robert Leiber, Kenneth Oye, and Donald Rothchild (Boston: Little, Brown, 1983).

26. See Joshua M. Epstein, "Soviet Vulnerabilities in Iran and the FDR Deterrent," *International Security* 6, no. 2, (Fall 1981), pp.126–50.

27. For advocacy of such procurement, see Jeffrey Record, *The Rapid Deployment Force and U.S. Military Intervention in the Persian Gulf,* Institute for Foreign Policy Analysis, Special Report (Cambridge, Massachusetts, 1981).

28. For a warning by a sophisticated defense analyst that the introduction of the RDF into an Arab country could be politically counterproductive, see Anthony H. Cordesman, "The Changing Military Balance in the Gulf and Middle East," *Armed Forces Journal,* September 1981, pp. 52–60. A defense of the potential usefulness of rapid deployment forces (especially maritime units) in a variety of Third World contingencies can be found in Stansfield Turner and George Thibault, "Preparing for the Unexpected: The Need for a New Military Strategy," *Foreign Affairs,* Fall 1982, pp.122–35. See also Department of Defense, *Annual Report FY1981* (Washington, D.C., 1980), pp. 115–17, 207.

29. Quoted in Leslie Gelb, "Reagan's Military Budget Puts Emphasis on a Buildup of U.S. Global Power," *New York Times,* 7 February 1982, p. 26.

30. Council of Economic Advisers, *Economic Report of the President, 1982* (Washington, D.C.: Government Printing Office, 1982), pp. 83, 85.

31. George Wilson, "Planners Say Defense Budget Is Insufficient," *Washington Post,* 8 March, 1982, p. 1.

32. William W. Kaufman, "The Defense Budget," in *Setting National Priorities: the 1983 Budget,* ed. Joseph A. Pechman (Washington, D.C.: Brookings Institution, 1982), pp. 51–100.

33. These "back of the envelope" estimates were provided in an interview with Posen and Van Evera. Among the casualties of their cuts would be one marine division, two army infantry divisions, and several air wings. These forces are considered either beyond what is required for containing the USSR in Europe and the Persian Gulf with a "moderate degree of confidence," and for protecting South Korea, or else they are the wrong kind of forces for accomplishing those objectives. An analysis by Posen and Van Evera of U.S. and Soviet intervention forces (which finds the Soviets far weaker) can be founded in "Overarming and Underwhelming," *Foreign Policy,* no. 40 (Fall 1980), pp.99-ND118.

Senator Gary Hart has also called for a reduction in land forces most suitable to "low density, Vietnam type" wars. He prefers smaller, modernized, sea-based forces required for intervening in extreme cases only. Hart would phase out the Army's 2nd Airborne and three infantry divisions, at an estimated savings of $60 billion over a ten-year period. See Robert Taft, Jr., and Gary Hart, "White Paper on Defense," mimeographed, Washington, D.C., 1978.

The savings foreseen by Posen and Van Evera and by Hart are modest compared to those calculated by other analysts who have estimated the reduced costs of a "non-interventionist" force structure. For example, Earl Ravenal estimated a 40 percent savings, in "After Schlesinger: Something Has to Give," *Foreign Policy,* no. 22 (Spring 1976), pp.71–95.

34. U.S., Department of Commerce, *National Income and Product Accounts* (Washington, D.C.: Government Printing Office, 1981).

35. It was the opinion of President Carter's Council of Economic Advisers that the United States would do well if, utilizing a wide range of instruments, its rate of investment increased by 1 percent. Council of Economic Advisers, *Economic Report of the President* (Washington, D.C.: Government Printing Office, 1980), pp. 136–40.

36. See Richard E. Feinberg, *Subsidizing Success: The Export-Import Bank in the U.S. Economy* (New York: Cambridge University Press, 1982), chap. 9.

37. For a critique of military procurement as a drag on civilian industry, see Robert Reich, "Making Industrial Policy," *Foreign Affairs,* Spring 1982, pp. 863–71.

38. Estimates from Data Resources, Inc., as published in *Business Week,* 8 February 1982, p. 94.

39. For a lucid discussion on the relative decline of productivity in the United States, see Ira Magaziner and Robert Reich, *Minding America's Business* (New York: Harcourt, Brace and Yuvonivich, 1982). The classic study is Edward F. Denison, *Accounting for Slower Economic Growth: The United States in the 1970s* (Washington, D.C.: The Brookings Institution, 1979).

40. William H. Branson, "Industrial Policy and U.S. International Trade," *Toward a New U.S. Industrial Policy?,* ed. Michael L. Wachter and Susan M. Wachter (Philadelphia: University of Pennsylvania Press, 1981), p. 383, table 16–2B.

41. For more detailed recommendations for U.S. industrial policy, see the Report of the Economic Policy Council of the United Nations Association-USA, "The Need for U.S. Industrial Objectives," 1982; Ronald Muller, *Revitalizing America: Politics for Prosperity* (New York: Simon and Schuster, 1980); Magaziner and Reich, *Minding America's Business;* and chapter 5.

CHAPTER 5

1. *Washington Post,* 3 March 1982, p. A1.

2. The international development banks can lend some $50 for every $1 paid in by the United States, since other countries match U.S. contributions, and the banks then leverage these donations by borrowing additional funds on private capital markets. Resources that the United States pays into the

International Monetary Fund continue to count as U.S. international reserves, and are not charged as a net outlay in U.S. budgetary calculations.

3. The following section on industrial policy relies heavily on the arguments developed in Magaziner and Reich, *Minding America's Business.*

4. For a discourse on "classical liberal" and "statist-nationalist" strands in Argentine foreign policy, see Milensky, *Argentina's Foreign Policies.*

5. Warren Christopher, "Lessons of Iran," speech delivered to the Los Angeles County Bar Association, 26 May 1981, reprinted in Warren Christopher, "Diplomacy: The Neglected Imperative," bound pamphlet, no date.

6. William Schneider, "Conservatism, not Interventionism: Trends in Foreign Policy Opinion, 1974–82," in *Eagle Defiant.*

7. Richard E. Feinberg, "The Rapid Redefinition of U.S. Interests and Diplomacy in Central America," in Feinberg, *Central America.*

8. For an explanation and evaluation of Carter's human rights policies, on humanitarian and other national interest criteria, see Richard E. Feinberg, *Human Rights: Latin America* (Washington, D.C.: Center for International Policy, 1980).

9. Samuel P. Huntington offers these and other suggestions for reducing political instability in the Persian Gulf states in "The Renewal of Strategy," *The Strategic Imperative,* ed. Samuel P. Huntington (Cambridge, Massachusetts: Ballinger, 1982), pp. 45–49.

Index

Dean Ac
George V
Larry Be
in V
Richard I
to U ... *ge*
Louis He
George F
1917
George F ... *ns,*
1917
Robert F ... *sis*
Henry A.
Henry A.
Walter L
Cen
Thomas I
Dankwar
Mid
John Stoc
John G. S
Ame
William

96349

E
840
.F44
1983

FEINBERG, RICHARD
THE INTEMPERATE ZONE.

DATE DUE

GAYLORD

PRINTED IN U.S.A.

Fernald Library
Colby-Sawyer College
New London, New Hampshire